Statement by the General Editors

The Anchor Series, "Documents in American Civilization," provides primary materials for the study of the history of the United States and for the understanding of American culture. In the belief that neither history nor culture can be properly studied without consideration of a variety of sources, the editors have adopted the interdisciplinary approach in the selection of documents. In our sense, a "document" is any idea, institution, or man-made object that provides a clue to the way in which subjective experience is organized at a specific moment in time.

The purpose of the series is twofold: to show the pervasiveness of those themes which are central to particular moments in history; and to underline the significance of cultural documents in their total historical context—and thus to illuminate problems or themes that characterize American society.

HENNIG COHEN is Professor of English at the University of Pennsylvania and editor of *American Quarterly*. He is also editor of *Selected Poems of Herman Melville* (Anchor Books, A375) and co-editor of *Folklore in America*.

JOHN WILLIAM WARD is Professor of History and American Studies at Amherst College. He is the author of *Andrew Jackson: Symbol for an Age* and editor of *Society, Manners, and Politics in the United States* by Michael Chevalier.

EDWIN C. ROZWENC was born in Dover, New Jersey. He received a Bachelor of Arts degree from Amherst College in 1937, and a Doctor of Philosophy degree from Columbia University in 1941. He was an instructor in History and Social Science at Cornell College and assistant professor of History at Clark University before being invited back to Amherst to join the faculty in 1946; at the present time, he is Chairman of the Department of American Studies at Amherst. His major interest has been to encourage students to find new ways of analyzing and organizing their knowledge of the history of American civilization. In this connection he has edited seven of the books in the "Amherst series" of *Problems in American Civilization.* In addition, he is director of a group of secondary school teachers who are preparing a series of new study units for secondary schools under the title, *Basic Concepts in History and Social Science.* He is also the author of numerous articles on various aspects of New England history and was co-editor and contributor to a collection of historical essays entitled *Teachers of History.*

Ideology and Power in the Age of Jackson

Edited with an Introduction by
Edwin C. Rozwenc

Anchor Books
Doubleday & Company, Inc.
Garden City, New York

Introduction

I

The concept "Jacksonian democracy" is a conventional term that most historians use without much conscious thought about its warrantability. No student of American historiography has been able to establish who invented this generalizing term, although such an inquiry into the origins of the concept might lead to some very revealing discoveries about American intellectual history. Whatever the origins of the concept, it is clear enough that historical writers in the twentieth century have been largely preoccupied with attempts to identify the social groups that supported the Jacksonian movement, and to explain the forces that shaped it. Thus, for example, Frederick Jackson Turner assumed that Jacksonian democracy was an outgrowth of the frontier and the political and social aspirations of Westerners; Arthur Meier Schlesinger, Jr., maintained that the goals of Jacksonian democracy were shaped by the social pressures of the rapidly changing economic order in the older states of the East; Bray Hammond contended that Jacksonian democracy received its main impetus from the entrepreneurial drive of state bankers and their business allies.[1]

There were some historical writers, however, who tried to move away from the conventional concept. Carl Russell Fish preferred "the age of the common man" as a more

[1] See Turner, *The United States, 1830–1850* (New York, 1935), Ch. 2; Schlesinger, *The Age of Jackson* (Boston, 1945), esp. Ch. 10; Hammond, *Banks and Politics in America from the Revolution to the Civil War* (Princeton, 1957), Ch. 12.

inclusive generalizing term for the great variety of forms in which the egalitarian urges of American life were expressed in the period from 1820 to 1850.[2] Louis Hartz saw the Jacksonian era as another phase in the liberal confusion that Americans must suffer because, in the often-quoted dictum of Tocqueville, they were "born equal" and did not have "to endure a democratic revolution."[3] Lee Benson has been more tendentious; he has explicitly proclaimed the necessity for discarding the concept of Jacksonian democracy and has proposed "the age of Egalitarianism" as a generalizing term less likely to lead the historian to distort "reality."[4]

There is no need to rehearse further the debates among historians concerning the meaning of Jacksonian democracy. The title of this book presupposes that the "age of Jackson" is still a useful generalizing term even though the egalitarian energies of the period were expressed in the rhetoric and the actions of groups other than those actually associated with the "Jackson party." The documents included in this volume reveal that an adequate historical explanation of this period is not possible if we try to remove Andrew Jackson and the Jacksonian party from the center of attention.

More particularly, we can begin to fashion a warrantable interpretation of the Jacksonian era best if we focus our inquiry by means of the concepts of wealth, status, and power. The usefulness of such a delimitation in the choice of documents should be obvious. When we apply such terms as "democracy," "egalitarianism," or "the age of the common man" to America in the second quarter of the nineteenth century, we are grouping together generalizing statements previously made about the distribution of such values as wealth, esteem, and power.

[2] Fish, *The Rise of the Common Man* (New York, 1927).
[3] Hartz, *The Liberal Tradition in America* (New York, 1955), esp. Ch. 5.
[4] See Benson, *The Concept of Jacksonian Democracy* (Princeton, 1961), esp. Ch. 15.

II

The enormous social energy devoted to the pursuit of material welfare was a frequent subject of comment by foreign travelers who visited America in the second quarter of the nineteenth century. The two most notable French visitors to America in the 1830s, Michel Chevalier and Alexis de Tocqueville, were struck by the feverish pursuit of wealth by Americans and the rapid progress in trade and manufactures. "The Americans," Tocqueville wrote, "arrived but as yesterday on the territory which they inhabit, and they have already changed the whole order of nature for their own advantage. They have joined the Hudson to the Mississippi and made the Atlantic Ocean communicate with the Gulf of Mexico. . . . The longest railroads which have been constructed, up to the present time, are in America. . . . The Americans make immense progress in productive industry, because they all devote themselves to it at once. . . ."[5]

The Jacksonian generation, however, did not need the observations of foreign travelers to make them aware of the rapid increase in national wealth taking place in the United States. Americans of all sorts and conditions were fully aware of the great increase in the volume of goods produced and of the unprecedented additions to capital equipment in roads, canals, steamboats, railroads, factories, and machines being made after 1820. Not only were they aware of this growth in wealth and income, they were also highly sensitive to the social and moral problems that accompanied such changes.

The most comprehensive study of population and wealth in the United States prepared during the Jacksonian era is George Tucker's *Progress of the United States in Population and Wealth*. Tucker's data came from insufficient census reports and his statistical methods were crude by modern standards. Yet, even his sketchy statisti-

[5] Unless otherwise indicated, all quotations in the Introduction are taken from the documents included in this volume.

cal measures enabled him to demonstrate that the proportion of labor employed in agriculture and commerce had
diminished between 1820 and 1840, while that employed
in manufactures had increased from 13.7 to 17.1 per cent
of the whole labor force. Tucker was able to show, also,
that wealth was increasing faster than population, and that
much of this increase resulted from the growing "stock of
labour-saving tools and machinery . . . [and] cheaper
and quicker modes of transportation." Moreover, his analysis of population growth between 1820 and 1840 revealed
that the increase of population in towns over 10,000 ex-
ceeded that of the whole population in the ratio of 50 to
32.

A professor of moral philosophy as well as a political
economist, Tucker was equally interested in the moral
aspect of these changes. Reared in Jefferson's Virginia, he
still clung to the Jeffersonian notion that the countryside
was the natural home of liberty and virtue. But, unlike
Jefferson, he could not go so far as to admit that cities
were wholly corrupt. Instead, he spoke of cities more am-
biguously as moral battlegrounds where vice wars with
virtue, liberty with domination, and where the outcome
may be the triumph of either good or evil.

To be sure, there were spokesmen in the Jacksonian
generation who did not fear the growth of cities or the
rapidity of change in the economic order. Daniel Webster,
for example, used his oratorical powers frequently to cele-
brate the new forms of motive power and the new technology. Yet, there is considerable evidence to indicate that
the Whig champions of industry and enterprise also had
their moments of anxiety about the moral effects of the
restless ambition and the pursuit of gain which the rapid
growth of the economy so intensified in Americans after
1820. The editors of the *American Whig Review*, for example, lamented the decline of such human values as grace
and kindliness. Similarly, Freeman Hunt, the editor of
Hunt's Merchant's Magazine, urged this maxim upon his
readers: "Do not be in a hurry to get rich. Gradual gains

are the only natural gains. . . . In morals, the inordinate
love of money is one of the most degrading of vices."[6]

Others in the Jacksonian generation were openly hostile
toward the new forces of change. James Fenimore Cooper
resented the emergence of new social types favored by the
conditions of rapid economic growth. The character of
Aristabulus Bragg in *Home as Found* represents the mix-
ture of enterprise, shrewdness, vulgarity, pretension, and
duplicity in the self-made man of Jacksonian America.
For Cooper, Aristabulus Bragg is the type most likely to
succeed in an America committed to the reckless pursuit
of material gain. Ralph Waldo Emerson, coming at the
same problem with his transcendentalist perspective, used
Napoleon as the symbol of the new man of the age. To
him, Napoleon was "the incarnate Democrat . . . the
agent . . . of the throng who fill the markets, shops, counting-houses, manufactories, ships, of the modern world,
aiming to be rich . . . the destroyer of the prescription,
the internal improver, the liberal, the radical, the inventor
of means, the opener of doors and markets, the subverter
of monopoly and abuse." That such a type is thoroughly
modern, Emerson readily admitted, but he warned that,
"As long as our civilization is essentially one of property,
of fences, of exclusiveness, it will be mocked by delusions.
Our riches will leave us sick; there will be bitterness in our
laughter, and our wine will burn in our mouth."

III

In our own time, we have learned from observing the
experience of undeveloped nations that a rapid pace of
economic growth and the rapid introduction of technical
innovations causes tremendous psychic and social strains
in traditional societies. Although America, in the second
quarter of the nineteenth century, was not a traditional
society in the sense that modern anthropologists use the

[6] Freeman Hunt, *Worth and Wealth, A Collection of Maxims,
Morals and Miscellanies for Merchants and Men of Business*
(New York, 1856), p. 105.

concept, it was a society that for two centuries had had a fairly stable social system and that had experienced only gradual changes during the previous generations. Hence, it is reasonable to assume that the quickened pace of social change between 1820 and 1850 created great strains for traditional norms in American society. Older ethical ideals and older conceptions of personal character were not always consonant with the emerging practices and institutional forms of a rapidly rising American capitalism. Hence Americans of all sorts and conditions were beset by inner conflicts and anxieties as they tried to adjust traditional conceptions of life to the new realities.

Emerson looked into the state of mind of the Jacksonian era and concluded that uncertainty was its distinguishing trait. "Every age," he wrote, "like every human body has its own distemper. . . . Our forefathers walked in the world and went to their graves, tormented with the fear of Sin, and the Terror of the Day of Judgment. These terrors have lost their force, and our torment is unbelief, the uncertainty as to what we ought to do."[7]

The uncertainties generated by rapid social change in Jacksonian America extended beyond the effort to adjust the traditional conceptions of individual morality. The multiplication of new enterprises, the emergence of new forms of technology and economic organization, the appearance of large numbers of newly enriched individuals, also deranged the previously established bases of personal identification and of social status.

We should not, however, assume that the problem of status in the Jacksonian era was a simple social drama in which an older aristocratic elite was displaced by vulgar and aggressive men on the make. While we can find such types of anxiety in Cooper's writings, the status system of a democratic society entering a dynamic stage of economic growth is much too complex to be elucidated by the lamentations of American "gentlemen." When John Calhoun boldly developed a theory of progress through

[7] *The Prose Works of Ralph Waldo Emerson* (Boston, 1870), I, 154.

exploitation, he reflected more than the psychic deprivation which the aristocratic planters may have sensed as
they watched the rise of the cotton snobs in the new states
of the lower South. He was building an ideological defense
for the whole system of caste and class throughout the
South and, indeed, his theory of exploitation was probably
more congenial to the newer and more aggressive members of the master class than to the older planting aristocracy of the South.

The anxieties expressed by social types within the middle class reveal further intricacies in the problem of status
in the Jacksonian era. The *Memoirs* of Charles Grandison
Finney, the greatest of the revivalist preachers in Jackson's
generation, gives us a clear picture of the antagonism of
the standing order of the Protestant ministry when they
found themselves caught in a throng of new prophets seeking to lead a restless people. At the same time, middle-
class leaders of educational reform like Horace Mann and
William Holmes McGuffey expressed fears for the traditional middle-class virtues and labored mightily to create
the moral mechanisms that would control the enormous
energies being released by the democratic upsurge in
American life.

The Jacksonian journalists and social theorists repeated
again and again the anxieties of small producers concerning the meaning of worth and wealth in the rapidly changing social conditions of their time. William Gouge, for
example, expressed his fear of those who had made the
way to wealth "a game of hap-hazard" instead of a moral
drama in which the virtues of industry, economy, enterprise and prudence were properly rewarded. In a similar
fashion, the resolutions of the first national convention of
the National Trades' Union in 1834 revealed the disquiet
of workingmen over the undermining of their moral independence by the new methods of manufacture and the
new practices of employers.

Tocqueville, viewing these anxieties in his lofty, philo-
sophic manner, assumed that uncertainties of esteem are

inevitable in a democratic society. The laws of honor in such a society are "less numerous, less precise, and . . . less vigorously obeyed" than in a feudal society. Michel Chevalier on the other hand, was more empirical and concrete in his observations. He emphasized the explosive character of the underlying tensions that had multiplied in the Jacksonian generation when he characterized the growing frequency of riots and other forms of mob violence in the 1830s as "symptoms of revolution." Clearly the age of egalitarianism was generating psychic and social conflicts of greater intensity than any since the American Revolution; and not even then had the systems of social esteem and the forms of social power been so unhinged.

IV

In a time of dynamic economic growth and of rapid shifts in the standards by which one part of society may be judged and tested by another, the relations of social power move toward new centers of focus. In the Jacksonian era, power seems to become more diffuse and abstract but, on closer examination, it appears also to be flowing into new channels of organization. Tocqueville developed the classic formulation of the diffuseness and abstractness of power in his conception of the "unlimited power of the majority." In his analysis, not only did the omnipotence of the majority include the making and the execution of laws, but the moral power of the majority also extended to the creation of public opinion. "As long as the majority is still undecided," Tocqueville declared, "discussion is carried on: but as soon as its decision is irrevocably pronounced, everyone is silent." Hence Tocqueville felt justified in concluding that the social power of the majority in America is *unlimited*: "When an individual or a party is wronged in the United States, to whom can he apply for redress? If to public opinion, public opinion constitutes the majority; if to the legislative, it represents the majority and implicitly obeys it; if to the executive power, it is appointed by the majority and serves as a passive tool in its hands. The public force consists of the majority under arms; the jury is the majority invested with the right of hearing judicial cases; and in certain states even the judges are elected by the majority."[8]

Tocqueville's concept of the unlimited power of the majority demonstrates a clear grasp of the significance of universal suffrage and the use of elective procedures in almost all areas of decision making in Jacksonian America. But the concept is too abstract; it is more useful for an understanding of the theory or, perhaps, the mythology of democracy in America than for the understanding of the actualities of the political process. A more concrete analysis of the uses of power is necessary if we are to understand the new relations of power in the age of Jackson.

When we reflect upon the political events of the Jacksonian era, it becomes clear that the uses of majority power were changing in character. In the early decades of the American republic, power was fractionated; decision making was largely decentralized and the governments of the states directed most of the affairs of society in America outside of the sphere of foreign policy. In the Jacksonian decade, however, the power of the majority was nationalized, its center of gravity began to shift from the state capitols to the national capitol, and its dynamism began to be expressed in executive power more than in legislative power.

No historical explanation of the new relations of power in the second quarter of the nineteenth century can be adequate unless it gives a central place to the role of Andrew Jackson. Unquestionably, Andrew Jackson had a charismatic appeal that was equaled by few other presidents in our history. He was a powerful symbol for his generation. The popular image of Old Hero as a man of iron will, a self-made man, and a man of untutored, natural genius made him a legendary figure even before he

[8] Alexis de Tocqueville, *Democracy in America*, Francis Bowen, ed. (Cambridge, Massachusetts, 1863), I, 332.

attained the powers of the presidency.[9] Jackson was a symbolic mirror of the ideals that composed the American consensus at the time.

Some of the more perceptive of President Jackson's contemporaries were fully aware of the symbolic power possessed by "Old Hero." William Holland, the campaign biographer of Martin Van Buren, emphasized the strong intuitive bond that existed between Andrew Jackson and the plain farmers and mechanics of America. Francis Grund, in his *Aristocracy in America,* concluded that Jackson was endowed with that peculiar genius of character, "a pure gift of Heaven," which belongs only to the great leaders of history.

Yet we cannot understand the nature of Jackson's leadership if we think of him as a passive receptacle for the symbolic values of the age. Jackson's power as a democratic leader must also be explained by reference to his actions in the presidency. By word and by deed, Jackson transformed the presidency and laid the foundations for the future expansion of executive power in the American political system. He extended the use of the veto power to include differences of opinion with Congress over the expediency of legislation. He developed the use of the removal power beyond anything that his predecessors had ever attempted. He articulated a theory of the presidency which asserted that the President was more directly representative of the American people than any member of Congress and that the President possessed a knowledge of the majority will superior to that of the elected representatives of both houses of Congress.

President Jackson's new uses of power enabled him to dramatize important social goals and values to a degree that no previous President had been able to do. His attack on South Carolina's ordinance of nullification made it possible for him to act out the theme that the symbol of the Union was superior to the symbol of State rights. His war

[9] See John William Ward, *Andrew Jackson, Symbol for an Age* (New York, 1955), for a full analysis of Jackson as a symbol for Americans in the early nineteenth century.

on the bank gave dramatic power to an image of conflict in which the honest farmer, the honest mechanic, and the honest capitalist were ranged against the speculators, the monopolists, and the seekers after economic privilege. Ineffective as many of his monetary policies were, Jackson's rhetoric and actions defined the terms, for his own day, of the great public dialogue which is so necessary for the democratic process in any day and age.

To be sure, Jackson could not have used executive power so successfully without the organized support of the masses of the people. The new techniques of organizing a mass electorate had already developed in some states, notably in New York, before Jackson came to the presidency. But, before the 1830s, national party organizations were still loose coalitions of various forms of state party organizations. Jackson, however, succeeded in nationalizing the new techniques of mass politics. By his use of patronage and by his manipulation of the party press, he was able to create a pattern of effective central party leadership. Factions in state organizations sought to strengthen themselves by obtaining presidential support. Jackson, as no President before him had done, asserted the fullness of the party principle. "I have labored," he wrote in 1835, "to reconstruct this great party and to bring the popular power to bear with full influence upon the government by securing its permanent ascendancy."[10]

There is a new degree of party discipline and a firmness of purpose in the Jackson party of the 1830s. We find a basic similarity of rhetoric whether the speaker is Jackson, Thomas Hart Benton in the Senate, Chief Justice Taney in the Supreme Court, or William Leggett in the editorial columns of a leading Democratic newspaper in New York. By the end of Jackson's administration all of the agencies of government, national and local, which the party organization controlled were enlisted in the ceaseless struggle against all forms of economic privilege in American life.

The new techniques of party leadership employed by

[10] As quoted in Leonard D. White, *The Jacksonians, a Study in Administrative History, 1829–1861* (New York, 1954), p. 14.

Andrew Jackson hastened the transformation of the party spirit in America. The manipulative skills of mass politics became the necessary requirement for political success in the 1830s. We can see how the arts of the demagogue became an accepted part of popular mythology as Americans chuckled over Davy Crockett's stories of his political cunning. In short, there is considerable truth in the rueful comment of the *Democratic Review* concerning the "Log Cabin and Hard Cider" campaign of 1840 conducted by the Whigs—"We have taught them how to conquer us."

v

Although the Jacksonian Democrats were more successful than the Whigs in winning elections, they were less successful in creating an ideology which could provide Americans with an adequate means of adjusting to the changing economic and social realities. There is much to be said for Marvin Meyers' assertion that the Jacksonians addressed themselves to the fears and resentments of their generation while the Whigs spoke to the explicit hopes of Americans.[11] An interpretation of experience which is based largely upon fears and resentments can easily lead to assumptions whose function is to conceal the meaning of reality rather than to reveal it.

The assertion that the Jacksonians spoke to the fears of their generation should not be pressed too far, however. There was a positive and optimistic side to the Jacksonian mental structure. In particular, the Jacksonians went much further than their Jeffersonian predecessors had been willing to go in their expressions of faith in the wisdom of the common man. Jefferson, at least, had still believed in the desirability of a natural aristocracy of merit and talent for a healthy republican society. Yet, even a talented Jacksonian writer like George Bancroft, trained at Harvard and Göttingen, could say with a tone of comfort and assurance, "It is hard for the pride of cultivated philosophy

[11] Meyers, *The Jacksonian Persuasion* (New York: Alfred A. Knopf, Inc., Vintage Books, 1960), p. 13.

to put its ear to the ground, and listen reverently to the voice of lowly humanity; yet the people collectively are wiser than the most gifted individual, for all his wisdom constitutes but a part of theirs." The same note of optimism pervades the fervent defense of majority rule which forms an essential part of the codification of democratic principles in the editorials of the *Democratic Review*.

There was much in this aspect of Jacksonian ideology which correctly interpreted the meaning of a broadened suffrage and an entrepreneurial struggle that was sweeping away the aristocratic pretensions of many of the older families whose scions had controlled political and social leadership throughout the Federalist and Jeffersonian eras. Yet there was also an excess of sentimentality in the typical Jacksonian utterances about the people and public opinion. There was little or no effort to codify the new lessons of experience in party organization or in the techniques of popular communication. Jackson revealed his grasp of these new realities only in his private correspondence, and anyone who looks hopefully to Martin Van Buren's *Inquiry into the Origin and Course of Political Parties in the United States* quickly discovers an astonishingly inchoate performance.

Even more important was the inability of the Jacksonians to develop a new interpretation of experience that was applicable to changing economic realities. The Jacksonian conception of a good society harked back to the comfortable values of an older and simpler society—one in which economic dealings were based on the virtues of personal character and in which the gathering of wealth was a prudent and gradual process. The Jacksonians did not seem able to accept very readily the new instrumentalities that provided for rapid capital formation in a period of quickening economic growth. Even when Jacksonian writers like Leggett endorsed a general law of incorporation, they seemed to imagine small, highly personalized "copartnerships" as the likely units of enterprise which would function in an economy that continued to operate on the basis of the virtues of personal character and the beneficent action of "natural law." Similarly, the radical rhetoric of Orestes Brownson seemed to point to little more than a restoration of an equality of opportunity by means of the abolition of laws of inheritance.

The Whigs, on the other hand, were more successful in creating a party ideology that was applicable to the changing social conditions of the Jacksonian era. To be sure there was a quotient of dread in the Whig mentality. The memory of a succession of humiliating political defeats at the hands of "King Andrew" was an ineradicable trauma in the Whig psyche. Hence, Henry Clay was willing to try to cure "executive usurpation" by emasculating the presidency, even though there was much in the Whig program of governmental support for rapid economic growth through tariffs and internal improvements that might need the initiative and energy of a strong executive. And when William Henry Harrison was swept into the presidency in 1840 by a landslide of popular voting and a tidal wave of popular symbol making, he willingly announced the unconditional surrender of the executive office to the legislative branch of the national government.

Yet this curious aberrancy in the Whig ideology was overshadowed by the striking success of the Whigs in fusing the new values of mass politics with the entrepreneurial values of the self-made man. This interesting marriage between democracy and capitalism was explicitly developed in the "Junius Tracts" of Calvin Colton. Where else in the literature of the Jacksonian era can we find a statement which sensed the spirit of the age as well as Calvin Colton's when he said:

> Ours is a country, where men start from an humble origin, and from small beginnings rise gradually in the world, as the reward of merit and industry, and where they can attain to the most elevated positions, or acquire a large amount of wealth, according to the pursuits they elect for themselves. No exclusive privileges of birth, no entailment of estates, no civil or political disqualifications, stand in their path; but

one has as good a chance as another, according to his talents, prudence, and personal exertions. This is a country of *self-made men*, than which nothing better could be said of any state of society.

Moreover, Colton was ready to accept all of the accessories of a rising capitalist order in America; in his opinion, corporations, banks, insurance companies, railroad and coal companies were "well adapted to a democratic state of society."

If the ethical norms and the conceptions of life presented in Colton's essay seem more fully applicable to the emergent forms of behavior than the typical articulations of the Jacksonian Democrats, one wonders why the Whigs were not more successful in American politics. To be sure, party ideologies are only one type of variable in the American political process, and other variables may have influenced the results of elections more strongly. Even so, it may still be possible to say that there was something about the Jacksonian generation that made it reluctant to cast off too quickly the comfortable values of the agrarian past. Perhaps Americans in the Jacksonian era were still too close to the agrarian modes of social experience to feel the need for any considerable reconstruction of their ideology. Or, perhaps, the yearning for the comfortable values of a simpler past is merely the manifestation of a more universal mode of thought among civilized men everywhere as they seek to adjust to the inevitable discontents of civilization.

Edwin C. Rozwenc

Amherst College

Contents

PART II. THE UNCERTAINTIES OF STATUS

PART III. THE NEW USES OF POWER

PART IV. THE RECONSTRUCTION OF IDEOLOGIES

PART I

The Restless Pursuit of Wealth

The Progress of the United States in Population and Wealth*

GEORGE TUCKER

The early career of George Tucker was shaped in the institutions of Jefferson's Virginia. His talents as a lawyer, legislator, and writer of political and moral essays attracted the notice of Jefferson and Madison, the elder statesmen of Virginia, and he was appointed Professor of Moral Philosophy at the University of Virginia when it was first opened in 1825. In his later career, Tucker was a prolific writer of books on history and political economy. He wrote a life of Jefferson and a history of the United States; he also turned out a considerable number of books on economic subjects, generally following the teachings of the English classical economists. As a true follower of Adam Smith and Thomas Malthus, Tucker was keenly interested in the growth of population and wealth in the United States, and his *Progress of the United States in Population and Wealth*, first published in 1843, clearly establishes him as the outstanding demographer of the Jacksonian generation.

The following selections from his work contain his statistical observations concerning the growth of cities, the changing distribution of occupational groups, and the growth of the national product. Although his estimates of national wealth are based upon crude calculations, Tucker's book gives us important clues about the way in which the Jacksonian generation measured the changes in American society.

* From George Tucker, *Progress of the United States in Population and Wealth in Fifty Years as Exhibited by the Decennial Census from 1790 to 1840* (New York, 1855), pp. 127–29, 135–42, 169–210, abridged.

All generations since the development of governmental statistics carry demographic pictures in their minds and these often affect their views of present and future possibilities. Consequently, we must ask ourselves: What shall we assume about the response of the Jacksonian generation to the knowledge that their wealth was growing faster than their population; that the industrial occupations were exerting the stronger pull among all the classes of occupations in American society; that the population of cities over 10,000 was increasing at a rate faster than that of the general population? Did this knowledge arouse feelings of hope or fear? Or did it create the deep-seated tensions of ambivalence? Jefferson had once assumed that the countryside was the natural home of virtue and that the cities were the inevitable centers of vice and corruption. What, then, are we to make of Tucker's assertion that "cities afford a wider field both for virtue and vice; and they are more prone to innovation, whether for good or evil"?

[The Growth of Cities]

The proportion between the rural and town population of a country is an important fact in its interior economy and condition. It determines, in a great degree, its capacity for manufactures, the extent of its commerce, and the amount of its wealth. The growth of cities commonly marks the progress of intelligence and the arts, measures the sum of social enjoyment, and always implies increased mental activity, which is sometimes healthy and useful, sometimes distempered and pernicious. If these congregations of men diminish some of the comforts of life, they augment others: if they are less favourable to health than the country, they also provide better defences against disease, and better means of cure. From causes both physical and moral, they are less favourable to the multiplication of the species. In the eyes of the moralist, cities afford a wider field both for virtue and vice; and they are more prone to innovation, whether for good or evil. The love of civil liberty is, perhaps, both stronger and more constant in the country than the town; and if it is guarded in the cities by a keener vigilance and a more far-sighted jealousy, yet law, order, and security, are also, in them, more exposed to danger, from the greater facility with which intrigue and ambition can there operate on ignorance and want. Whatever may be the good or evil tendencies of populous cities, they are the result to which all countries, that are at once fertile, free, and intelligent, inevitably tend.

The following table shows the population of the towns in the United States, of 10,000 inhabitants and upwards, in 1820, 1830, and 1840; their decennial increase, and the present ratio of the town population, in each State, to its whole population:

TOWNS	STATES	POPULATION OF TOWNS IN			DECENNIAL INCREASE		Ratio of Town population per cent
		1820	1830	1840	1830	1840	
Portland........	Maine	8,581	12,601	 15,218	63.9	20.8	3.
Boston..........	Massachusetts	43,298	61,392	93,383	41.8	52.1	....
Lowell*	Massachusetts	....	6,474	20,796	....	221.2	....
Salem	Massachusetts	11,346	13,836	15,082	21.9	9.1	....
New Bedford..	Massachusetts	3,947	7,592	12,087	92.3	59.2	....
Charlestown ..	Massachusetts	6,591	8,783	11,484	33.3	30.7	....
Springfield	Massachusetts	3,914	6,784	10,985	73.3	61.9	22.2
				163,817			
Providence....	Rhode Island..	11,767	16,833	 23,171	43.1	37.7	21.3
New Haven	Connecticut....	7,147	10,180	 12,960	63.8	44.7	4.18
New York......	New York......	123,706	202,589	312,710	114.6	135.3	....
Brooklyn	New York......	7,175	15,396	36,233	91.9	39.1	....
Albany	New York......	12,630	24,238	33,721	92.3	....	....
Rochester	New York......	1,767	9,207	20,191	421.	119.	....
Troy	New York......	5,264	11,405	19,334	116.6	69.6	....
Buffalo	New York......	2,095	8,668	18,213	313.7	110.	....
Utica	New York......	2,972	10,183	12,782	242.6	25.5	18.6
				453,184			
Newark........	New Jersey....	6,507	10,953	 17,290	68.3	57.8	4.6
Philadelphia...	Pennsylvania..	119,325	161,427	205,580	36.1	25.6	....
Pittsburg & Alleghany	Pennsylvania..	10,000	18,000	31,204	80.	73.3	13.7
				237,054			
Baltimore......	Maryland	62,738	80,625	 102,313	28.5	26.8	21.7
Richmond......	Virginia	12,067	16,060	20,153	33.1	25.5	....
Petersburg....	Virginia	6,690	8,322	11,136	20.6	33.8	....
Norfolk.........	Virginia	8,478	9,816	10,920	18.4	11.2	3.4
				42,209			
Charleston	S. Carolina	24,780	30,289	.... †29,261	22.2	....	4.9
Savannah	Georgia	7,523	†7,423	 11,214	....	51.	1.8
Mobile	Alabama	1,500	3,914	 12,672	112.9	296.7	2.1
New-Orleans ..	Louisiana	27,118	46,082	 102,193	68.6	121.7	29.
Louisville	Kentucky......	4,012	10,196	 21,210	154.	108.	2.7
St. Louis	Missouri.......	4,123	6,694	 16,469	62.4	146.	4.3
Cincinnati	Ohio	9,642	24,831	 46,338	157.5	86.6	3.
Washington	Dist. of Col. ..	13,247	18,227	 23,364	40.8	28.2	....
31 Towns	16 States	570,010	878,300	 1,329,937	54.	51.3	7.79

* Lowell had no existence before 1822.

† The decline of population here indicated, was the effect of very destructive fires.

It appears, from the preceding table, that the population in all the towns of the United States, containing 10,000 inhabitants and upwards, is something more than one-thirteenth (10/123) of the whole number; that ten of the States, whose united population exceeds 4,000,000, have, as yet, no town of that rank; and that, in the other sixteen States, the ratio of their town population to their whole population, varies from something less than one-third, to less than a sixteenth part. It further appears, that the increase of those towns has been nearly the same, from 1830 to 1840, as from 1820 to 1830; and that, in both decennial periods, it exceeds that of the whole population, nearly as 50 to 32. . . .

[THE DISTRIBUTION OF THE INDUSTRIOUS CLASSES]

In 1820, for the first time, the census took an account of the number of persons who were severally employed in agriculture, commerce, and manufactures. In the succeeding census, no notice was taken of the occupations of the people; but that of 1840 gave a fuller enumeration of the industrious classes, distinguishing them under the several heads of mining, agriculture, commerce, manufactures, navigating the ocean, internal navigation, and the learned professions. The result of each census may be seen in the tables on the facing page.

. . . Whilst all civilized countries are so much alike as to the amount of labour put in requisition to satisfy human wants, they differ very greatly as to the distribution of that labour among the three principal branches of industry; and the difference is very great in this respect, not only between the several States, but in the whole United States, in 1820 and 1840. It is seen by Table I that the proportion of labour employed in agriculture and commerce had diminished; while that employed in manufactures had, in twenty years, increased from 13.7 per cent to 17.1 per cent of the whole. The positive increase in

TABLE I. Comparative view of the number of persons employed in Agriculture, Commerce, and Manufactures, in the five great divisions of the United States, in 1820 and 1840, and the relative proportions of each class.

GEOGRAPHICAL DIVISIONS		Number of persons employed in			Total	Centesimal proportions		
		Agriculture	Commerce	Manufactures		Agriculture	Commerce	Manufactures
New England S..	1820	283,903	24,184	81,922	391,010	72.8	6.2	21.
	1840	414,138	17,757	187,258	619,153	66.7	2.9	30.2
Middle States....	1820	522,508	23,842	159,839	706,189	74.	3.4	22.6
	1840	808,633	50,077	333,947	1,192,657	67.8	4.2	28.
Southern States.	1820	718,510	11,883	54,484	784,877	91.6	1.5	6.9
	1840	955,729	12,962	87,955	1,056,646	90.5	1.2	8.3
Southwestern S.	1820	212,148	7,958	16,142	236,248	89.8	3.4	6.8
	1840	650,546	14,496	37,899	702,941	92.5	2.1	5.4
Northwestern S.	1820	332,577	4,625	37,119	364,321	88.5	1.3	10.2
	1840	890,905	22,315	144,690	1,057,910	84.2	2.2	13.6
Total U. States...	1820	2,070,646	72,493	349,506	2,483,645	83.4	2.9	13.7
	1840	3,719,951	117,607	791,749	4,629,307	80.4	2.5	17.1

TABLE II. Showing the proportions in which the several industrious classes of the Union, according to the census of 1840, are distributed among its great geographical divisions.

GEOGRAPHICAL DIVISIONS	Per centage of persons employed in							Total
	Mining	Agriculture	Commerce	Manufactures	Navigating the Ocean	Internal navigation	Learned professions	
New England States......	5.3	11.1	15.1	23.6	75.3	5.8	16.9	14.1
Middle States	46.7	21.7	42.6	42.2	17.3	53.2	37.6	26.1
Southern States	21.1	24.8	11.	11.1	3.5	5.6	12.1	22.3
Southwestern States	1.6	18.5	12.3	4.8	3.	12.5	9.8	14.9
Northwestern States	25.3	23.9	19.	18.3	.9	22.9	23.6	22.6
	100.	100.	100.	100.	100.	100.	100.	100.

TABLE III. Showing the ratio which the number of persons in the several industrious classes of each great geographical division of the States bears to the whole population of such division, according to the census of 1840.

GEOGRAPHICAL DIVISIONS	Number of persons employed in							Whole laboring class as 1 to
	Mining as 1 to	Agriculture as 1 to	Commerce as 1 to	Manufactures as 1 to	Navigating the Ocean as 1 to	Internal navigation as 1 to	Learned professions as 1 to	
New England States ..	2755	5.4	126	12.	53	1161	202	3.31
Middle States	723	6.3	102	15.3	528	291	209	4.08
Southern States........	1038	3.5	257	37.9	1677	802	422	3.01
Southwestern States..	8806	3.4	155	56.6	1345	1206	351	3.14
Northwestern States .	1075	4.6	185	28.5	8336	546	267	3.8
	1122	4.58	145	21.5	304	516	261	3.55

that time was from 349,506 persons employed in 1820, to 791,749 employed in 1840.

This increase was greatest in the New England States, whose manufacturing population had enlarged from 21 per cent, in 1820, to 30.2 per cent in 1840; in which time the same class of population had nearly trebled in Massachusetts, and more than trebled in Rhode Island. In the Southwestern States, alone, the proportion of the agricultural class had increased; in all the others it had diminished. In the Middle and Northwestern States, the proportion employed in commerce experienced a small increase. In several of the States, not only was the proportion less in 1840 than it had been in 1820, but the number of persons actually employed in commerce was less. This was the case in Maine, Massachusetts, Connecticut, Maryland, and to a smaller extent, in Delaware, North Carolina, and South Carolina. Is this falling off to be attributed solely to the loss of our legitimate share of the West India trade since 1830, or, in part, also, to some difference in the mode of taking the census, by which a portion of the seamen, who, in 1840, were separately numbered, were, in 1820, reckoned among the persons employed in commerce? The first cause seems quite adequate to the effect produced.

If we suppose that the whole labour of Great Britain is distributed among the several departments of industry in the same proportions as the labour of the males above twenty years of age, the difference of distribution in that country and this is very striking. In that country, agricultural labour is but 31.5 per cent of the whole; here, it is 77.5 per cent. In that country, manufactures and trade employ 28.8 per cent of the whole labour; here, they employ but 18.9 per cent. Each country employs its industry in that way which is most profitable, and best suited to its circumstances.

Table II shows how the different departments of productive industry are distributed among the five great divisions of the States, in centesimal proportions. Two-thirds of the mining labour is in the Middle and Southern States. The Southern States stand foremost in agricultural labour, though they hold but the third rank in population. The Middle States employ the least labour in agriculture, in proportion to their numbers. In commerce, however, they employ the most, and next to them, the New England States. The same two divisions take the lead in manufactures, they contributing nearly two-thirds of the labour employed in this branch of industry. Three-fourths of the seamen are furnished by New England, of which nine-tenths belong to Massachusetts and Maine. More than half the labour employed in inland navigation is in the Middle States, and, next to them, are the Northwestern States.

Of that department in industry which comprehends the learned professions, and which is at once the best fruit of civilization, and the most powerful agent of its further advancement, the New England and Middle States have the largest proportion, though there is less diversity in this than in any other class of industry.

Of the individual States, New York, Pennsylvania, and Virginia employ the greatest number in mining; in agriculture, New York, Virginia, and Ohio; in commerce, New York, Pennsylvania, Louisiana, and Massachusetts; in ocean navigation, next to Massachusetts and Maine, but far behind, is New York; in internal navigation, New York, Pennsylvania, Ohio, and Virginia furnish 20,000 out of the 30,000 employed.

In Table III we see the various ratios which the persons employed in the several branches of industry bear to the whole population in the several divisions of the States. According to this table, without regarding local diversities, and taking the whole United States together, the great classes of occupation range themselves in the following order, viz:

Persons employed in agriculture,	1 out of	4½
Persons employed in manufactures,	1 out of	21½
Persons employed in commerce,	1 out of	145
Persons employed in the learned professions,	1 out of	261
Persons employed in navigating the ocean,	1 out of	304
Persons employed in internal navigation,	1 out of	516
Persons employed in mining,	1 out of	1122

Taking all the employments together, the number engaged is 355 out of every 1,000 of the whole population; which implies, on the grounds already stated, that there can be but a very small proportion of males who are not occupied in some mode of profitable industry. . . .

[The Increase of Wealth]

The census of 1840 has thus given us a mass of materials for estimating the annual income of the United States, which has been rarely if ever, afforded to seventeen millions of people. Yet, with all this valuable aid, precise accuracy is still unattainable; for those diversities and fluctuations of price, from which no country is exempt, are particularly great in this country. Articles of raw produce, which vary in price, from year to year, far more than manufactures, constitute here the unusually large proportion of more than two-thirds of the whole annual product. In a country, moreover, of such large extent as the United States, differing so widely in soil, climate, density of numbers, and easy access to market, the price of the same commodity varies considerably among the different States in the same year. Nay, more—with the larger States, the same local diversities apply to different parts of the same State, and often make the price of the more bulky commodities, at one place of production, more than twice as high as the price they bear at another. To make, then, a fair average, it is necessary to take into account the quantities produced in the several parts, as well as the difference of price. There are also sources of revenue, in which the census has not given the annual product, but the whole value of the capital invested, as in the case of live stock, and of the capitals employed in commerce; in which items, there being room for further difference of opinion, there is a further source of uncertainty. Even in those manufactures of which the census has determined their gross values, we may expect, in deducting the value of the raw materials which have been estimated under other heads, somewhat of the same difference of opinion, and the same uncertainty. The most careful estimate practicable must therefore rest, in part, on conjecture and probability. Yet, if the estimate be cautiously made, and be founded on the opinion of judicious persons, who look not beyond their own experience and observation, the unavoidable errors will probably so balance and compensate each other, that the result will afford an approximation to the truth, which is all that the subject admits of, and, indeed, all that it is important for us to know. . . .

Summary of the Annual Products of Industry in the several States, with the proportional amount to each individual of the whole of the free population in each State.

STATES AND TERRITORIES	VALUE OF ANNUAL PRODUCTS FROM							PROP. TO EACH PERSON	
	Agriculture	Manufactures	Commerce	Mining	Forest	Fisheries	Total	Whole pop.	Free pop.
	Dollars	Dollars	Dollars	Dollars	Dollars	Dollars	Dollars	Dollars	Dollars
Maine.........	15,856,270	5,615,303	1,505,380	327,376	1,877,663	1,280,713	26,462,705	52	52
N. Hamp....	11,377,752	6,545,811	1,001,533	88,373	449,861	92,811	19,556,141	68	68
Vermont....	17,879,155	5,685,425	758,899	389,488	430,224		25,143,191	85	85
Mass.	16,065,627	43,518,057	7,004,691	2,020,572	377,354	6,483,996	75,470,297	103	102
R. Island....	2,199,309	8,640,626	1,294,956	162,410	44,610	659,312	13,001,223	110	119
Connecticut.	11,371,776	12,778,963	1,963,281	820,419	181,575	907,723	28,023,737	90	90
N. Eng. S. ..	74,749,889	82,784,185	13,528,740	3,808,638	3,361,287	9,424,555	187,657,294	84	84
N. York....	106,275,281	47,454,514	24,311,715	7,408,070	5,040,781	1,316,072	193,806,433	79	79
N. Jersey...	16,209,853	10,696,257	1,206,929	1,073,921	361,326	124,140	29,672,426	79	79
Pennsylvania	68,180,924	33,354,279	10,593,368	17,666,146	1,203,578	35,360	131,033,655	76	76
Delaware ...	3,198,440	1,538,879	266,257	54,555	13,119	181,285	5,252,535	67	70
Maryland....	17,586,720	6,212,677	3,499,087	1,056,210	241,194	225,773	28,821,661	61	76
D. of Col. ...	176,942	904,526	802,725			87,400	1,971,593	45	50
Middle S. ...	213,628,160	100,161,132	40,680,081	27,258,902	6,859,998	1,970,030	390,558,303	76	77
Virginia	59,085,821	8,349,218	5,299,451	3,321,629	617,760	95,173	76,769,053	62	97
N. Carolina..	26,975,831	2,053,697	1,322,284	372,486	1,446,108	251,792	32,422,198	44	63
S. Carolina..	21,553,691	2,248,915	2,632,421	187,608	.549,626	1,275	27,173,536	45	101
Georgia	31,466,271	1,953,950	2,248,488	191,631	117,439	584	35,980,363	52	87
Florida	1,834,237	434,544	464,637	2,700	27,350	213,219	2,976,687	54	103
Southern S...	140,917,851	15,040,324	11,967,281	4,076,054	2,758,283	562,043	175,321,836	52	87
Alabama	24,696,513	1,732,770	2,273,267	81,310	177,465		28,961,325	49	103
Mississippi..	26,494,565	1,585,790	1,453,686		205,297		29,739,338	79	164
Louisiana...	22,851,375	4,087,655	7,868,898	165,280	71,751		35,044,959	99	189
Arkansas....	5,086,757	1,145,309	420,635	18,225	217,469		6,888,395	70	88
Tennessee...	31,660,180	2,477,193	2,239,478	1,371,331	225,179		37,973,360	45	58
S'western S..	110,789,390	11,028,717	14,255,964	1,636,146	897,161		138,607,378	61	97
Missouri	10,484,263	2,360,708	2,349,245	187,669	448,559		15,830,444	41	48
Kentucky ...	29,226,545	5,092,353	2,580,575	1,539,919	184,799		38,624,191	49	64
Ohio	37,802,001	14,588,091	8,050,316	2,442,682	1,013,063	10,525	63,906,678	42	42
Indiana	17,247,743	3,676,705	1,868,155	660,836	80,000	1,192	23,532,631	34	34
Illinois	13,701,466	3,243,981	1,493,425	293,272	249,841		18,981,965	39	39
Michigan....	4,502,889	1,376,249	622,822	56,790	467,540		7,026,390	33	33
Wisconsin...	568,105	304,692	189,957	384,603	430,580	27,663	1,905,600	47	47
Iowa	769,295	179,087	136,525	13,250	83,949		1,132,106	27	27
N'western S.	114,302,307	30,821,866	17,289,090	5,579,011	2,958,331	39,380	170,989,925	41	44
Total......	654,387,597	239,836,224	79,721,086	42,358,761	16,835,060	11,996,008	1,063,134,736	62	73

If we distribute the whole annual product in 1840—1,063 millions of dollars—among the whole population, we find that the proportion to each inhabitant is greatest in the New England States, where it is $84; in the Middle States, it is $76; in the Southern, $52; in the Southwestern, $61; and in the Northwestern, $41. The causes of this diversity are to be found yet more in the different densities of population, different degrees of fertility, and different distances from market, than in the existence or absence of slavery, though that also has its influence. It is the difference of distance from market which makes the industry of an individual in the Southwestern States 50 per cent greater than in the Northwestern. It is the difference of fertility which makes the same industry worth $79 in Mississippi, and but $49 in Alabama. The same cause makes the industry of the Southwestern States more productive than that of the Southern States. It is the greater density of numbers in Massachusetts and Rhode Island, and their consequent success in manufactures, which makes industry more productive in those States than it is in New York and Pennsylvania. In the two former, the proportion to an individual is greater than in any other State. In Rhode Island, it is $110, and in Massachusetts, $103. The annual product from manufactures in Rhode Island is very nearly four times that derived from her agriculture.

If we distribute the annual product among the free population exclusively, then the proportion to each individual will be greater in the slaveholding than in the free States, for in several of them the proportion will then be more than doubled. Thus, in South Carolina, it will be raised from $45 to $101; in Mississippi, from $79 to $164; and in Louisiana, from $99 to $189; then the highest proportion in the Union. . . .

Having ascertained the amount of the national income, it would on many accounts be desirable to ascertain also its ratio of increase, and more especially whether it increases at the same rate as the population or at a different rate.

There are obvious reasons why the wealth of an industrious and prosperous community should increase faster than its population. Every year adds to its stock of labour-saving tools and machinery, as well as improves their usefulness. Lands, too, are made more productive by draining, ditching, manuring, and better modes of culture. Both science and practical art are constantly enlarging the quantity of manufactured commodities, and yet more improving their quality. By means of cheaper and quicker modes of transportation, much of that labour which, in every country is expended, not in producing, but in transferring products from place to place, is saved and rendered directly productive: and lastly, the small excess of annual income over annual expense is constantly adding to the mass of capital, which is so efficient an agent of production.

But we must bear in mind that so far as this improvement in the sources of wealth are shared by the whole civilized world, it is not manifested in pecuniary estimates of annual products, supposing the value of the precious metals to be unchanged, since the same portion of them will be constantly representing a greater and greater amount of what is useful and convenient to man. It is only where the increase of wealth of a country is faster or slower than the average that it will be shown in the money value of its annual products compared with its population. It is, then, the relative and not the positive increase of wealth in the United States which we propose to consider.

Had each preceding census furnished the information afforded by the census of 1840, this question had been of easy solution. But this not being the case, we are left to infer the progress of national wealth from such partial indications of it as we are able to derive from other statistical facts. . . .

The result of [all] . . . comparisons may be seen in the following summary:

Decennial increase of land, 10 States,	68%. Of pop.	30.80%
Decennial increase of land, Virginia,	31%. Of pop.	7.00%
Decennial increase of land, New York,	27%. Of pop.	37.00%
Decennial increase of imports, 50 years,	47%. Of pop.	33.50%
Decennial increase of exports, 50 years,	51%. Of pop.	33.33%
Decennial increase of imports, 20 years,	33%. Of pop.	33.33%
Decennial increase of exports, 20 years,	33%. Of pop.	33.33%
Decennial increase of imports of tea,	61%. Of pop.	33.33%
Decennial increase of imports of coffee,	81%. Of pop.	33.33%
Decennial increase of imports of wine,	46%. Of pop.	33.33%
Decennial increase of manufactures,	46%. Of pop.	33.33%
Decennial increase of specie,	82%. Of pop.	33.33%
[Ratio of capital and wealth to population]		
	601	371.94

Which shows the decennial increase of capital and wealth to have been to that of population as 601 to 371.94 or nearly as 50 to 31; and supposing the decennial increase of population to have averaged 33⅓ per cent, that of wealth has been 53 per cent.

See page 86 for description of Plates 1–8.

[1] Arcadian or Pastoral State. By Thomas Cole. Photograph by courtesy of The New-York Historical Society, New York City.

[2] *Consummation of Empire*. By Thomas Cole. Photograph by courtesy of The New-York Historical Society, New York City.

[3] Destruction of Empire. By Thomas Cole. Photograph by courtesy of The New-York Historical Society, New York City.

[4] *View of Meredith (New Hampshire).* Engraved by W. H. Bartlett.

[5] *East View of Lowell, Mass. Engraved by E. L. Barber.*

[6] *View of the City of Boston.* Engraver unknown.

[7] Lockport, Erie Canal. Engraved by W. H. Bartlett.

[8] *First of May in New York*. Engraver unknown. Courtesy of Forbes Library, Northampton, Massachusetts.

2

Agriculture, Mechanics, and Manufactures: On These Depends the Prosperity of Our Nation

Rensselaer Bentley was one of the energetic enterprisers who made the publication of new educational textbooks a flourishing activity in the Jacksonian era. Bentley was particularly notable for the copious use of illustrations and his books were sold under such titles as *The Pictorial Primer*, *The Pictorial Speller*, and *The Pictorial Reader*. He was also concerned to develop reading materials that were relevant to the new conditions of American economic development. His *Pictorial Reader* contained selections that explained the operations of various economic pursuits in American society—farming, mechanical labor, and manufactures. In Bentley's words, "The instruments used in various trades, and the articles manufactured, have been illustrated by accurate engravings with explanations, designed to produce a favorable impression on the minds of children. . . ."

The illustration that follows is the emblematic frontispiece for *The Pictorial Reader*. In this engraving, the Goddess of Liberty is pointing to a banner on which is inscribed "Agriculture, Mechanics, *and Manufactures*: on these Depends the Prosperity of our Nation." In this way, Bentley sought to impress upon the minds of school children in the Jacksonian age the value of the new combination of forces that composed the political economy of America.

From Rensselaer Bentley, *The Pictorial Reader:* Containing a Variety of Useful and Instructive Lessons upon Familiar Subjects. (New York, 1847).

3

What Causes Almost All Americans to Follow Industrial Callings*

ALEXIS DE TOCQUEVILLE

Alexis de Tocqueville's *Democracy in America* won instant recognition as a political treatise of the first order when the two volumes first appeared in 1835 and 1840. In America, the merits of the work were warmly debated by the Jacksonian generation and controversy about Tocqueville's judgments and methods has continued among historians and social scientists down to the present day. Nevertheless, Tocqueville's commentary has provided valuable insights to those seeking to interpret the Jacksonian period and, indeed, for many recent historians and sociologists, his work has become the touchstone for generalizations about the American character.

Because of the abstractness of many of Tocqueville's explanations of democracy, there are difficulties in using *Democracy in America* as a historical source, especially for a limited period like the Jacksonian years. Throughout the two volumes, a larger conceptual scheme of democracy drawn from a broader sweep of historical experience is elaborated in conjunction with the particular observations of American life made during Tocqueville's visit to America in 1831–32. Yet, it is usually possible for a perceptive reader to bring Tocqueville's abstractions and empirical observations into focus.

George Tucker's work on population and wealth provided us with statistical measures of the increase in industrial occupations between 1820 and 1840. Tocque-

* From Alexis de Tocqueville, *Democracy in America*, Francis Bowen, ed. (Cambridge, Massachusetts, 1863), II, 187–92, unabridged.

ville, on the other hand, is more concerned to explain why it is that Americans are so prone to pursue industrial and commercial callings. In an earlier chapter, Tocqueville noted "It is strange to see with what feverish ardor the Americans pursue their own welfare." This restless pursuit of worldly welfare, according to Tocqueville, finds its natural fulfillment in commercial and industrial occupations. In the chapter below, Tocqueville is trying to explain the cause of this pervasive behavior by "the equality of conditions" that exists in America.

Agriculture is, perhaps, of all the useful arts, that which improves most slowly amongst democratic nations. Frequently, indeed, it would seem to be stationary, because other arts are making rapid strides towards perfection. On the other hand, almost all the tastes and habits which the equality of condition produces naturally lead men to commercial and industrial occupations.

Suppose an active, enlightened, and free man, enjoying a competency, but full of desires: he is too poor to live in idleness; he is rich enough to feel himself protected from the immediate fear of want, and he thinks how he can better his condition. This man has conceived a taste for physical gratifications, which thousands of his fellowmen indulge in around him; he has himself begun to enjoy these pleasures, and he is eager to increase his means of satisfying these tastes more completely. But life is slipping away, time is urgent;—to what is he to turn? The cultivation of the ground promises an almost certain result to his exertions, but a slow one; men are not enriched by it without patience and toil. Agriculture is therefore only suited to those who have already large superfluous wealth, or to those whose penury bids them only seek a bare subsistence. The choice of such a man as we have supposed is soon made; he sells his plot of ground, leaves his dwelling, and embarks in some hazardous but lucrative calling.

Democratic communities abound in men of this kind;

and in proportion as the equality of conditions becomes greater, their multitude increases. Thus, democracy not only swells the number of working-men, but it leads men to prefer one kind of labor to another; and, whilst it diverts them from agriculture, it encourages their taste for commerce and manufactures.

This spirit may be observed even amongst the richest members of the community. In democratic countries, however opulent a man is supposed to be, he is almost always discontented with his fortune, because he finds that he is less rich than his father was, and he fears that his sons will be less rich than himself. Most rich men in democracies are therefore constantly haunted by the desire of obtaining wealth, and they naturally turn their attention to trade and manufactures, which appear to offer the readiest and most efficient means of success. In this respect, they share the instincts of the poor without feeling the same necessities; say, rather, they feel the most imperious of all necessities, that of not sinking in the world.

In aristocracies, the rich are at the same time the governing power. The attention which they unceasingly devote to important public affairs diverts them from the lesser cares which trade and manufactures demand. But if an individual happens to turn his attention to business, the will of the body to which he belongs will immediately prevent him from pursuing it; for, however men may declaim against the rule of numbers, they cannot wholly escape it; and even amongst those aristocratic bodies which most obstinately refuse to acknowledge the rights of the national majority, a private majority is formed which governs the rest.

In democratic countries, where money does not lead those who possess it to political power, but often removes them from it, the rich do not know how to spend their leisure. They are driven into active life by the inquietude and the greatness of their desires, by the extent of their resources, and by the taste for what is extraordinary, which is almost always felt by those who rise, by whatsoever means, above the crowd. Trade is the only road open to them. In democracies, nothing is more great or more brilliant than commerce: it attracts the attention of the public, and fills the imagination of the multitude; all energetic passions are directed towards it. Neither their own prejudices nor those of anybody else can prevent the rich from devoting themselves to it. The wealthy members of democracies never form a body which has manners and regulations of its own; the opinions peculiar to their class do not restrain them, and the common opinions of their country urge them on. Moreover, as all the large fortunes which are found in a democratic community are of commercial growth, many generations must succeed each other before their possessors can have entirely laid aside their habits of business.

Circumscribed within the narrow space which politics leave them, rich men in democracies eagerly embark in commercial enterprise: there they can extend and employ their natural advantages; and indeed, it is even by the boldness and the magnitude of their industrial speculations that we may measure the slight esteem in which productive industry would have been held by them, if they had been born amidst an aristocracy.

A similar observation is likewise applicable to all men living in democracies, whether they be poor or rich. Those who live in the midst of democratic fluctuations have always before their eyes the image of chance; and they end by liking all undertakings in which chance plays a part. They are therefore all led to engage in commerce, not only for the sake of the profit it holds out to them, but for the love of the constant excitement occasioned by that pursuit.

The United States of America have only been emancipated for half a century from the state of colonial dependence in which they stood to Great Britain: the number of large fortunes there is small, and capital is still scarce. Yet no people in the world have made such rapid progress in trade and manufactures as the Americans: they constitute at the present day the second maritime nation in the world; and although their manufactures have to struggle with almost insurmountable natural impediments, they are not prevented from making great and daily advances.

In the United States, the greatest undertakings and speculations are executed without difficulty, because the whole population are engaged in productive industry, and because the poorest as well as the most opulent members of the commonwealth are ready to combine their efforts for these purposes. The consequence is, that a stranger is constantly amazed by the immense public works executed by a nation which contains, so to speak, no rich men. The Americans arrived but as yesterday on the territory which they inhabit, and they have already changed the whole order of nature for their own advantage. They have joined the Hudson to the Mississippi and made the Atlantic Ocean communicate with the Gulf of Mexico, across a continent of more than five hundred leagues in extent which separates the two seas. The longest railroads which have been constructed, up to the present time, are in America.

But what most astonishes me in the United States is not so much the marvellous grandeur of some undertakings, as the innumerable multitude of small ones. Almost all the farmers of the United States combine some trade with agriculture; most of them make agriculture itself a trade. It seldom happens that an American farmer settles for good upon the land which he occupies; especially in the districts of the Far West, he brings land into tillage in order to sell it again, and not to farm it: he builds a farm-house on the speculation, that, as the state of the country will soon be changed by the increase of population, a good price may be obtained for it.

Every year, a swarm of people from the North arrive in the Southern States, and settle in the parts where the cotton-plant and the sugar-cane grow. These men cultivate the soil in order to make it produce in a few years enough to enrich them; and they already look forward to the time when they may return home to enjoy the competency thus acquired. Thus the Americans carry their business-like qualities into agriculture; and their trading passions are displayed in that, as in their other pursuits.

The Americans make immense progress in productive industry, because they all devote themselves to it at once; and for this same reason, they are exposed to unexpected and formidable embarrassments. As they are all engaged in commerce, their commercial affairs are affected by such various and complex causes, that it is impossible to foresee what difficulties may arise. As they are all more or less engaged in productive industry, at the least shock given to business, all private fortunes are put in jeopardy at the same time, and the state is shaken. I believe that the return of these commercial panics is an endemic disease of the democratic nations of our age. It may be rendered less dangerous, but it cannot be cured; because it does not originate in accidental circumstances, but in the temperament of these nations.

4

Speculations in Land, Railroads, and Banks*

MICHEL CHEVALIER

Michel Chevalier was in the United States for two years, from 1833 to 1835. He was sent to America by the French government to inquire into the construction of canals and railroads and, like Alexis de Tocqueville, he used the occasion for developing a broader analysis of American society. His *Lettres sur l'Amerique du Nord,* first printed in France in 1836, was published in Boston three years later in an English translation under the title, *Society, Manners, and Politics in the United States; Being a Series of Letters on North America.*

We could get at most of the essential characteristics of American society in the age of Jackson if we proceeded with nothing more than the books of Tocqueville and Chevalier in either hand. Indeed, Chevalier's book is the necessary complement to Tocqueville's *Democracy in America.* While Tocqueville is usually philosophical and abstract, Chevalier is nearly always concrete and descriptive. To be sure, Chevalier has certain ruling conceptions in his analysis that are derived from the Saint-Simonian movement in France, but these are always developed through an empirical style of reporting. Moreover, the Saint-Simonian influence has obviously prepared Chevalier for the sharper and more specific conceptions of economic organization and social power which are so strikingly evident in his writing.

The chapter on "Speculations," which follows, extends Tocqueville's observations about the restless pur-

* From Michael Chevalier, *Society, Manners, and Politics in the United States,* John W. Ward, ed. (Garden City, New York: Doubleday & Co., Inc., Anchor Books, 1961), pp. 295–302, abridged.

suit of wealth by Americans. Chevalier helps us to see that much of this feverish social energy in the 1830's is being specifically directed toward speculations in railroads and banks and toward land speculations associated with the growth of cities—not only older cities like New York and New Orleans, but also burgeoning new cities, like Chicago, in the inland wilderness. Can we not say that there is much in Chevalier's description to remind us that the American economy in the Jacksonian decade was entering what W. W. Rostow has called the "take-off" period of economic growth? This is to be seen not only in the transportation boom, but more particularly, as Chevalier's chapter suggests, in the emergence of a social framework that exploits the impulses to expansion and gives to the economy a dynamic, on-going character.

. . . Everybody is speculating and everything has become an immense *rue Quincampoix*. Thus far everyone has made money, as is always the case when speculation is in the ascendant. Since with money it is easy come, easy go, spending is enormously increased and Lyons feels the effect.

I said that everything has become an object of speculation; I was mistaken. The American, essentially practical in his views, will never speculate in tulips, even at New York although the inhabitants of that city have Dutch blood in their veins. The principal objects of speculation are those subjects which chiefly occupy the calculating minds of the Americans, that is to say, cotton, land, city and town lots, banks, railroads.

The lovers of land in the North contest with each other for valuable timberlands; in the deep South, for Mississippi swamps and Alabama and Red River cotton lands; in the far West, for the cornfields and pastures of Illinois and Michigan. The unparalleled growth of some new towns has turned people's heads and there is a general rush to any location which is fortunately situated; as if, before ten years, three or four Londons, as many Parises, and a dozen Liverpools were about to display their streets, their monuments, their quays crowded with warehouses, and their harbors bristling with masts in the American wilderness. In New York enough building lots (a lot is generally from 22 to 25 feet front, and from 80 to 100 feet deep) have been sold for a population of two million; at New Orleans, for at least a million. Pestilential marshes and naked precipices of rock have been bought and sold as places to build. In Louisiana, the quagmires, the bottomless haunts of alligators, the lakes and cypress swamps, with ten feet of water or slime, and in the North, the bed of the Hudson with twenty, thirty, or fifty feet of water, have found numerous purchasers.

Take the map of the United States; place yourself on the shore of Lake Erie, which twenty years ago was a solitary wilderness; ascend it to its head; pass thence to Lake St. Clair and from that lake push on toward the north, across Lake Huron; go forward still, thread your way through Lake Michigan and advance southward till the water fails you; here you will find a little town by the name of Chicago, one of the outposts of our indefatigable countrymen when they had possession of America. Chicago seems destined at some future period to enjoy an extensive trade; it will occupy the head of a canal which will connect the Mississippi with the Lakes and the St. Lawrence; but at present it hardly numbers two or three thousand inhabitants. Chicago has behind it a country of amazing fertility; but this country is yet an uncultivated wilderness. Nevertheless the land for twenty-five miles around has been sold, resold and sold again in small sections, not, however, at Chicago, but at New York which by the route actually traveled is two thousand miles away. There you may find plans of enough Chicago lots for three hundred thousand inhabitants; this is more than any city of the New World at present contains. Surely, more than one buyer will count himself fortunate if, on examination, he finds no more than six feet of water on his purchase.

Speculations in railroads have been hardly less wild than those in land. The American has a perfect passion for railroads; he loves them, to use Camille Desmoulins' expression in reference to Mirabeau, as a lover loves his mistress. It is not merely because his supreme happiness consists in that speed which annihilates time and space; it is also because he sees, for the American always reasons, that this mode of communication is admirably adapted to the vast extent of his country, to its great maritime plain and to the level surface of the Mississippi valley, and because he sees all around him in the native forest abundant materials for executing these works at a cheap rate. This is the reason why railroads are multiplied in such profusion, competing not only with each other but entering into a rivalry with the rivers and canals. If the works now in process of construction are completed (and I think that they will be), there will be within two years three distinct routes between Philadelphia and Baltimore, exclusive of the old post route; namely, two lines consisting wholly of railroads, and a third consisting in part of steamboats and in part of railroad. The line that has the advantage of half an hour over its rivals will be sure to crush them.

The manner of establishing banks, universally adopted here (it is the same for all enterprises which affect the public welfare, even when they are handed over to private enterprise), is this: a legislative act authorizes the opening of books for public subscription of stock and all persons have the right to subscribe on payment of a certain sum, say five, ten, or twenty per cent on the amount of stock taken by them. The day the books are opened is a matter of great moment. In France, we queue up at the doors of the theaters; but in the United States, this year, lines of deeply anxious people form at the doors of those special places where the books for subscription to bank stocks are deposited. In Baltimore the books were opened for a new bank, the Merchants' Bank, with a capital of 2 million; the amount subscribed was nearly 50 million. At Charleston, for a bank of the same capital, 90 million was subscribed and, as the act in this instance required the advance of 25 per cent, the sum actually paid in, in paper money to be sure, but yet in current bills at par, amounted to 22½ million, or more than 11 times the capital required. This rage for bank stock is easily explained. Most of the banks here are, in fact, irresponsible establishments which have the privilege of coining money from paper. The shareholders, by means of a series of ingenious contrivances, realize 8, 9, 10, and 12 per cent interest on capital which they do not actually hold; and this in a country where the 5 per cents of Pennsylvania and New York and the 6 per cents of Ohio are at 110 to 115. The Ohio sixes! What would the heroes of Fort Duquesne think of that, if they should come back?

Most of these speculations are imprudent, many of them are foolish. The boom today may and must be followed by a crisis tomorrow. Great fortunes, and many of them too, have sprung out of the earth since the spring; others will, perhaps, return to it before the fall. The American does not worry about that. Violent sensations are necessary to stir his vigorous nerves. Public opinion and the pulpit forbid sensual gratifications, wine, women, and the display of princely luxury; cards and dice are equally prohibited; the American, therefore, has recourse to business for the strong emotions which he requires to make him feel life. He launches with delight into the ever-moving sea of speculation. One day, the wave raises him to the clouds; he enjoys in haste the moment of triumph. The next day he disappears between the crests of the billows; he is little troubled by the reverse; he bides his time coolly and consoles himself with the hope of better fortune. In the midst of all this speculation, while some enrich and some ruin themselves, banks spring up and diffuse credit; railroads and canals extend themselves over the country; steamboats are launched into the rivers, the lakes, and the sea; the career of the speculators is ever enlarging, the field for railroads, canals, steamers, and banks goes on expanding. Some individuals lose, but the country is a gainer; the country is peopled, cleared, cultivated; its resources are unfolded, its wealth increased. Go ahead!

If movement and the quick succession of sensations and

ideas constitute life, here one lives a hundredfold more than elsewhere; here, all is circulation, motion, and boiling agitation. Experiment follows experiment; enterprise follows enterprise. Riches and poverty follow on each other's traces and each in turn occupies the place of the other. While the great men of one day dethrone those of the past, they are already half overturned themselves by those of the morrow. Fortunes last for a season; reputations for the twinkling of an eye. An irresistible current sweeps everything away, grinds everything to powder and deposits it again under new forms. Men change their houses, their climate, their trade, their condition, their party, their sect; the States change their laws, their officers, their constitutions. The soil itself, or at least the houses, partake in the universal instability. The existence of social order in the bosom of this whirlpool seems a miracle, an inexplicable anomaly. One is tempted to think that such a society, formed of heterogeneous elements, brought together by chance, each following its own orbit according to the impulse of its own caprice or interest—one would think that after rising for one moment to the heavens, like a waterspout, such a society would inevitably fall flat in ruins the next; such is not, however, its destiny. Amid this general change there is one fixed point; it is the domestic fireside, or to speak more clearly, the conjugal bed. An austere watchman, sometimes harsh even to fanaticism, wards off from this sacred spot, everything that can disturb its stability; that guardian is religious sentiment. While that fixed point shall remain untouched, while that sentinel shall persist in his vigilant watch over it, the social system may make new somersaults and undergo new changes without serious risk; it may be pelted by the storm, but while it is made fast to that anchorage, it will neither split nor sink. It may even be broken up into different groups nearly independent of one another, but it will expand across the earth, it will still grow in energy, in resources, in extent.

The influence of the democracy is so universal in this

country that it was quite natural for it to raise its head among speculators. There have, therefore, been strikes on the part of workmen who wish to share in the profits of speculation and who have demanded higher wages and less work. The demand for higher pay is just since all provisions, all articles of consumption, have risen in price. These coalitions are by no means timid in this country; the English practice of haranguing in public and getting up processions prevails here and the working class feels its strength, is conscious of its power, and knows how to make use of it. The different trades have held meetings in Philadelphia, New York, and other places, discussed their affairs publicly, and set forth their demands. The women have had their meeting as well as the men. That of the seamstresses of Philadelphia attracted notice; Matthew Carey, known as a political writer, presided, assisted by two clergymen. Among the various demands one might point out is that of the journeymen bakers who, by virtue of the rights of man and the sanctity of the seventh day, would not make bread Sundays. The principal trades have decided that all work shall be suspended until the masters, if this name can be applied here except in derision, have acceded to their ultimatum. That everyone may know this, they have published their resolutions in the newspapers, signed by the president and secretaries of the meeting. These resolutions declare that those workmen who shall refuse to conform to their provisions will have to abide the consequences of their refusal. The consequences have been that those refractory workmen who persisted in working have been driven with stones and clubs from their workshops without any interference on the part of the magistrates. The consequence is that, at this very moment, a handful of boatmen on the Schuylkill Canal prevent the coal boats from descending to the sea, lay an embargo upon them, and thus interrupt one of the most lucrative branches of the Pennsylvania trade, deprive the mariners and shipowners who transport the coal to all parts of the coast of wages and freights and expose the miners to the danger of being dismissed from the mines. Meanwhile the militia looks on; the sheriff stands with folded arms. If this minority of boatmen—for these acts of disorder are the work of a small minority—persists in their plans, a fight between them and the miners is conceivable. In Philadelphia, the consequence has been that the carpenters in order to reduce some contractors to terms have set fire to several houses which were being built. This time the authorities at length interfered, the mayor issued a proclamation reciting that, whereas there is reason to believe these fires to be the work of some evil-minded persons, he offers $1,000 reward to whoever shall disclose the authors of the same. But it is too late. The municipal authorities, for the purpose, it is said, of gaining a few votes on the side of the Opposition, instead of interposing their power between the workmen and the masters, hastened from the first to comply with all the demands of the former, who were employed on the municipal works.

The philosopher, in whose eyes the present is but a point, may find reason to rejoice in considering these facts. Workmen and domestics in Europe live in a state of nearly absolute dependence which is favorable only to him who commands. Monarchists, republicans, the classes in between, all comport themselves toward the worker they employ or the domestic in their service as if he were a being of an inferior nature who owes his master all his zeal and all his efforts, but who has no claim on any return beyond a miserable pittance of wages. One may be permitted to wish for the establishment of a juster scale of rights and duties. In the United States—the absolute principle of the popular sovereignty having been applied to the relations of master and servant, of employer and operative—the manufacturer, the contractor, and the entrepreneur, to whom the workmen give the law, endeavor to dispense with their aid as much as possible by substituting more and more machinery for human force; thus the most painful processes in the arts become less burdensome to the human race. The master, whose domestics obey him when they please and who pays dear for being badly and ungraciously served, favors, to the extent of his power, the introduction of mechanical contrivances for simplifying work in order to spare himself the inconveniences of such a dependence. . . .

5

"There are certain causes which have acted with peculiar energy in our generation . . ."*

DANIEL WEBSTER

Webster was known to later Americans primarily as the greatest orator of the Jacksonian generation and, in particular, as the celebrant of the themes of Nationalism and Union. Indeed, Webster's reply to Hayne in the famous debate over the nature of the Union in 1830 became a documentary cliché in the textbooks of American rhetoric even in Webster's lifetime. If the American schoolboy remembered anything about Webster, he remembered the famous closing words of the Second Reply to Hayne—"Liberty and Union, now and forever, one and inseparable." Oratory was a great popular art in Webster's lifetime and Webster certainly exploited this manipulative skill more successfully than any other man of his generation.

Yet we must not make the mistake of dismissing Webster as the "quasi-official rhapsodist of American nationalism." Webster was much sought after as a lecturer, and he appeared not only before meetings of the Whig faithful, but also before agricultural fairs, mechanics' institutes, college and literary societies. His addresses reveal a preoccupation with other themes as well as the theme of nationalism. Once he had made his agonizing decision in 1828 to support a protective tariff, Webster celebrated Technology, Capital, and Enterprise as the forces which would improve the condition of American society.

The selection which follows is from an address that Webster made to the Society for the Diffusion of Useful

* From *The Writings and Speeches of Daniel Webster*, National Edition (Boston, 1903), XIII, 66–77, abridged.

Knowledge, in Boston, in November of 1836. In it he raises the question—what are the causes of the "unprecedented augmentation of general wealth" and the "improvement in the condition of the mass of society" which are to be seen in America? In his Olympian style, he argues that it is "the successful application of science to art." Much of his lecture is a celebration of the steam engine as the symbol of the new forces. Everywhere this new motive force is increasing the productive power of society with factories, steamboats, railroads, and printing presses. Although he reminds his listeners that "the factories, the steamboats, the railroads . . . require capital, and aggregate capital," he insists that these new establishments "are yet general and popular in all the good they produce."

. . . There has been in the course of half a century an unprecedented augmentation of general wealth. Even within a shorter period, and under the actual observation of most of us, in our own country and our own circles, vastly increased comforts have come to be enjoyed by the industrious classes, and vastly more leisure and time are found for the cultivation of the mind. It would be easy to prove this by detailed comparisons between the present and the past, showing how far the present exceeds the past, in regard to the shelter, food, clothing, and fuel enjoyed by laboring families. But this is a truth so evident and so open to common observation as matter of fact, that proof by particular enumeration of circumstances becomes unnecessary. We may safely take the fact to be, as it certainly is, that there are certain causes which have acted with peculiar energy in our generation, and which have improved the condition of the mass of society with a degree of rapidity heretofore altogether unknown.

What, then, are these causes? This is an interesting question. It seems to me the main cause is the successful application of science to art; or, in other words, the progress of scientific art.

It is the general doctrine of writers on political econ-

omy, that labor is the source of wealth. This is undoubtedly true. The materials of wealth are in the earth, and
in the seas, or in their productions; and it is labor only
which obtains them, works upon them, and fashions them
to the uses of man. The fertility of the soil is nothing, till
labor cultivates it; the iron in the mountain rock is of no
value, till the strong hand of labor has drawn it forth,
separated it from the neighboring earths, and melted and
forged it into a manufactured article.

The great agent, therefore, that procures shelter, and
food, and raiment for man, is labor; that is to say, it is
an active agency, it is some moving power, it is something
which has action and effort, and is capable of taking hold
of the materials, with which the world supplies us, and
of working them into shapes and forms such as shall administer to the wants and comforts of mankind.

The proposition of the philosophers, therefore, is true,
that labor is the true source, and the only source of wealth;
and it necessarily follows, that any augmentation of labor,
augments, to the same degree, the production of wealth.
But when Adam Smith and his immediate followers laid
down this maxim, it is evident that they had in view,
chiefly, either the manual labors of agriculturists and artisans, or the active occupations of other productive classes.
It was the toil of the human arm that they principally
regarded. It was labor, as distinct from capital. But it
seems to me that the true philosophy of the thing is,
that any labor, any active agency, which can be brought
to act usefully on the earth, or its materials, is the source
of wealth. The labor of the ox, and the horse, as well as
that of man, produces wealth. That is to say, this labor,
like man's labor, extracts from the earth the means of
living, and these constitute wealth in its general political
sense.

Now it has been the purpose, and a purpose most successfully and triumphantly obtained, of scientific art, to
increase this active agency, which, in a philosophical point
of view, is, I think to be regarded as labor, by bringing the
powers of the elements into active and more efficient op-

eration, and creating millions of automatic laborers, all diligently employed for the benefit of man. The powers are principally steam, and the weight of water. The automatic machinery are mechanisms of infinitely various kinds. Two classes: first—when a series of operations is carried through by one power, till a perfect result is had, like factories. Second—more [powers,] single or united, steamboats, cars, and printing presses. We commonly speak of mechanic inventions as labor-saving machines; but it would be more philosophical to speak of them as labor-doing machines; because they, in fact, are laborers. They are made to be active agents, to have motion, and effect, and though without intelligence, they are guided by those laws of science which are exact and perfect, and they produce results, therefore, in general, more exact and accurate than the human hand is capable of producing. When one sees Mr. Whittemore's carding machine in operation and looks at the complexity and accuracy of its operations, their rapidity, and yet their unbroken and undisturbed succession, he will see that in this machine (as well as in the little dog that turns it) man has a fellow laborer, and this fellow laborer is of immense power, of mathematical accuracy and precision, and of un-wearied effort. And while he is thus a most skilful and productive laborer, he is, at the same time, a non-consumer. His earnings all go to the use of man. It is over such engines, even with more propriety than on the apiary, that the motto might be written, *vos, non vobis, laborastis.*

It is true that the machinery, in this and similar cases, is the purchase of capital. But human labor is the purchase of capital also; though the free purchase, and in communities less fortunate than ours, the human being himself, who performs the labor, is the purchase of capital. The work of machinery is certainly labor in all sense, as much as slave service, and in an enlarged sense, it is labor in [there is a blank space here in the manuscript] and regarding labor as a mere active power of production; whether that power be the hand of man, or the automatic movement of machinery, the general result is the same.

It is thus that the successful application of science to art increases the productive power and agency of the human race. It multiplies laborers without multiplying consumers, and the world is precisely as much benefited as if Providence had provided for our use millions of men, like ourselves in external appearance, who would work and labor and toil, and who yet required for their own subsistence neither shelter, nor food, nor clothing. These automata in the factories and the workshops are as much our fellow laborers, as if they were automata wrought by some Maelzel into the form of men, and made capable of walking, moving, and working, of felling the forest or cultivating the fields.

It is well known that the era of the successful application of science to arts, especially in the production of the great article of human subsistence, clothing, commenced about half a century ago. H. Arkwright predicted how productive human industry would become when no longer proportioned in its results to muscular strength. He had great sagacity, boldness, judgment, and power of arrangement. In 1770, England consumed four million pounds of cotton in manufactures—[the] United States none. The aggregate consumption of Europe and America is now five millions. Arkwright deserves to be regarded as a benefactor of mankind. From the same period we may date the commencement in the general improvement in the condition of the mass of society, in regard to wealth and the means of living; and to the same period also we may assign the beginning of that spread of popular knowledge which now stamps such an imposing character on the times.

What is it, then, but this increased laboring power, what is it but these automatic allies and co-operators, who have come with such prodigious effect to man's aid in the great business of procuring the means of living, of comfort, and of wealth, out of the materials of the physical universe, which has so changed the face of society?

And this mighty agency, this automatic labor whose ability cannot be limited nor bounded, is the result of the successful application of science to art. Science has thus reached its greatest excellence, and achieved its highest attainment, in rendering itself emphatically, conspicuously, and in the highest degree useful to men of all classes and conditions. Its noblest attainment consists in conferring practical and substantial blessings on mankind.

"Practical mechanics," says a late ingenious and able writer, "is, in the pre-eminent sense, a scientific art." It is indeed true, that the arts are growing every day more and more perfect, from the prosecution of scientific researches. And it ought to put to the blush all those who decry any department of science, or any field of knowledge, as barren and unproductive, that man has, as yet, learned nothing that has not been, or may not be, capable of useful application. If we look to the unclouded skies, when the moon is riding among the constellations, it might seem to us, that the distance of that luminary from any particular star could be of no possible importance, or its knowledge of no practical use to man. Yet it is precisely the knowledge of that distance, wrought out and applied by science, that enables the navigator to decide, within a few miles, his precise place on the ocean, not having seen land in many months. The high state of navigation, its safety and its despatch, are memorials of the highest character in honor of science, and the application of science to the purposes of life. The knowledge of conic sections, in like manner, may appear quite remote from practical utility, yet there are mechanical operations, of the highest importance, entirely dependent on an accurate knowledge, and a just application of the scientific rules pertaining to that subject. Therefore he who studied astronomy and explores the celestial system, a La Place or Bowditch; or he who constructs tables for finding the longitude, or works out results and proportions applicable to machinery from conic sections, or other branches of mathematics; or he who fixes by precise rule the vibration of the pendulum, or applies to use the counterbalancing and mutually adjusting centripetal and centrifugal force of bodies, are laborers for the human race of the highest character and the greatest merit.

It is unnecessary to multiply instances or examples. We are surrounded on all sides by abundant proofs of the utility of scientific research applied to the purposes of life. Every ship that swims the sea exhibits such proof; every factory exhibits it; every printing office and almost every workshop exhibits it; agriculture exhibits it; household comforts exhibit it. On all sides, wherever we turn our eyes, innumerable facts attest the great truth, that knowledge is not barren.

It is false in morals to say that good principles do not tend to produce good practice; it is equally false in matters of science and of art to declare that knowledge produces no fruit.

Perhaps the most prominent instance of the application of science to art, in the production of things necessary to man's subsistence, is the use of the elastic power of steam, applied to the operations of spinning and weaving and dressing fabrics for human wear. All this mighty discovery bears directly on the means of human subsistence and human comfort. It has greatly altered commerce, agriculture, and even the habits of life among nations. It has affected commerce by creating new objects, or vastly increasing the importance of those before hardly known; it has affected agriculture by giving new value to its products; —what would now be the comparative value of the soil of our Southern and Southwestern States if the spinning of cotton by machinery, the power loom, and the cotton gin, were struck out of existence? And it has affected habits by giving a new direction to labor and creating a multitude of new pursuits.

Bearing less on the production of the objects necessary to man's subsistence, but hardly inferior in its importance, is the application of the power of steam to transportation and conveyance by sea and by land. Who is so familiarized to the sight even now, as to look without wonder and amazement on the long train of cars, full of passengers and merchandise, drawn along our valleys, and the sides of our mountains themselves with a rapidity which holds competition [with] the winds?

This branch of the application of steam power is younger. It is not yet fully developed; but the older branch, its application to manufacturing machinery, is perhaps to be regarded as the more signal instance marking the great and glorious epoch of the application of science to the useful arts. From the time of Arkwright to our own days, and in our own country, from a period a little earlier than the commencement of the late war with England, we see the successive and astonishing effects of this principle, not new-born, indeed, in our time, but awakened, animated, and pushed forward to most stupendous results. It is difficult to estimate the amount of labor performed by machinery, compared with manual labor. It is computed that in England, on articles exported it is thirty millions sterling per year. It would be useful, if one with competent means should estimate the products of the annual labor of Massachusetts in manufactured articles carried from the State.

If these, and other considerations may suffice to satisfy us that the application of science to art is the main cause of the sudden augmentation of wealth and comfort in modern times, a truth remains to be stated of the greatest magnitude, and the highest practical importance, and that is, that this augmentation of wealth and comfort is general and diffusive, reaching to all classes, embracing all interests, and benefiting, not a part of society, but the whole. There is no monopoly in science. There are no exclusive privileges in the workings of automatic machinery, or the powers of natural bodies. The poorest, as well as the richest man in society, has a direct interest, and generally the poor a far greater interest than the rich, in the successful operation of these arts, which make the means of living, clothing especially, abundant and cheap. The advantages conferred by knowledge in increasing our physical resources, from their very nature, cannot be enjoyed by a few only. They are all open to the many, and to be profitable, the many must enjoy it.

The products of science applied to art in mechanical inventions, are made, not to be hoarded, but to be sold. Their successful operation requires a large market. It requires that the great mass of society should be able to buy and to consume. The improved condition of all classes, more ability to buy food and raiment, better modes of living, and increased comforts of every kind, are exactly what is necessary and indispensable in order that capital invested in automatic operations should be productive to the owners. Some establishments of this kind necessarily require large capital, such as the woollen and cotton factories. And in a country like ours, in which the spirit of our institutions, and all our laws, tend so much to the distribution and equalization of property, there are few individuals of sufficient wealth to build and carry on an establishment by their own means. This renders a union of capitals necessary, and this among us is conveniently effected by corporations which are but partnerships regulated by law. And this union of many to form capital for the purpose of carrying on those operations by which science is applied to art, and comes in aid of man's labor in the production of things essential to man's existence, constitutes that aggregated wealth of which complaint is sometimes heard. It would seem that nothing could be plainer than that whatever reduces the price, whether of food or of clothing, must be in the end beneficial to the laboring classes. Yet it has not unfrequently happened, that machinery has been broken and destroyed in England, by workmen, by open and lawless violence. Most persons in our country see the folly as well as the injustice and barbarism of such proceedings; but the ideas in which these violences originated are no more unfounded and scarcely more disreputable, than those which would represent capital, collected, necessarily, in large sums, in order to carry on useful processes in which science is applied to art, in the production of articles useful to all, as being hostile to the common good, or having an interest separate from that of the majority of the community. All such representations, if not springing from sinister design, must be the result of great ignorance or great prejudice. It has been found by long experience in England, that large capitalists can produce cheaper than small ones, especially in the article of cotton. Greater savings can be made and these savings enable the proprietor to go on, when he must otherwise stop. There is no doubt that it is to her abundant capital, England is now indebted for whatever power of competition with the United States she now sustains, in producing cheap articles.

There are modes of applying wealth, useful principally to the owner, and not otherwise beneficial to the community than as they employ labor. Such are the erection of expensive houses, the embellishment of ornamental grounds, the purchase of costly furniture and equipages. These modes of expenditure, although entirely lawful and sometimes very proper, are yet not such as directly benefit the whole community. Not so with aggregate wealth employed in producing articles of general consumption. This mode of employment is, peculiarly and in an emphatic sense, an application of capital to the benefit of all. Any one who complains of it, or decries it, acts against the greatest good of the greatest number. The factories, the steamboats, the railroads, and other similar establishments, although they require capital, and aggregate capital, are yet general and popular in all the good they produce.

The unquestionable operation of all these things has been not only to increase property, but to equalize it, to diffuse it, to scatter its advantages among the many, and to give content, cheerfulness, and animation to all classes of the social system. In New England, more particularly, has this been the result. What has enabled us to be rich and prosperous, notwithstanding the barrenness of our soil and the rigor of our climate? What has diffused so much comfort, wealth, and happiness among all classes, but the diligent employment of our citizens, in these processes and mechanical operations in which science comes in aid of handicraft? Abolish the use of steam and the application of water power to machinery, and what would at this moment be the condition of New England? And yet steam and water power have been employed only, and can be employed only, by what is called aggregated wealth. Far distant be the day then, when the people of New England shall be deceived by the specious fallacy, that there are different and opposing interests in our community; that what is useful to one, is hurtful to the rest; that there is one interest for the rich, and another interest for the poor; that capital is the enemy of labor, or labor the foe of capital. And let every laboring man, on whose understanding such a fallacy is attempted to be imposed, stop the mouth of the false reasoner at once, by stating the plain and evident fact, that while aggregated wealth has for years, in Massachusetts, been most skilfully and steadily employed in the productions which result from the application of science to art; thereby reducing the cost of many of the articles most essential to human life in all conditions; labor, meantime, has been constantly rising, and is at this very moment, notwithstanding the present scarcity of money, and the constant pressure on capital, higher than it ever was before in the history of the country. These are, indeed, facts which baffle all former dogmas of political economy. In some of our most agricultural districts in the midst of our mountains, on whose tops the native forests still wave and where agricultural labor is high, in an unprecedented degree, even here automatic processes are carried on by water, and fabrics wrought out of materials which have been transported hundreds and thousands of miles, by sea and by land, and which fabrics go back again, some of them, for sale and consumption to the places where the raw material was produced. Carolina cotton is carried to the County of Berkshire, and Berkshire cotton goods are sold in Carolina. Meanwhile labor in Berkshire is not only in money price, but in comparison with the cost of the main articles of human subsistence, higher than it was ever known before. Writers on political economy may, perhaps, on facts like these see occasion to qualify their theories; meantime, it becomes every man to question and scrutinize severely, if not the motives, yet the reasoning and the logic of those who would persuade us that capital, employed in the most efficient modes of producing things useful, is hurtful to society. It would be quite as reasonable to insist, that the weaving of paper, if that be the proper term, in consequence of recent most valuable mechanical inventions, should be [suppressed], and the power press, and the hydrostatic machine taken out of the printing houses, as being all hurtful and injurious, although they may have reduced the price of books for general circulation one half.

The truth, in my opinion, rather is, that such is the enterprise of our people, such the astonishing amount of labor which they perform, and which they perform cheerfully because it is free and because it is profitable, and such the skill with which capital is used, that still more capital would be useful and that its introduction would be advantageous, and most of all to the busy and industrious classes. And let it never be forgotten, that with us labor is free, intelligent, respecting itself, and respected by other interests; that it accumulates; that it is provident; that it lays up for itself; and that these savings become capital, and their owners in time capitalists.

I cannot omit to notice, here, another fact peculiar to this country, and which should cause us to hesitate in applying to ourselves, and our condition, European maxims respecting capital and labor. In Europe, generally speaking, the laborer is always a laborer. He is destined to no better condition on earth, ordinarily he rises no higher. We see proofs, melancholy proofs, of this truth often in the multitudes who come to our own shores from foreign countries for employment. It is not so with the people of New England. Capital and labor are much less distinctly divided with us. Few are they, on the one hand, who have need to perform no labor; few are they, on the other, who have no property or capital of their own. Or if there be those of the latter class among the industrious and the sober, they are young men who, though they are laborers to-day, will be capitalists to-morrow. A career of usefulness and enterprise is before them. If without moneyed capital, they have a capital in their intelligence, their knowledge, and their good habits. Around them are a thousand collections of automatic machinery, requiring the diligence of skilful and sober [laborers]; before them is the ocean, always inviting to deeds of hardihood and enterprise; behind them are the fertile [prairies] of the West, soliciting cultivation; and over them all is the broad banner of free institutions, of mild laws, and parental Government. Would [an] American young man of good health and good habits need say that he is without capital? Or why should he [discredit] his own understanding by listening to the absurdity, that they who have earned property, and they who have not yet lived long enough to earn it, must be enemies? The proportion of those who have not capital, such as to render them independent without personal labor, and who are yet not without some capital, is vastly larger in this community than any other. They form indeed the great mass of our society. They are its life and muscle; and long may they continue free, moral, intelligent, and prosperous as they now are. . . .

6

Machinery, for Machine Making

Graham's Lady's and Gentleman's Magazine offered to both ladies and gentlemen the same type of sentimental and moralizing literary fare that appeared in *Godey's Lady's Book*. Indeed most of the essays, stories, and illustrations were obviously aimed at a female audience. There were, however, frequent travel adventures and historical sketches of wars and kings which must have appealed to the men as well. Occasionally, also, there were articles of an economic character that were aimed primarily at male readers. Among these were some excellent articles on the new technological advances in American industry. The following illustration appeared with a long descriptive article on the manufacture of machine tools. From such illustrations we can begin to get some idea of the degree of technological sophistication that had been achieved in America by the end of the Jacksonian generation.

MACHINERY, FOR MACHINE MAKING.

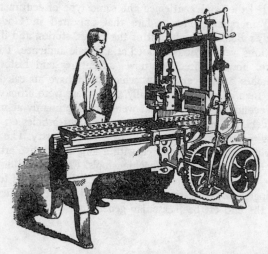

NO. 1.—IMPROVED POWER PLANER

From "Machinery, for Machine Making" in *Graham's Lady's and Gentleman's Magazine* (1852), XLI, 469.

7

The Influence of the Trading Spirit
on the Social and Moral Life in America*

THE AMERICAN WHIG REVIEW

Although Daniel Webster was a leading spokesman for the values of technology and industrial capitalism, he loved his Marshfield farm and his rides afield among his cattle, horses, and crops. Even Vernon Louis Parrington, in *The Romantic Revolution in America*, makes this love of the homely things at his country estate in Marshfield a saving element in a generally unflattering portrait of Webster. There was a part of Webster that hated to let go the simpler virtues of the yeoman farmer which had been bred into him in his New Hampshire boyhood. Yet Webster was not unique among his Whiggish contemporaries in feeling a sense of loss amid the social improvements being wrought by industry and science, as many articles in *The American Whig Review* attest.

The American Review: A Whig Journal of Politics, Literature, Art and Science was launched in New York late in the Jacksonian era and in a very real sense it was a product of the social upheavals associated with Jacksonian politics. Its leaders saw the necessity of a Whig magazine to compete with the *Democratic Review* which had operated as an important organ of Democratic opinion since 1837. Moreover, George Hooker Colton, the first editor, conceived of American Whiggery as a response to the erroneous principles and destructive actions of the Democratic party as they were formed under the leadership of Andrew Jackson.

As an exponent of Whig principles, *The American Whig Review* celebrated the themes of Capital, Enter-

* From *The American Review*, I (January 1845), 95–98, abridged.

prise, and Industry. Yet, often enough, the editorial
writers for the new magazine regretted the price which
was being paid for so much commercial and industrial
progress. The editorial writer of the selection that follows notes that the restless ambition and the love of
gain which is so pervasive in America seems to be accompanied by a loss of kindliness and grace in human
relations. These deep-seated feelings of anxiety and guilt
concerning the pursuit of wealth among the Whig
champions of industrial enterprise raise a perplexing
problem for the historian seeking to explain thought and
behavior in American society during the Jacksonian
period.

. . . All strangers who come among us remark the excessive anxiety written in the American countenance. The
widespread comfort, the facilities for livelihood, the
spontaneous and cheap lands, the high price of labor are
equally observed, and render it difficult to account for these
lines of painful thoughtfulness. It is not poverty, nor
tyranny, nor over-competition which produces this anxiety;
that is clear. It is the concentration of the faculties
upon an object, which in its very nature is unattainable—
the perpetual improvement of the outward condition.
There are no bounds among us to the restless desire to be
better off; and this is the ambition of all classes of society.
We are not prepared to allow that wealth is more valued
in America than elsewhere, but in other countries the successful pursuit of it is necessarily confined to a few, while
here it is open to all. No man in America is contented to
be poor, or expects to continue so. There are here no
established limits within which the hopes of any class
of society must be confined, as in other countries. There is
consequently no condition of hopes realized, in other
words, of contentment. In other lands, if children can
maintain the station and enjoy the means, however moderate, of their father, they are happy. Not so with us. This is
not the spirit of our institutions. Nor will it long be otherwise in other countries. That equality, that breaking down

of artificial barriers which has produced this universal ambition and restless activity in America, is destined to prevail throughout the earth. But because we are in advance of the world in the great political principle, and are now experiencing some of its first effects, let us not mistake these for the desirable fruits of freedom. Commerce is to become the universal pursuit of men. It is to be the first result of freedom, of popular institutions everywhere. Indeed, every land not steeped in tyranny is now feeling this impulse. But while trade is destined to free and employ the masses, it is also destined to destroy for the time much of the beauty and happiness of every land. This has been the result in our own country. We are free. It is a glorious thing that we have no serfs, with the large and unfortunate exception of our slaves—no artificial distinctions—no acknowledged superiority of blood—no station which merit may not fill—no rounds in the social ladder to which the humblest may not aspire. But the excitement, the commercial activity, the restlessness, to which this state of things has given birth, is far from being a desirable restlessness or a natural condition. It is natural to the circumstances, but not natural to the human soul. It is good and hopeful to the interests of the race, but destructive to the happiness, and dangerous to the virtue of the generation exposed to it.

Those unaccustomed, by reading or travel, to other states of society, are probably not aware how very peculiar our manner of life here is. The laboriousness of Americans is beyond all comparison, should we except the starving operatives of English factories. And when we consider that here, to the labor of the body is added the great additional labor of mental responsibility and ambition, it is not to be wondered at that as a race, the commercial population is dwindling in size, and emaciated in health, so that *palor* is the national complexion. If this devotion to business were indispensable to living, it would demand our pity. It is unavoidable, we know, in one sense. That is, it is customary—it is universal. There is no necessity for the custom; but there is a necessity, weakly constituted as

men are, that every individual should conform greatly to
the prevailing habits of his fellows, and the expectations of
the community in and with which he deals. It is thus that
those who deeply feel the essentially demoralizing and
wretched influences of this system are yet doomed to be
victims of it. Nay, we are all, no matter what our occupations, more or less, and all greatly, sufferers from the
excessive stimulus under which every thing is done. We are
all worn out with thought that does not develop our thinking faculties in a right direction, and with feeling expended upon poor and low objects. There is no profession
that does not feel it. The lawyer must confine himself to
his office, without vacation, to adjust a business which
never sleeps or relaxes. The physician must labor day and
night to repair bodies, never well from over-exertion, over-
excitement, and over-indulgence. The minister must stimulate himself to supply the cravings of diseased moral
appetites, and to arouse the attention of men deafened
by the noise, and dizzy with the whirl in which they constantly live.

We call our country a *happy* country; happy, indeed, in
being the home of noble political institutions, the abode
of freedom; but very far from being happy in possessing
a cheerful, light-hearted, and joyous people. Our agricultural regions even are infected with the same anxious spirit
of gain. If ever the curse of labor was upon the race, it is
upon us; nor is it simply now "by the sweat of thy brow
thou shalt earn thy bread." Labor for a livelihood is dignified. But we labor for bread, and labor for pride, and *labor*
for pleasure. A man's life with us *does* consist of the
abundance of the things which he possesseth. To get, and
to have the reputation of possessing, is the ruling passion.
To it are bent all the energies of nine-tenths of our population. Is it that our people are so much more miserly and
earth-born than any other? No, not by any constitutional
baseness; but circumstances have necessarily given this
direction to the American mind. In the hard soil of our
common mother, New England—the poverty of our ancestors—their early thrift and industry—the want of other

distinctions than those of property—the frown of the Puritans upon all pleasures; these circumstances combined, directed our energies from the first into the single channel of trade. And in that they have run till they have gained a tremendous head, and threaten to convert our whole people into mere money-changers and producers. Honor belongs to our fathers, who in times of great necessity met the demand for a most painful industry with such manly and unflinching hearts. But what was their hard necessity we are perpetuating as our willing servitude! what they bore as evil we seek as good. We cannot say that the destiny of this country did not demand that the spirit of trade should rule it for centuries. It may be that we are now carrying out only the decree of Providence. But if so, let us consider ourselves as in the wilderness, and not in the promised land. Let us bear the dispensation of God, but not glory in our bondage. If we are doomed to be tradesmen, and nothing but tradesmen—if money, and its influences and authority, are to reign for a season over our whole land, let us not mistake it for the kingdom of heaven, and build triumphal arches over our avenues of trade, as though the Prince of Peace and the Son of God were now and thus to enter in.

It is said that we are not a happy people. And it is true; for we most unwisely neglect all those free fountains of happiness which Providence has opened for all its children. Blessed beyond any people with the means of living, supplied to an unparalleled extent with the comforts and luxuries of life, our American homes are sombre and cheerless abodes. There is even in the air of comfort which their well-furnished apartments wear something uncomfortable. They are the habitations of those who do not live at home. They are wanting in a social and cheerful aspect. They seem fitted more to be admired than to be enjoyed. The best part of the house is for the occasional use of strangers, and not to be occupied by those who might, day by day, enjoy it, which is but one proof among many that we love to appear comfortable rather than to be so. Thus miserable pride hangs like a mill-stone about our hospitality. "We sacrifice the hospitality of a year to the prodigality of a night." We are ashamed of any thing but affluence, and when we cannot make an appearance, or furnish entertainments as showy as the richest, we will do nothing. Thus does pride close our doors. Hospitality becomes an event of importance. It is not our daily life, one of our chiefest enjoyments, but a debt, a ceremony, a penance. And not only pride, but anxiety of mind, interferes with sociality. Bent upon one aim, the merchant grudges his thoughts. He cannot expend his energies in social enjoyment. Nay, it is not enjoyment to him; society has nothing of the excitement of business. The excessive pursuit of gain begets a secrecy of thought, a contradiction of ideas, a barrenness of interest, which renders its votary any thing but social or companionable. Conversation incessantly takes an anxious and uninteresting turn; and the fireside becomes only a narrower exchange, and the parlor a more private news-room.

It is rare to see a foreigner without some taste for amusement, some power of relaxing his mind, some interest in the arts, or in literature. This is true even of the less privileged classes. It is rare, on the contrary, to find a *virtuous* American past middle life, who does not regard amusements of all sorts either as childish or immoral; who possesses any acquaintance with or taste for the arts, except it be a natural and rude taste for music; or who reads any thing except newspapers, and only the political or commercial columns of those. It is the want of tastes for other things than business which gives an anxious and unhappy turn to our minds. It cannot be many years before the madness of devoting the whole day to the toils of the counting-house will be acknowledged; before the claim of body and mind to relaxation and cheerful, exhilarating amusement will be seen. We consider the common suspicion which is felt of amusements among thoughtful people to be one of the most serious evils to which our community is exposed. It outlaws a natural taste, and violates and ruins the consciences of the young, by stamping as sinful what they have not the force to refrain from. It makes our places of amusement low, divides the thoughtful and the careless, the grave and the gay, the old and the young, in their pleasures. Children are without the protection of their parents in their enjoyments. And thus, too, is originated one of the greatest curses of our social state—the great want of intimacy and confidence between children and their parents, especially between fathers and sons.

The impulses that incline to pleasure, if opposed, tend to vice. Nature finds a vent for her pent-up forces. Alas! for what are called *strict morals* in this view; when, by an unnatural restriction, innocent and open pleasures make way for secret vices or sins of the heart.

While the commercial spirit in this extravagant form gives a certain sobriety and moral aspect to society, it occasions an excessive barrenness of real moral excellencies. This is a very difficult and delicate distinction to render popularly apparent, although of the most vital and substantial reality. There is a very great difference between what are called strict morals that are really profound in their sources, and pervading in their influence. We are more strict in our morals in these Northern States than anywhere in the world, but it is questionable whether our morality is not of a somewhat inferior quality, and in a too narrow view. It is artificial, conventional. There is no quarter of the earth where the Sabbath is more scrupulously observed —where religious institutions are so well supported, or where more abstinence from pleasure is practised. The great virtue of industry prevails. Overt sins are more rare here than elsewhere. As far as morality is restrictive in its nature, it has accomplished a great work in America. The vices or sins which are reducible to statute, or known by name, are generally restrained. We have a large class of persons of extraordinary propriety and faultlessness of life. Our view of morals has a tendency to increase this class. Our pursuits are favorable to it. The love of gain is one of the most sober of all desires. The seriousness of a miser surpasses the gravity of a devotee. Did not every commercial city draw a large body of strangers to it, and attract many reckless and vicious persons, it would wear a very solemn aspect. The pleasure-seeking, the gay, the disorderly, are never the trading population. Large commercial cities tend to great orderliness and decency of manners and morals. But they also tend to very low and barren views of moral excellence. And the American spirit of our own day illustrates this. Our moral sense operates only in one direction. Our virtues are the virtues of merchants, and not of men. We run all to honesty, and mercantile honesty. We do not cultivate the graces of humanity. We have more conscience than heart, and more propriety than either. The fear of evil consequences is more influential than the love of goodness. There is nothing hearty, gushing, eloquent, in the national virtue. You do not see goodness leaking out from the full vessel at every motion it feels. Our goodness is formal, deliberate, premeditated. The upright man is not benevolent, and the just man is not generous. The good man is not cheerful. The religious man is not agreeable. In other words, our morals are partial, and therefore barren. It is not generally understood how great scrupulousness of character may be united with great selfishness, and, how along with a substantial virtue, there may exist the most melancholy deficiencies. This seems to be very common with us, and to be the natural result of our engrossing pursuits. Every one minds his own business, to the extreme peril of his own soul. The apostolic precept, Mind not thine own things, but also the things of another, is in danger of great neglect. Our social condition makes us wary, suspicious, slow to commit ourselves too far in interest for others. The shyness of the tradesman communicates itself to the manners of the visitor; we learn to live within ourselves; we grow unsocial, unfraternal in feeling; and the sensibility, the affection, the cordiality, the forth-putting graces of a warm and virtuous heart, die of disuse. For our part, we are ready to say, let us have more faults and more virtues; more weaknesses and more graces; less punctilio, and more affluence of heart. Let us be less dignified and more cordial; less sanctimonious and more unselfish; less thriving and more cheerful; less toilsome and more social. . . .

8

The Absorbing Desire for Gain: Two Scenes

JAMES FENIMORE COOPER

James Fenimore Cooper was America's literary giant in the Jacksonian era. When Jackson became President, Cooper had already written a half-dozen novels, among them some of the enormously popular Leather-stocking Tales. After his return to Jacksonian America in 1833, he turned out novels, essays, and travel sketches at a furious pace as if driven by some compelling need to take a stand against the tremendous social changes that had transformed America during the seven years that he had lived in France.

Henry Nash Smith has taught us to recognize that, in the Leather-stocking Tales, Cooper was mythicizing some basic conceptions in the American mind. Hence we are able to assume that, when Cooper's generation read the romances of Leather-stocking so avidly, they were responding with emotionally weighted values which accepted Nature as a beneficent force and The Natural Man as the symbol of virtue and freedom. On the other hand, Cooper's novels dealing with his contemporary society, such as *Homeward Bound* and *Home as Found,* often enraged his readers and reviewers. In these novels, Cooper is attempting to give emotive power to the Jeffersonian conception of natural aristocracy—to the idea that leadership in a republican society should come from men of talent. He is attempting to restore a standard of excellence in America that depends on knowledge, dignity, habits of refinement, and liberal attainments in every direction. Either angle of vision offers a basis for criticism of the restless ambition and the desire for gain that Cooper found in Jacksonian America: the natural virtue of a mythical Leather-stock-

ing can stand against the rapaciousness of the settlements
of civilization; the gentility of the Effinghams stands in
graceful contrast to the vulgar man on the make.

The two scenes that follow are taken from two novels
that bracket chronologically the career of Andrew Jackson in national politics—*The Pioneers* (1823) and
Home as Found (1838). In the scene from *The Pioneers*
that describes the slaughter of the pigeons while Leather-
stocking watches disapprovingly, we experience a pre-
monitory sense of the exploitive energies that are about
to burst forth in American life. In the scene from *Home
as Found*, we are introduced to Aristabulus Bragg, a
new social type created by the circumstances and conditions of Jacksonian America and summarized elsewhere
in the novel as—"a compound of shrewdness, impu-
dence, common-sense, pretension, humility, cleverness,
vulgarity, kind-heartedness, duplicity, selfishness, law-
honesty, moral fraud, and mother-wit, mixed up with a
smattering of learning and much penetration in practical
things."

A historian is always on dangerous ground when he
presumes to guess what takes place in the unspoken
dialogue between a novelist and his readers. Nevertheless we are not risking too much in the use of our
historical imagination if we speculate about the response
of the Jacksonian generation to their most widely read
writer. If we can assume that the Leather-stocking
Tales appealed to the readers of the Jacksonian generation because they liked to identify themselves with all
of the natural virtue and anarchic freedom of Natty
Bumppo, then can we not assume, also, that they disliked *Home as Found* because it contained a truth that
hurt? It was impossible within the conditions of Jacksonian America to recreate a society of Effinghams—
but it was equally impossible for most Americans to be
like Leather-stocking. Was it not true, then, that most
Americans were being made in the image of Aristabulus
Bragg?

[LEATHER-STOCKING AND THE SLAUGHTER OF THE PIGEONS]

From James Fenimore Cooper, *The Pioneers* (New York, n.d.), Ch. 22, unabridged.

From this time to the close of April the weather continued to be a succession of great and rapid changes. One day, the soft airs of spring seemed to be stealing along the valley, and in unison with an invigorating sun, attempting covertly to rouse the dormant powers of the vegetable world; while on the next, the surly blasts from the north would sweep across the lake, and erase every impression left by their gentle adversaries. The snow, however, finally disappeared, and the green wheat-fields were seen in every direction, spotted with the dark and charred stumps that had, the preceding season, supported some of the proudest trees of the forest. Ploughs were in motion, wherever those useful implements could be used, and the smokes of the sugar-camps were no longer seen issuing from the woods of maple. The lake had lost the beauty of a field of ice, but still a dark and gloomy covering concealed its waters, for the absence of currents left them yet hidden under a porous crust, which, saturated with the fluid, barely retained enough strength to preserve the contiguity of its parts. Large flocks of wild geese were seen passing over the country, which hovered, for a time, around the hidden sheet of water apparently searching for a resting-place; and then, on finding themselves excluded by the chill covering, would soar away to the north, filling the air with discordant screams, as if venting their complaints at the tardy operations of nature.

For a week, the dark covering of the Otsego was left to the undisturbed possession of two eagles, who alighted on the center of its field, and sat eying their undisputed territory. During the presence of these monarchs of the air, the flocks of migrating birds avoided crossing the plain of ice, by turning into the hills, apparently seeking the protection of the forests, while the white and bald heads of the

tenants of the lake were turned upward with a look of
contempt. But the time had come when even these kings of
birds were to be dispossessed. An opening had been gradually increasing at the lower extremity of the lake, and
around the dark spot where the current of the river prevented the formation of ice, during even the coldest
weather; and the fresh southerly winds, that now breathed
freely upon the valley, made an impression on the waters.
Mimic waves began to curl over the margin of the frozen
field, which exhibited an outline of crystallizations that
slowly receded toward the north. At each step the power of
the winds and the waves increased, until, after a struggle of
a few hours, the turbulent little billows succeeded in setting the whole field in motion, when it was driven beyond
the reach of the eye, with a rapidity that was as magical as
the change produced in the scene by this expulsion of the
lingering remnant of winter. Just as the last sheet of
agitated ice was disappearing in the distance, the eagles
rose, and soared with a wide sweep above the clouds, while
the waves tossed their little caps of snow into the air, as if
rioting in their release from a thraldom of five months'
duration.

The following morning Elizabeth was awakened by the
exhilarating sounds of the martins, who were quarrelling
and chattering around the little boxes suspended above
her windows, and the cries of Richard, who was calling
in tones animating as the signs of the season itself—

"Awake! awake! my fair lady! the gulls are hovering over
the lake already, and the heavens are alive with pigeons.
You may look an hour before you can find a hole through
which to get a peep at the sun. Awake! awake! lazy ones!
Benjamin is overhauling the ammunition, and we only
wait for our breakfasts, and away for the mountains and
pigeon shooting."

There was no resisting this animated appeal, and in a
few minutes Miss Temple and her friend descended to the
parlor. The doors of the hall were thrown open, and the
mild, balmy air of a clear spring morning was ventilating
the apartment where the vigilance of the ex-steward had

been so long maintaining an artificial heat with such un-
remitted diligence. The gentlemen were impatiently
waiting for their morning's repast, each equipped in the
garb of a sportsman. Mr. Jones made many visits to the
southern door, and would cry—

"See, cousin Bess! see, 'duke, the pigeon-roosts of the
south have broken up! They are growing more thick every
instant. Here is a flock that the eye cannot see the end of.
There is food enough in it to keep the army of Xerxes for a
month, and feathers enough to make beds for the whole
country. Xerxes, Mr. Edwards, was a Grecian king who—no,
he was a Turk, or a Persian, who wanted to conquer
Greece, just the same as these rascals will overrun our
wheat-fields, when they come back in the fall. Away! away!
Bess; I long to pepper them."

In this wish both Marmaduke and young Edwards
seemed equally to participate, for the sight was exhilarating to a sportsman; and the ladies soon dismissed the party
after a hasty breakfast.

If the heavens were alive with pigeons, the whole village
seemed equally in motion, with men, women, and children.
Every species of fire-arms, from the French ducking-gun
with a barrel near six feet in length, to the common horseman's pistol, was to be seen in the hands of the men and
boys; while bows and arrows, some made of the simple stick
of a walnut sapling, and others in a rude imitation of the
ancient cross-bows, were carried by many of the latter.

The houses and the signs of life apparent in the village,
drove the alarmed birds from the direct line of their flight,
toward the mountains, along the sides and near the bases
of which they were glancing in dense masses, equally wonderful by the rapidity of their motion, and their incredible
numbers.

We have already said, that across the inclined plane
which fell from the steep ascent of the mountain to the
banks of the Susquehanna, ran the highway, on either side
of which a clearing of many acres had been made at a
very early day. Over those clearings, and up the eastern
mountain, and along the dangerous path that was cut into

its side, the different individuals posted themselves, and in a few moments the attack commenced.

Among the sportsmen was the tall, gaunt form of Leather-stocking, walking over the field, with his rifle hanging on his arm, his dogs at his heels; the latter now scenting the dead or wounded birds, that were beginning to tumble from the flocks, and then crouching under the legs of their master, as if they participated in his feelings at this wasteful and unsportsmanlike execution.

The reports of the fire-arms became rapid, whole volleys rising from the plain, as flocks of more than ordinary numbers darted over the opening, shadowing the field like a cloud; and then the light smoke of a single piece would issue from among the leafless bushes on the mountain, as death was hurled on the retreat of the affrighted birds, who were rising from a volley, in a vain effort to escape. Arrows, and missiles of every kind, were in the midst of the flocks; and so numerous were the birds, and so low did they take their flight, that even long poles, in the hands of those on the sides of the mountain, were used to strike them to the earth.

During all this time, Mr. Jones, who disdained the humble and ordinary means of destruction used by his companions, was busily occupied, aided by Benjamin, in making arrangements for an assault of more than ordinarily fatal character. Among the relics of the old military excursions, that occasionally are discovered throughout the different districts of the western part of New York, there had been found in Templeton, at its settlement, a small swivel, which would carry a ball of a pound weight. It was thought to have been deserted by a war party of the whites, in one of their inroads into the Indian settlements, when, perhaps, convenience or their necessity induced them to leave such an incumbrance behind them in the woods. This miniature cannon had been released from the rust, and being mounted on little wheels, was now in a state for actual service. For several years it was the sole organ for extraordinary rejoicings used in those mountains. On the mornings of the Fourths of July, it would be heard ringing among the hills; and even Captain Hollister, who was the highest authority in that part of the country on all such occasions, affirmed that, considering its dimensions, it was no despicable gun for a salute. It was somewhat the worse for the service it had performed, it is true, there being but a trifling difference in size between the touch-hole and the muzzle. Still, the grand conceptions of Richard had suggested the importance of such an instrument in hurling death at his nimble enemies. The swivel was dragged by a horse into a part of the open space that the Sheriff thought most eligible for planting a battery of the kind, and Mr. Pump proceeded to load it. Several handfuls of duck-shot were placed on top of the powder, and the major-domo announced that his piece was ready for service.

The sight of such an implement collected all the idle spectators to the spot, who, being mostly boys, filled the air with cries of exultation and delight. The gun was pointed high, and Richard, holding a coal of fire in a pair of tongs, patiently took his seat on a stump, awaiting the appearance of a flock worthy of his notice.

So prodigious was the number of the birds, that the scattering fire of the guns, with the hurling of missiles, and the cries of the boys, had no other effect than to break off small flocks from the immense masses that continued to dart along the valley, as if the whole of the feathered tribe were pouring through that one pass. None pretended to collect the game, which lay scattered over the fields in such profusion as to cover the very ground with the fluttering victims.

Leather-stocking was a silent, but uneasy spectator of all these proceedings, but was able to keep his sentiments to himself until he saw the introduction of the swivel into the sports.

"This comes of settling a country!" he said; "here have I known the pigeons to fly for forty long years, and, till you made your clearings, there was nobody to skear or to hurt them. I loved to see them come into the woods, for they were company to a body; hurting nothing; being, as it was, as harmless as a garter-snake. But now it gives me sore thoughts when I hear the frighty things whizzing through the air, for I know it's only a motion to bring out all the brats in the village. Well! the Lord won't see the waste of his creatures for nothing, and right will be done to the pigeons, as well as others, by and by. There's Mr. Oliver, as bad as the rest of them, firing into the flocks, as if he was shooting down nothing but Mingo warriors."

Among the sportsmen was Billy Kirby, who, armed with an old musket, was loading and without even looking into the air, was firing and shouting as his victims fell even on his own person. He heard the speech of Natty, and took upon himself to reply—

"What! old Leather-stocking," he cried, "grumbling at the loss of a few pigeons! If you had to sow your wheat twice, and three times, as I have done, you wouldn't be so massyfully feeling'd toward the divils.—Hurrah, boys! scatter the feathers. This is better than shooting at a turkey's head and neck, old fellow."

"It's better for you, maybe, Billy Kirby," replied the indignant old hunter, "and all them that don't know how to put a ball down a rifle barrel, or how to bring it up again with a true aim; but it's wicked to be shooting into flocks in this wasty manner; and none do it, who know how to knock over a single bird. If a body has a craving for pigeon's flesh, why, it's made the same as all other creatures, for man's eating; but not to kill twenty and eat one. When I want such a thing I go into the woods till I find one to my liking, and then I shoot him off the branches, without touching the feather of another, though there might be a hundred on the same tree. You couldn't do such a thing, Billy Kirby—you couldn't do it, if you tried."

"What's that, old corn-stalk? you sapless stub!" cried the wood-chopper. "You have grown wordy, since the affair of the turkey; but if you are for a single shot, here goes at that bird which comes on by himself."

The fire from the distant part of the field had driven a single pigeon below the flock to which it belonged, and, frightened with the constant reports of the muskets, it was approaching the spot where the disputants stood, darting first from one side and then to the other, cutting the air with the swiftness of lightning, and making a noise with its wings not unlike the rushing of a bullet. Unfortunately for the wood-chopper, notwithstanding his vaunt, he did not see this bird until it was too late to fire as it approached, and he pulled his trigger at the unlucky moment when it was darting immediately over his head. The bird continued its course with the usual velocity.

Natty lowered the rifle from his arm when the challenge was made, and waiting a moment, until the terrified victim had got in a line with his eye, and had dropped near the bank of the lake, he raised it again with uncommon rapidity, and fired. It might have been chance, or it might have been skill, that produced the result; it was probably a union of both; but the pigeon whirled over in the air, and fell into the lake, with a broken wing. At the sound of his rifle, both his dogs started from his feet, and in a few minutes the "slut" brought out the bird, still alive.

The wonderful exploit of Leather-stocking was noised through the field with great rapidity, and the sportsmen gathered in, to learn the truth of the report.

"What!" said young Edwards, "have you really killed a pigeon on the wing, Natty, with a single ball?"

"Haven't I killed loons before now, lad, that dive at the flash?" returned the hunter. "It's much better to kill only such as you want, without wasting your powder and lead, than to be firing into God's creatures in this wicked manner. But I came out for a bird, and you know the reason why I like small game, Mr. Oliver, and now I have got one I will go home, for I don't relish to see these wasty ways that you are all practising as if the least thing wasn't made for use, and not to destroy."

"Thou sayest well, Leather-stocking," cried Marmaduke, "and I begin to think it time to put an end to this work of destruction."

"Put an ind, Judge, to your clearings. An't the woods his work as well as the pigeons? Use, but don't waste. Wasn't the woods made for the beasts and birds to harbor in? and when man wanted their flesh, their skins, or their feathers, there's the place to seek them. But I'll go to the hut with my own game, for I wouldn't touch one of the harmless things that cover the ground here, looking up with their eyes on me, as if they only wanted tongues to say their thoughts."

With this sentiment in his mouth, Leather-stocking threw his rifle over his arm, and followed by his dogs, stepped across the clearing with great caution, taking care not to tread on one of the wounded birds in his path. He soon entered the bushes on the margin of the lake, and was hid from view.

Whatever impression the morality of Natty made on the Judge, it was utterly lost on Richard. He availed himself of the gathering of the sportsmen, to lay a plan for one "fell swoop" of destruction. The musket men were drawn up in battle array, in a line extending on each side of his artillery, with orders to await the signal of firing from himself.

"Stand by, my lads," said Benjamin, who acted as an aide-de-camp on this occasion; "stand by, my hearties, and when Squite Dickens heaves out the signal to begin firing, d'ye see, you may open upon them in a broadside. Take care and fire low, boys, and you'll be sure to hull the flock."

"Fire low!" shouted Kirby:—"hear the old fool! If we fire low, we may hit the stumps, but not ruffle a pigeon."

"How should you know, you lubber?" cried Benjamin, with a very unbecoming heat for an officer on the eve of battle—"how should you know, you grampus? Haven't I sailed aboard of the Boadishy for five years? and wasn't it a standing order to fire low, and to hull your enemy? Keep silence at your guns, boys, and mind the order that is passed."

The loud laughs of the musket men were silenced by the more authoritative voice of Richard, who called for attention and obedience to his signals.

Some millions of pigeons were supposed to have already passed, that morning, over the valley of Templeton; but nothing like the flock that was now approaching had been seen before. It extended from mountain to mountain in one solid blue mass, and the eye looked in vain, over the southern hills, to find its termination. The front of this living column was distinctly marked by a line but very slightly indented, so regular and even was the flight. Even Marmaduke forgot the morality of Leather-stocking as it approached, and, in common with the rest, brought his musket to a poise.

"Fire!" cried the Sheriff, clapping a coal to the priming of the cannon. As half of Benjamin's charge escaped through the touch-hole, the whole volley of the musketry preceded the report of the swivel. On receiving this united discharge of small-arms, the front of the flock darted upward, while, at the same instant, myriads of those in the rear rushed with amazing rapidity into their places, so that when the column of white smoke gushed from the mouth of the little cannon, an accumulated mass of objects was gliding over its point of direction. The roar of the gun echoed along the mountains, and died away to the north, like distant thunder, while the whole flock of alarmed birds seemed, for a moment, thrown into one disorderly and agitated mass. The air was filled with their irregular flight, layer rising above layer, far above the tops of the highest pines, none daring to advance beyond the dangerous pass; when, suddenly, some of the leaders of the feathered tribe shot across the valley, taking their flight directly over the village, and hundreds of thousands in their rear followed the example, deserting the eastern side of the plain to their persecutors and the slain.

"Victory!" shouted Richard, "victory! we have driven the enemy from the field."

"No so, Dickon," said Marmaduke: "the field is covered with them; and, like the Leather-stocking, I see nothing but eyes, in every direction, as the innocent sufferers turn their heads in terror. Full one-half of those that have fallen are yet alive; and I think it is time to end the sport, if sport it be."

"Sport!" cried the Sheriff; "it is princely sport! There

are some thousands of the blue-coated boys on the ground, so that every old woman in the village may have a pot-pie for the asking."

"Well, we have happily frightened the birds from this side of the valley," said Marmaduke, "and the carnage must of necessity end, for the present. Boys, I will give you six-pence a hundred for the pigeons' heads only; so go to work and bring them into the village."

This expedient produced the desired effect, for every urchin on the ground went industriously to work to wring the necks of the wounded birds. Judge Temple retired toward his dwelling with that kind of feeling that many a man has experienced before him, who discovers, after the excitement of the moment has passed, that he has purchased pleasure at the price of misery to others. Horses were loaded with the dead; and, after this first burst of sporting, the shooting of pigeons became a business, with a few idlers, for the remainder of the season. Richard, however, boasted for many a year, of his shot with the "cricket;" and Benjamin gravely asserted, that he thought they killed nearly as many pigeons on that day, as there were Frenchmen destroyed on the memorable occasion of Rodney's victory.

[ARISTABULUS BRAGG]

From James Fenimore Cooper, *Home As Found* (New York, n.d.), Ch. 2, abridged.

. . . The service at Mr. Effingham's table was made in the quiet but thorough manner that distinguishes a French dinner. Every dish was removed, carved by the domestics, and handed in turn to each guest. But there were a delay and a finish in this arrangement that suited neither Aristabulus's go-ahead-ism, nor his organ of acquisitiveness. Instead of waiting, therefore, for the more graduated movements of the domestics, he began to take care of himself, an office that he performed with a certain dexterity that he had acquired by frequenting ordinaries—a school, by the way, in which he had obtained most of his notions of the proprieties of the table. One or two slices were obtained in the usual manner, or by means of the regular service; and then, like one who had laid the foundation of a fortune by some lucky windfall in the commencement of his career, he began to make accessions, right and left, as opportunity offered. Sundry *entremets*, or light dishes that had a peculiarly tempting appearance, came first under his grasp. Of these he soon accumulated all within his reach, by taxing his neighbors, when he ventured to send his plate here and there, or wherever he saw a dish that promised to reward his trouble. By such means, which were resorted to, however, with a quiet and unobtrusive assiduity that escaped much observation, Mr. Bragg contrived to make his own plate a sample epitome of the first course. It contained in the centre, fish, beef, and ham; and around these staple articles he had arranged croquettes, rognons, râgouts, vegetables, and other light things, until not only was the plate completely covered, but it was actually covered in double and triple layers; mustard, cold butter, salt, and even pepper garnishing its edges. These different accumulations were the work of time and address, and most of the company had repeatedly changed their plates before Aristabulus had eaten a mouthful, the soup excepted. The happy moment when his ingenuity was to be rewarded had now arrived, and the land agent was about to commence the process of mastication, or of deglutition rather, for he troubled himself very little with the first operation, when the report of a cork drew his attention toward the champagne. To Aristabulus this wine never came amiss, for, relishing its piquancy, he had never gone far enough into the science of the table to learn which were the proper moments for using it. As respected all the others at table, this moment had in truth arrived, though, as respected himself, he was no nearer to it, according to a regulated taste, than when he first took his seat. Perceiving that Pierre was serving it, however, he offered his own glass, and enjoyed a delicious instant as he swallowed a beverage that much surpassed anything he had ever known to issue out of the waxed and leaded nozzles that, pointed like so many enemies' batteries loaded with headaches and disordered stomachs, garnished sundry village bars of his acquaintance.

Aristabulus finished his glass at a draught, and when he took breath he fairly smacked his lips. That was an unlucky instant; his plate, burdened with all its treasures, being removed at this unguarded moment; the man who performed this unkind office fancying that a dislike to the dishes could alone have given rise to such an *omnium-gatherum*.

It was necessary to commence *de novo*, but this could no longer be done with the "first course," which was removed, and Aristabulus set to with zeal forthwith on the game. Necessity compelled him to eat, as the different dishes were offered; and such was his ordinary assiduity with the knife and fork, that, at the end of the second remove, he had actually disposed of more food than any other person at the table. He now began to converse, and we shall open the conversation at the precise point in the dinner when it was in the power of Aristabulus to make one of the interlocutors.

Unlike Mr. Dodge, he had betrayed no peculiar interest in the baronet, being a man too shrewd and worldly to set his heart on trifles of any sort; and Mr. Bragg no more hesitated about replying to Sir George Templemore or Mr. Effingham, than he would have hesitated about answering one of his own nearest associates. With him age and experience formed no particular claims to be heard, and, as to rank, it is true he had some vague ideas about there being such a thing in the militia, but as it was unsalaried rank, he attached no great importance to it. Sir George Templemore was inquiring concerning the recording of deeds, a regulation that had recently attracted attention in England; and one of Mr. Effingham's replies contained some immaterial inaccuracy, which Aristabulus took occasion to correct, as his first appearance in the general discourse.

"I ask pardon, sir," he concluded his explanations by saying, "but I ought to know these little niceties, having served a short part of a term as a county clerk, to fill a vacancy occasioned by a death."

"You mean, Mr. Bragg, that you were employed to write in a county clerk's office," observed John Effingham, who so much disliked untruth, that he did not hesitate much about refuting it, or what he now fancied to be an untruth.

"As county clerk, sir. Major Pippin died a year before his time was out, and I got the appointment. As regular a county clerk, sir, as there is in the fifty-six counties of New York."

"When I had the honor to engage you as Mr. Effingham's agent, sir," returned the other, a little sternly, for he felt his own character for veracity involved in that of the subject of his selection, "I believed, indeed, that you were writing in the office, but I did not understand it was as the clerk."

"Very true, Mr. John," returned Aristabulus, without discovering the least concern, "I was then engaged by my successor as a clerk; but a few months earlier, I filled the office myself."

"Had you gone on, in the regular line of promotion, my dear sir," pithily inquired Captain Truck, "to what preferment would you have risen by this time?"

"I believe I understand you, gentlemen," returned the unmoved Aristabulus, who perceived a general smile. "I know that some people are particular about keeping pretty much on the same level, as to office: but I hold to no such doctrine. If one good thing cannot be had, I do not see that it is a reason for rejecting another. I ran that year for sheriff, and finding I was not strong enough to carry the county, I accepted my successor's offer to write in the office, until something better might turn up."

"You practised all this time, I believe, Mr. Bragg," observed John Effingham.

"I did a little in that way too, sir; or as much as I could. Law is flat with us of late, and many of the attorneys are turning their attention to other callings."

"And pray, sir," asked Sir George, "what is the favorite pursuit with most of them just now?"

"Some our way have gone into the horse line; but much the greater portion are just now dealing in western cities."

"In western cities!" exclaimed the baronet, looking as if he distrusted a mystification.

"In such articles, and in mill-seats, and railroad lines, and other expectations."

"Mr. Bragg means that they are buying and selling lands on which it is hoped all these conveniences may exist, a century hence," explained John Effingham.

"The hope is for next year, or next week even, Mr. John," returned Aristabulus with a sly look, "though you may be very right as to the reality. Great fortunes have been made on a capital of hopes, lately, in this country."

"And have you been able yourself to resist these temptations?" asked Mr. Effingham. "I feel doubly indebted to you, sir, that you should have continued to devote your time to my interests, while so many better things were offering."

"It was my duty, sir," said Aristabulus, bowing so much the lower, from the consciousness that he had actually deserted his post for some months, to embark in the western speculations that were then so active in the country, "not to say my pleasure. There are many profitable occupations in this country, Sir George, that have been overlooked in the eagerness to embark in the town-trade——"

"Mr. Bragg does not mean trade in town, but trade in towns," explained John Effingham.

"Yes, sir, the traffic in cities. I never come this way without casting an eye about me, in order to see if there is anything to be done that is useful; and I confess that several available opportunities have offered, if one had capital. Milk is a good business."

"*Le lait!*" exclaimed Mademoiselle Viefville, involuntarily.

"Yes, ma'am, for ladies as well as gentlemen. Sweet potatoes I have heard well spoken of, and peaches are really making some rich men's fortunes."

"All of which are honester and better occupations than the traffic in cities, that you have mentioned," quietly observed Mr. Effingham.

Aristabulus looked up in a little surprise for with him everything was eligible that returned a good profit, and all things honest that the law did not actually punish. Perceiving, however, that the company was disposed to listen, and having by this time recovered the lost ground, in the way of food, he cheerfully resumed his theme.

"Many families have left Otsego, this and the last summer, Mr. Effingham, as emigrants for the west. The fever has spread far and wide."

"The fever! Is old Otsego," for so its inhabitants loved to call a county of half a century's existence, it being venerable by comparison, "is old Otsego losing its well-established character for salubrity?"

"I do not allude to an animal fever, but to the western fever."

"*Ce pays de l'ouest, est-il bien malsain?*" whispered Mademoiselle Viefville.

"*Apparemment, Mademoiselle, sur plusieurs rapports.*"

"The western fever has seized old and young, and it has carried off many active families from our part of the world," continued Aristabulus, who did not understand the little aside just mentioned, and who, of course, did not need it; "most of the counties adjoining our own have lost a considerable portion of their population."

"And they who have gone, do they belong to the permanent families, or are they merely the floating inhabitants?" inquired Mr. Effingham.

"Most of them belong to the regular movers."

"Movers!" again exclaimed Sir George—"is there any material part of your population who actually deserve this name?"

"As much so as the man who shoes a horse ought to be called a smith, or the man who frames a house a carpenter," answered John Effingham.

"To be sure," continued Mr. Bragg, "we have a pretty considerable leaven of them in our political dough, as

well as in our active business. I believe, Sir George, that
in England men are tolerably stationary."

"We love to continue for generations on the same spot.
We love the tree that our forefathers planted, the roof
that they built, the fireside by which they sat, the sods
that cover their remains."

"Very poetical, and I dare say there are situations in
life in which such feelings come in without much effort.
It must be a great check to business operations, however,
in your part of the world, sir!"

"Business operations! what is business, as you term it,
sir, to the affections, to the recollections of ancestry, and
to the solemn feelings connected with history and
tradition?"

"Why, sir, in the way of history, one meets with but few
encumbrances in this country, but he may do very much
as interest dictates, so far as that is concerned, at least.
A nation is much to be pitied that is weighed down by
the past, in this manner, since its industry and enterprise
are constantly impeded by obstacles that grow out of its
recollections. America may, indeed, be termed a happy
and a free country, Mr. John Effingham, in this, as well
as in all other things!"

Sir George Templemore was too well-bred to utter all
he felt at that moment, as it would unavoidably wound
the feelings of his hosts, but he was rewarded for his
forbearance by intelligent smiles from Eve and Grace,
the latter of whom the young baronet fancied, just at that
moment, was quite as beautiful as her cousin, and if less
finished in manners, she had the most interesting naïveté.

"I have been told that most old nations have to struggle
with difficulties that we escape," returned John Effingham,
"though I confess this is a superiority on our part that
never before presented itself to my mind."

"The political economists, and even the geographers,
have overlooked it, but practical men see and feel its
advantages every hour in the day. I have been told, Sir
George Templemore, that in England there are difficulties in running highways and streets through homesteads

and dwellings; and that even a railroad or a canal is obliged to make a curve to avoid a church-yard or a tombstone?"

"I confess to the sin, sir."

"Our friend Mr. Bragg," put in John Effingham, "considers life as all means and no end."

"An end cannot be got at without the means, Mr. John Effingham, as I trust you will yourself admit. I am for the end of the road at least, and must say that I rejoice in being a native of a country in which as few impediments as possible exist to onward impulses. The man who should resist an improvement in our part of the country, on account of his forefathers, would fare badly among his contemporaries." . . .

9

*Napoleon, or the Man of the World**

RALPH WALDO EMERSON

Ralph Waldo Emerson began to acquire a considerable reputation as a lecturer and writer in the later years of the Jacksonian decade. In 1836, his first book, a slim volume of ninety-five pages, entitled *Nature,* was published. Although not enthusiastically received at the time, the essay attracted the attention of some notable reviewers in America and England. Modern scholars accept it as an opening manifesto in the movement of thought which Emerson and his contemporaries called "transcendentalism."

In *Nature,* Emerson proclaims the necessity and the virtue of change. "Our age is retrospective," he writes. "Why should not we also enjoy an original relation to the Universe? Why should not we have a poetry and philosophy of insight and not of tradition, and religion by revelation to us? . . . Let us demand our own works and laws and worship." Yet the changes which Emerson calls for are not the material inventions of an industrial society. The catalogue of these is endless, and Emerson describes them only as "a mercenary benefit . . . which has respect to a farther good." And this farther good is spiritual in quality, containing such values as Beauty and Justice and Truth and Freedom. These spiritual values can be discovered intuitively when man understands that Nature is the symbol of spirit, and that particular natural facts are the symbols of spiritual facts. In some respects then, a transcendentalist is a sophisticated Natty Bumppo who has given up his hut in the wilderness for a book-lined study in Concord and who

* From Ralph Waldo Emerson, *Representative Men* (Cambridge, Massachusetts, 1903), pp. 223–56, abridged.

reads the signs of Nature with the help of Plato rather than of Chingachgook.

It should not surprise us, then, that Emerson had misgivings about the rapid social changes of his own time. His essay on "Napoleon, or the Man of the World" written in 1845, is a disturbing parable about democracy and the age of the common man. The Jacksonians mythicized Jefferson as the Father of Democracy. To the Jacksonians, the Jefferson image was the touchstone by which to register the progress of democracy and the rise of the common man. For Emerson, Napoleon—not Jefferson—represents the "incarnate Democrat." Napoleon is the symbol of the democratic class of men—a class which "is selfish . . . , encroaching, bold, self-relying. . . . It desires to keep open every avenue to the competition of all, and to multiply avenues: the class of business men in America, in England, in France and throughout Europe."

Emerson's essay on Napoleon contains a remarkable perception of the enormous power of the new social and economic forces that are at work in America and Europe. The new men of means and of power are carrying all before them. "Men give way before such men as before natural events." By means of this essay we get an unusual kind of insight into the social tensions that "the destroyer of prescription, the internal improver . . . the inventor of means, the opener of doors and markets" had brought to America and to Europe in the age of the common man.

Among the eminent persons of the nineteenth century, Bonaparte is far the best known and the most powerful; and owes his predominance to the fidelity with which he expresses the tone of thought and belief, the aims of the masses of active and cultivated men. It is Swedenborg's theory that every organ is made up of homogeneous particles; or as it is sometimes expressed, every whole is made of similars; that is, the lungs are composed of infinitely small lungs; the liver, of infinitely small livers; the kidney, of little kidneys, etc. Following this analogy, if any man is found to carry with him the power and affections of vast numbers, if Napoleon is France, if Napoleon is Europe, it is because the people whom he sways are little Napoleons.

In our society there is a standing antagonism between the conservative and the democratic classes; between those who have made their fortunes, and the young and the poor who have fortunes to make; between the interests of dead labor,—that is, the labor of hands long ago still in the grave, which labor is now entombed in money stocks, or in land and buildings owned by idle capitalists, —and the interests of living labor, which seeks to possess itself of land and buildings and money stocks. The first class is timid, selfish, illiberal, hating innovation, and continually losing numbers by death. The second class is selfish also, encroaching, bold, self-relying, always outnumbering the other and recruiting its numbers every hour by births. It desires to keep open every avenue to the competition of all, and to multiply avenues: the class of business men in America, in England, in France and throughout Europe; the class of industry and skill. Napoleon is its representative. The instinct of active, brave, able men, throughout the middle class every where, has pointed out Napoleon as the incarnate Democrat. He had their virtues and their vices; above all, he had their spirit or aim. That tendency is material, pointing at a sensual success and employing the richest and most various means to that end; conversant with mechanical powers, highly intellectual, widely and accurately learned and skilful, but subordinating all intellectual and spiritual forces into means to a material success. To be the rich man, is the end. "God has granted," says the Koran, "to every people a prophet in its own tongue." Paris and London and New York, the spirit of commerce, of money and material power, were also to have their prophet; and Bonaparte was qualified and sent.

Every one of the million readers of anecdotes or memoirs or lives of Napoleon, delights in the page, because he studies in it his own history. Napoleon is thoroughly modern, and, at the highest point of his fortunes, has the very spirit of the newspapers. He is no saint,—to use his own word, "no capuchin," and he is no hero, in the high sense. The man in the street finds in him the qualities and powers of other men in the street. He finds him, like himself, by birth a citizen, who, by very intelligible merits, arrived at such a commanding position that he could indulge all those tastes which the common man possesses but is obliged to conceal and deny: good society, good books, fast travelling, dress, dinners, servants without number, personal weight, the execution of his ideas, the standing in the attitude of a benefactor to all persons about him, the refined enjoyments of pictures, statues, music, palaces and conventional honors,—precisely what is agreeable to the heart of every man in the nineteenth century, this powerful man possessed.

It is true that a man of Napoleon's truth of adaptation to the mind of the masses around him, becomes not merely representative but actually a monopolizer and usurper of other minds. Thus Mirabeau plagiarized every good thought, every good word that was spoken in France. Dumont relates that he sat in the gallery of the Convention and heard Mirabeau make a speech. It struck Dumont that he could fit it with a peroration, which he wrote in pencil immediately, and showed it to Lord Elgin, who sat by him. Lord Elgin approved it, and Dumont, in the evening, showed it to Mirabeau. Mirabeau read it, pronounced it admirable, and declared he would incorporate it into his harangue to-morrow, to the Assembly. "It is impossible," said Dumont, "as, unfortunately, I have shown it to Lord Elgin." "If you have shown it to Lord Elgin and to fifty persons beside, I shall still speak it to-morrow:" and he did speak it, with much effect, at the next day's session. For Mirabeau, with his over-powering personality, felt that these things which his presence inspired were as much his own as if he had said them, and that his adoption of them gave them their weight. Much more absolute and centralizing was the successor to Mirabeau's popularity and to much more than his predominance in France. Indeed, a man of Napoleon's stamp almost ceases to have a private speech and opinion. He is so largely receptive, and is so placed, that he comes to be a bureau for all the intelligence, wit and power of the age and country. He gains the battle; he makes the code; he makes the system of weights and measures; he levels the Alps; he builds the road. All distinguished engineers, savants, statists, report to him: so likewise do all good heads in every kind: he adopts the best measures, sets his stamp on them, and not these alone, but on every happy and memorable expression. Every sentence spoken by Napoleon and every line of his writing, deserves reading, as it is the sense of France.

Bonaparte was the idol of common men because he had in transcendent degree the qualities and powers of common men. There is a certain satisfaction in coming down to the lowest ground of politics, for we get rid of cant and hypocrisy. Bonaparte wrought, in common with that great class he represented, for power and wealth,—but Bonaparte, specially, without any scruple as to the means. All the sentiments which embarrass men's pursuit of these objects, he set aside. The sentiments were for women and children. Fontanes, in 1804, expressed Napoleon's own sense, when in behalf of the Senate he addressed him,— "Sire, the desire of perfection is the worst disease that ever afflicted the human mind." The advocates of liberty and of progress are "ideologists;"—a word of contempt often in his mouth;—"Necker is an ideologist:" "Lafayette is an ideologist."

An Italian proverb, too well known, declares that "if you would succeed, you must not be too good." It is an advantage, within certain limits, to have renounced the dominion of the sentiments of piety, gratitude and generosity; since what was an impassable bar to us, and still is to others, becomes a convenient weapon for our purposes; just as the river which was a formidable barrier, winter transforms into the smoothest of roads.

Napoleon renounced, once for all, sentiments and affections, and would help himself with his hands and his head. With him is no miracle and no magic. He is a worker in brass, in iron, in wood, in earth, in roads, in buildings, in money and in troops, and a very consistent and wise master-workman. He is never weak and literary, but acts with the solidity and the precision of natural agents. He has not lost his native sense and sympathy with things. Men give way before such a man, as before natural events. To be sure there are men enough who are immersed in things, as farmers, smiths, sailors and mechanics generally; and we know how real and solid such men appear in the presence of scholars and grammarians: but these men ordinarily lack the power of arrangement, and are like hands without a head. But Bonaparte superadded to this mineral and animal force, insight and generalization, so that men saw in him combined the natural and the intellectual power, as if the sea and land had taken flesh and begun to cipher. Therefore the land and sea seem to presuppose him. He came unto his own and they received him. This ciphering operative knows what he is working with and what is the product. He knew the properties of gold and iron, of wheels and ships, of troops and diplomatists, and required that each should do after its kind.

The art of war was the game in which he exerted his arithmetic. It consisted, according to him, in having always more forces than the enemy, on the point where the enemy is attacked, or where he attacks: and his whole talent is strained by endless manoeuvre and evolution, to march always on the enemy at an angle, and destroy his forces in detail. It is obvious that a very small force, skilfully and rapidly manoeuvring so as always to bring two men against one at the point of engagement, will be an overmatch for a much larger body of men.

The times, his constitution and his early circumstances combined to develop this pattern democrat. He had the virtues of his class and the conditions for their activity. That commonsense which no sooner respects any end than it finds the means to effect it; the delight in the use of means; in the choice, simplification and combining of means; the directness and thoroughness of his work; the prudence with which all was seen and the energy with which all was done, make him the natural organ and head of what I may almost call, from its extent, the *modern* party.

Nature must have far the greatest share in every success, and so in his. Such a man was wanted, and such a man was born; a man of stone and iron, capable of sitting on horseback sixteen or seventeen hours, of going many days together without rest or food except by snatches, and with the speed and spring of a tiger in action; a man not embarrassed by any scruples; compact, instant, selfish, prudent and of a perception which did not suffer itself to be baulked or misled by any pretences of others, or any superstition or any heat or haste of his own. "My hand of iron," he said, "was not at the extremity of my arm, it was immediately connected with my head." He respected the power of nature and fortune, and ascribed to it his superiority, instead of valuing himself, like inferior men, on his opinionativeness, and waging war with nature. His favorite rhetoric lay in allusion to his star; and he pleased himself, as well as the people, when he styled himself the "Child of Destiny." "They charge me," he said, "with the commission of great crimes: men of my stamp do not commit crimes. Nothing has been more simple than my elevation, it is in vain to ascribe it to intrigue or crime; it was owing to the peculiarity of the times and to my reputation of having fought well against the enemies of my country. I have always marched with the opinion of great masses and with events. Of what use then would crimes be to me?" Again he said, speaking of his son, "My son can not replace me; I could not replace myself. I am the creature of circumstances."

He had a directness of action never before combined with so much comprehension. He is a realist, terrific to all talkers and confused truth-obscuring persons. He sees where the matter hinges, throws himself on the precise point of resistance, and slights all other considerations. He is strong in the right manner, namely by insight. He never blundered into victory, but won his battles in his head before he won them on the field. His principal means are in himself. He asks counsel of no other. In 1796 he writes to the Directory: "I have conducted the campaign without consulting any one. I should have done no good if I had been under the necessity of conforming to the notions of another person. I have gained some advantages over superior forces and when totally destitute of every thing, because, in the persuasion that your confidence was reposed in me, my actions were as prompt as my thoughts."

. . . To these gifts of nature, Napoleon added the advantage of having been born to a private and humble fortune. In his later days he had the weakness of wishing to add to his crowns and badges the prescription of aristocracy; but he knew his debt to his austere education, and made no secret of his contempt for the born kings, and for "the hereditary asses," as he coarsely styled the Bourbons. He said that "in their exile they had learned nothing, and forgot nothing." Bonaparte had passed through all the degrees of military service, but also was citizen before he was emperor, and so has the key to citizenship. His remarks and estimates discover the information and justness of measurement of the middle class. Those who had to deal with him found that he was not to be imposed upon, but could cipher as well as another man. This appears in all parts of his Memoirs, dictated at St. Helena. When the expenses of the empress, of his household, of his palaces, had accumulated great debts, Napoleon examined the bills of the creditors himself, detected overcharges and errors, and reduced the claims by considerable sums.

His grand weapon, namely the millions whom he directed, he owed to the representative character which clothed him. He interests us as he stands for France and for Europe; and he exists as captain and king only as far as the Revolution, or the interest of the industrious masses, found an organ and a leader in him. In the social interests, he knew the meaning and value of labor, and threw himself naturally on that side. I like an incident mentioned by one of his biographers at St. Helena. "When walking with Mrs. Balcombe, some servants, carrying heavy boxes, passed by on the road, and Mrs. Balcombe desired them, in rather an angry tone, to keep back. Napoleon interfered, saying 'Respect the burden, Madam.'" In the time of the empire he directed attention to the improvement and embellishment of the markets of the capital. "The market-place," he said, "is the Louvre of the common people." The principal works that have survived him are his magnificent roads. He filled the troops with his spirit, and a sort of freedom and companionship grew up between him and them, which the forms of his court never permitted between the officers and himself. They performed, under his eye, that which no others could do. The best document of his relation to his troops is the order of the day on the morning of the battle of Austerlitz, in which Napoleon promises the troops that he will keep his person out of reach of fire. This declaration, which is the reverse of that ordinarily made by generals and sovereigns on the eve of a battle, sufficiently explains the devotion of the army to their leader.

But though there is in particulars this identity between Napoleon and the mass of the people, his real strength lay in their conviction that he was their representative in his genius and aims, not only when he courted, but when he controlled, and even when he decimated them by his conscriptions. He knew, as well as any Jacobin in France, how to philosophize on liberty and equality; and when allusion was made to the precious blood of centuries, which was spilled by the killing of the Duc d'Enghien, he suggested, "Neither is my blood ditch-water." The people felt that no longer the throne was occupied and the land sucked of its nourishment, by a small class of legitimates, secluded from all community with the children of the soil, and holding the ideas and superstitions of a long-forgotten state of society. Instead of that vampyre, a man of themselves held, in the Tuileries, knowledge and ideas like their own, opening of course to them and their children all places of power and trust. The day of sleepy, selfish policy, ever narrowing the means and opportunities of young men, was ended, and a day of expansion and demand was come. A market for all the powers and productions of man was opened; brilliant prizes glittered in the eyes of youth and talent. The old, iron-bound, feudal France was changed into a young Ohio or New York; and those who smarted under the immediate rigors of the new monarch, pardoned them as the necessary severities of the military system which had driven out the oppressor. And even when the majority of the people had begun to ask whether they had really gained any thing under the exhausting levies of men and money of the new master, the whole talent of the country, in every rank and kindred, took his part and defended him as its natural patron. In 1814, when advised to rely on the higher classes, Napoleon said to those around him, "Gentlemen, in the situation in which I stand, my only nobility is the rabble of the Faubourgs."

. . . I call Napoleon the agent or attorney of the middle class of modern society; of the throng who fill the markets, shops, counting-houses, manufactories, ships, of the modern world, aiming to be rich. He was the agitator, the destroyer of the prescription, the internal improver, the liberal, the radical, the inventor of means, the opener of doors and markets, the subverter of monopoly and abuse. Of course the rich and aristocratic did not like him. England, the centre of capital, and Rome and Austria, centres of tradition and genealogy, opposed him. The consternation of the dull and conservative classes, the terror of the foolish old men and old women of the Roman conclave, who in their despair took hold of any thing, and would cling to red-hot iron,—the vain attempts of statists to amuse and deceive him, of the emperor of Austria to bribe him; and the instinct of the young, ardent and active men every where, which pointed him out as the giant of the middle class, make his history bright and commanding. He had the virtues of the masses of his constituents: he had also their vices. I am sorry that the brilliant picture has its reverse. But that is the fatal quality which we discover in our pursuit of wealth, that it is treacherous, and is bought by the breaking or weakening of the sentiments; and it is inevitable that we should find the same fact in the history of this champion, who proposed to himself simply a brilliant career, without any stipulation or scruple concerning the means.

Bonaparte was singularly destitute of generous sentiments. The highest-placed individual in the most cultivated age and population of the world,—he has not the merit of common truth and honesty. He is unjust to his generals; egotistic and monopolizing; meanly stealing the credit of their great actions from Kellermann, from Bernadotte; intriguing to involve his faithful Junot in hopeless bankruptcy, in order to drive him to a distance from Paris, because the familiarity of his manners offends the new pride of his throne. He is a boundless liar. The official paper, his "Moniteur," and all his bulletins, are proverbs for saying what he wished to be believed; and worse,— he sat, in his premature old age, in his lonely island, coldly falsifying facts and dates and characters, and giving to history a theatrical *éclat*. Like all Frenchmen he has a passion for stage effect. Every action that breathes of generosity is poisoned by this calculation. His star, his love of glory, his doctrine of the immortality of the soul, are all French. "I must dazzle and astonish. If I were to give the liberty of the press, my power could not last three days." To make a great noise is his favorite design. "A great reputation is a great noise: the more there is made, the farther off it is heard. Laws, institutions, monuments, nations, all fall; but the noise continues, and resounds in after ages." His doctrine of immortality is simply fame. His theory of influence is not flattering. "There are two levers for moving men,—interest and fear. Love is a silly infatuation, depend upon it. Friendship is but a name. I love nobody. I do not even love my brothers: perhaps Joseph a little, from habit, and because he is my elder; and Duroc, I love him too; but why?—because his character pleases me: he is stern and resolute, and I believe the fellow never shed a tear. For my part I know very well that I have no true friends. As long as I continue to be what I am, I may have as many pretended friends as I please. Leave sensibility to women; but men should be firm in heart and purpose, or they should have nothing to do with war and government." He was thoroughly unscrupulous. He would steal, slander, assassinate, drown and poison, as his interest dictated. He had no generosity, but mere vulgar hatred; he was intensely selfish; he was perfidious; he cheated at cards; he was a prodigious gossip, and opened letters, and delighted in his infamous police, and rubbed his hands with joy when he had intercepted some morsel of intelligence concerning the men and women about him, boasting that "he knew every thing;" and interfered with the cutting [of] the dresses of the women; and listened after the hurrahs and the compliments of the street, incognito. His manners were coarse. He treated women with low familiarity. He had the habit of pulling their ears and pinching their cheeks when he was in good humor, and of pulling the ears and whiskers of men, and of striking and horse-play with them, to his last days. It does not appear that he listened at key-holes, or at least that he was caught at it. In short, when you have penetrated through all the circles of power and splendor, you were not dealing with a gentleman, at last; but with an impostor and a rogue; and he fully deserves the epithet of *Jupiter Scapin*, or a sort of Scamp Jupiter. . . .

10

The Course of Civilization: Allegory and Reality

(See Plates 1–8 following page 14.)

Thomas Cole has sometimes been called one of the founders of the Hudson River school of landscape painters. His works depicting the Catskills or the rich fertility of the Connecticut River Valley are among the best paintings of American rivers and mountains done in the Jacksonian era. Later in his career, Cole turned to more mystical and moral themes in his art, undoubtedly influenced by his visits to Europe where he acquired a fascination for crumbling towers and the ruins of ancient Rome. Between 1836 and 1848, he created such strange worlds in his own imagination as the *Course of Empire* series. N. P. Willis believed that Cole had succumbed to the "poetry of decay" which was fashionable in Europe, but the moralizing in the *Course of Empire* paintings is quite American even if the landscapes are not. The *Course of Empire* paintings represent a morality play which composed one of the figured patterns in the mythology of the Jacksonian generation. Plates 1–3 state the essential themes in this moral drama.

PLATE 1. *Arcadian or Pastoral State.* By Thomas Cole.
In this painting we are shown a pastoral scene with sheep and shepherds, a village by the lake, and a temple of worship on the hill above the village. The whole representation suggests such themes as plenty, piety, virtue, and serenity.

PLATE 2. *Consummation of Empire.* By Thomas Cole.
This painting has a very different tone and mood. We see the magnificent architectural structures and the

monumental sculptures of a great city. The streets are teeming with people and the harbor is filled with ships of trade. The whole representation suggests power, pomp, luxury, and extravagance as well as commercial and technological sophistication.

PLATE 3. *Destruction of Empire.* By Thomas Cole.
This painting depicts the doom of empire with warfare and social chaos as the main conditions of life. Somehow, this seems to be the inevitable outcome of the departure from the simplicity and virtue of the arcadian state.

If Thomas Cole's *Course of Empire* can be taken as an allegorical representation of the Jacksonian fears about the corrupting influence of wealth and power, the succeeding illustrations in this group—Plates 4–8—give us a more direct representation of the changing realities of the American landscape. These engravings were familiar to many Americans of the Jacksonian generation since they appeared in the pictorial books and magazines that were becoming so popular in the second half of the nineteenth century.

PLATE 4. *View of Meredith (New Hampshire).* Engraved by W. H. Bartlett. From N. P. Willis, *American Scenery: or Land, Lake and River Illustrations of Transatlantic Nature* (London, 1840), I, 125.
This scene parallels Thomas Cole's representation of the arcadian state. There are sheep, an oxcart, and yeoman farmers, a village and a church by the quiet lake. Such pastoral scenes suggesting simplicity and plenty can be seen again and again in the pictorial books of this period.

PLATE 5. *East View of Lowell, Mass.* Engraved by E. L. Barber. From John Warner Barber, *Historical Collections. Being a General Collection of Interesting Facts, Traditions, Biographical Sketches, Anecdotes, etc., Relating to the History and Antiquities of Every Town in Massachusetts* (Worcester, 1839), p. 405.
This engraving discloses the changes that are taking

place with the course of civilization in America. Not
monumental works of architecture and sculpture, but
monotonous rows of many-storied factory buildings
dominate the physical form of the village becoming an
industrial town.

PLATE 6. *View of the City of Boston*. Engraver unknown.
From Robert Sears, *A Pictorial Description of the United
States; embracing the History, Geographical Position, Agri-
cultural and Mineral Resources, Population, Manufacture,
Commerce, and Sketches of Cities, Towns, Public Build-
ings, etc. etc. of Each State and Territory in the Union*
(New York, 1852), p. 58.

This scene reveals the physical transformations that are
taking place in the old colonial cities of America as they
begin to reach into the great inland market with the
tentacular lines of railroad transportation.

PLATE 7. *Lockport, Erie Canal*. Engraved by W. H. Bartlett. From N. P. Willis, *American Scenery*, I, 110.

This remarkable Bartlett engraving, depicting the
shanty-town characteristics of Lockport on the Erie
Canal, reveals the lack of taste and the loss of any
reverence for time and place which became typical of
so many hastily built towns as Americans moved across
the continent in their restless pursuit of material gain.

PLATE 8. *First of May in New York*. Engraver unknown.
From *Gleason's Pictorial Drawing Room Companion*
(1851), I, 21.

This street scene on the customary spring moving-day in
New York suggests the noise and tumult, and the restless mobility, which were taking the Americans of Jacksonian America further and further away from the pastoral serenity of village life.

PART II

The Uncertainties of Status

11

Of Honor in the United States and in Democratic Communities*

ALEXIS DE TOCQUEVILLE

We have already seen some evidence of the anxiety and guilt that accompanied the remarkable increase of wealth, the rapid development of industry and transportation, and the significant growth of cities in America between 1820 and 1840. The Jacksonian generation wrestled mightily with the perplexing problems of adjusting older ideologies and loyalties to the new social necessities created by the forces of change. And it is never easy for a people to change from the habits and values of an agrarian society to the techniques and goals of a society moving rapidly into an industrial stage of economy, even when there is a reasonably fluid system of social stratification as in the United States in the early nineteenth century.

Many of the anxieties that were articulated by the Jacksonian generation revealed a broadly based consensus —the nostalgia for the comfortable values in the earlier agrarian mythology can be discovered among Whigs as well as Democrats, among merchants as well as poets. But the social changes between 1820 and 1840 generated more specific uncertainties—uncertainties about social status and personal identification that were as troublesome as the unhinging of commonly shared values and ideals.

Tocqueville's *Democracy in America* makes a good starting point for the investigation of the uncertainties of status that existed in Jacksonian America. Tocqueville is

* From Alexis de Tocqueville, *Democracy in America*, Francis Bowen, ed. (Cambridge, Massachusetts, 1863), II, 281–93, abridged.

always sensitive to the fact that America lacked feudal institutions and, therefore, was creating a different kind of social system. In the selection that follows, he is using a conception of systems of esteem and disesteem which seems surprisingly modern. In particular, he is contrasting the American system of esteem with the earlier feudal system of Europe. In addition to noting the differences in the American notions of honor, Tocqueville argues that in America, where "all men are in constant motion, and where society, transformed daily by its own operations, changes its opinions together with its wants," the laws of honor are "more obscure" and "it must often be difficult to distinguish them."

If Tocqueville is right, then we can assume that the American in the Jacksonian generation had a peculiar problem of self-identification and self-esteem. Tocqueville believes this is so and tries elsewhere in the *Democracy* to describe the form of this anxiety when he writes, "Among democratic nations, men easily attain a certain equality of condition, but they can never attain as much as they desire. It perpetually retires before them, yet without hiding itself from their sight, and retiring draws them on. At every moment they think they are about to grasp it; it escapes at every moment from their hold. They are near enough to see its charms, but too far off to enjoy them; and before they have fully tasted its delights, they die."

It would seem that men employ two very distinct methods in the judgment which they pass upon the actions of their fellow-men; at one time, they judge them by those simple notions of right and wrong which are diffused all over the world; at another, they appreciate them by a few very special rules which belong exclusively to some particular age and country. It often happens that these two standards differ; they sometimes conflict: but they are never either entirely identified or entirely annulled by one another. . . .

Honor is simply that peculiar rule founded upon a peculiar state of society, by the application of which a people or a class allot praise or blame. Nothing is more unproductive to the mind than an abstract idea; I therefore hasten to call in the aid of facts and examples to illustrate my meaning.

I select the most extraordinary kind of honor which has ever been known in the world, and that which we are best acquainted with,—viz. aristocratic honor springing out of feudal society. I shall explain it by means of the principle already laid down, and explain the principle by means of this illustration.

I am not here led to inquire when and how the aristocracy of the Middle Ages came into existence, why it was so deeply severed from the remainder of the nation, or what founded and consolidated its power. I take its existence as an established fact, and I am endeavoring to account for the peculiar view which it took of the greater part of human actions.

The first thing that strikes me is, that, in the feudal world, actions were not always praised or blamed with reference to their intrinsic worth, but were sometimes appreciated exclusively with reference to the person who was the actor or the object of them, which is repugnant to the general conscience of mankind. Thus, some of the actions which were indifferent on the part of a man in humble life, dishonored a noble; others changed their whole character according as the person aggrieved by them belonged, or did not belong, to the aristocracy.

When these different notions first arose, the nobility formed a distinct body amidst the people, which it commanded from the inaccessible heights where it was ensconced. To maintain this peculiar position, which constituted its strength, it not only required political privileges, but it required a standard of right and wrong for its own special use.

That some particular virtue or vice belonged to the nobility rather than to the humble classes,—that certain actions were guiltless when they affected the villain, which were criminal when they touched the noble,—these were often arbitrary matters; but that honor or shame should be attached to a man's actions according to his condition, was a result of the internal constitution of an aristocratic community. This has been actually the case in all the countries which have had an aristocracy; as long as a trace of the principle remains, these peculiarities will still exist: to debauch a woman of color scarcely injures the reputation of an American,—to marry her dishonors him.

In some cases, feudal honor enjoined revenge, and stigmatized the forgiveness of insults; in others, it imperiously commanded men to conquer their own passions, and required forgetfulness of self. It did not make humanity or kindness its law, but it extolled generosity; it set more store on liberality than on benevolence; it allowed men to enrich themselves by gambling or by war, but not by labor; it preferred great crimes to small earnings; cupidity was less distasteful to it than avarice; violence it often sanctioned, but cunning and treachery it invariably reprobated as contemptible.

These fantastical notions did not proceed exclusively from the caprice of those who entertained them. A class which has succeeded in placing itself above all others, and which makes perpetual exertions to maintain this lofty position, must especially honor those virtues which are conspicuous for their dignity and splendor, and which may be easily combined with pride and the love of power. Such men would not hesitate to invert the natural order of conscience in order to give these virtues precedence over all others. It may even be conceived that some of the more bold and brilliant vices would readily be set above the quiet, unpretending virtues. The very existence of such a class in society renders these things unavoidable.

The nobles of the Middle Ages placed military courage foremost amongst virtues, and in lieu of many of them. This, again, was a peculiar opinion, which arose necessarily from the peculiar state of society. Feudal aristocracy existed by war and for war; its power had been founded by arms, and by arms that power was maintained: it therefore required nothing more than military courage, and that quality was naturally exalted above all others; whatever denoted it, even at the expense of reason and humanity, was therefore approved and frequently enjoined by the manners of the time. Such was the main principle; the caprice of man was to be traced only in minuter details. That a man should regard a tap on the cheek as an unbearable insult, and should be obliged to kill in single combat the person who struck him thus lightly, is an arbitrary rule; but that a noble could not tranquilly receive an insult, and was dishonored if he allowed himself to take a blow without fighting, were direct consequences of the fundamental principles and the wants of a military aristocracy.

Thus it was true, to a certain extent, that the laws of honor were capricious; but these caprices of honor were always confined within certain necessary limits. The peculiar rule which was called honor by our forefathers is so far from being an arbitrary law in my eyes, that I would readily engage to ascribe its most incoherent and fantastical injunctions to a small number of fixed and invariable wants inherent in feudal society.

If I were to trace the notion of feudal honor into the domain of politics, I should not find it more difficult to explain its dictates. The state of society and the political institutions of the Middle Ages were such, that the supreme power of the nation never governed the community directly. That power did not exist in the eyes of the people: every man looked up to a certain individual whom he was bound to obey; by that intermediate personage he was connected with all the others. Thus, in feudal society, the whole system of the commonwealth rested upon the sentiment of fidelity to the person of the lord; to destroy that sentiment was to fall into anarchy. Fidelity to a political superior was, moreover, a sentiment of which all the members of the aristocracy had constant opportunities of estimating the importance; for every one of them was a vassal as well as a lord, and had to command as well as to obey. To remain faithful to the lord, to sacrifice one's self for him if called upon, to share his good or evil fortunes, to stand by him in his undertakings whatever they might be,—such were the first injunctions of feudal honor in re-lation to the political institutions of those times. The treachery of a vassal was branded with extraordinary severity by public opinion, and a name of peculiar infamy was invented for the offence; it was called *felony*. . . .

Any nation would furnish us with similar grounds of observation; for, as I have already remarked, whenever men collect together as a distinct community, the notion of honor instantly grows up amongst them; that is to say, a system of opinions peculiar to themselves as to what is blamable or commendable; and these peculiar rules always originate in the special habits and special interests of the community.

This is applicable to a certain extent to democratic communities as well as to others, as we shall now proceed to prove by the example of the Americans.

Some loose notions of the old aristocratic honor of Europe are still to be found scattered amongst the opinions of the Americans; but these traditional opinions are few in number, they have but little root in the country, and but little power. They are like a religion which has still some temples left standing, though men have ceased to believe in it. But amidst these half-obliterated notions of exotic honor some new opinions have sprung up, which consti-tute what may be termed in our days American honor.

I have shown how the Americans are constantly driven to engage in commerce and industry. Their origin, their social condition, their political institutions, and even the region they inhabit, urge them irresistibly in this direc-tion. Their present condition, then, is that of an almost exclusively manufacturing and commercial association, placed in the midst of a new and boundless country, which their principal object is to explore for purposes of profit. This is the characteristic which most distinguishes the American people from all others at the present time.

All those quiet virtues which tend to give a regular move-ment to the community, and to encourage business, will therefore be held in peculiar honor by that people, and to neglect those virtues will be to incur public contempt.

All the more turbulent virtues, which often dazzle, but more frequently disturb society, will, on the contrary, occupy a subordinate rank in the estimation of this same people; they may be neglected without forfeiting the esteem of the community; to acquire them would perhaps be to run a risk of losing it.

The Americans make a no less arbitrary classification of men's vices. There are certain propensities which appear censurable to the general reason and the universal conscience of mankind, but which happen to agree with the peculiar and temporary wants of the American community: these propensities are lightly reproved, sometimes even encouraged; for instance, the love of wealth and the secondary propensities connected with it may be more particularly cited. To clear, to till, and to transform the vast uninhabited continent which is his domain, the American requires the daily support of an energetic passion; that passion can only be the love of wealth; the passion for wealth is therefore not reprobated in America, and, provided it does not go beyond the bounds assigned to it for public security, it is held in honor. The American lauds as a noble and praiseworthy ambition what our own forefathers, in the Middle Ages, stigmatized as servile cupidity, just as he treats as a blind and barbarous frenzy that ardor of conquest and martial temper which bore them to battle.

In the United States, fortunes are lost and regained without difficulty; the country is boundless, and its resources inexhaustible. The people have all the wants and cravings of a growing creature; and, whatever be their efforts, they are always surrounded by more than they can appropriate. It is not the ruin of a few individuals, which may be soon repaired, but the inactivity and sloth of the community at large, which would be fatal to such a people. Boldness of enterprise is the foremost cause of its rapid progress, its strength, and its greatness. Commercial business is there like a vast lottery, by which a small number of men continually lose, but the state is always a gainer; such a people ought therefore to encourage and do honor to

boldness in commercial speculations. But any bold speculation risks the fortune of the speculator and of all those
who put their trust in him. The Americans, who make a
virtue of commercial temerity, have no right in any case
to brand with disgrace those who practise it. Hence arises
the strange indulgence which is shown to bankrupts in the
United States; their honor does not suffer by such an accident. In this respect the Americans differ, not only from
the nations of Europe, but from all the commercial nations
of our time; and accordingly they resemble none of them in
their position or their wants.

In America, all those vices which tend to impair the purity of morals, and to destroy the conjugal tie, are treated
with a degree of severity which is unknown in the rest of
the world. At first sight, this seems strangely at variance
with the tolerance shown there on other subjects, and one
is surprised to meet with a morality so relaxed and also so
austere amongst the self-same people. But these things are
less incoherent than they seem to be. Public opinion in the
United States very gently represses that love of wealth
which promotes the commercial greatness and the prosperity of the nation, and it especially condemns that laxity of
morals which diverts the human mind from the pursuit of
well-being, and disturbs the internal order of domestic life
which is so necessary to success in business. To earn the
esteem of their countrymen, the Americans are therefore
constrained to adapt themselves to orderly habits; and it
may be said in this sense that they make it a matter of
honor to live chastely.

On one point, American honor accords with the notions
of honor acknowledged in Europe; it places courage as
the highest virtue, and treats it as the greatest of the moral
necessities of man; but the notion of courage itself assumes
a different aspect. In the United States, martial valor is but
little prized; the courage which is best known and most
esteemed is that which emboldens men to brave the
dangers of the ocean, in order to arrive earlier in port,—to
support the privations of the wilderness without complaint, and solitude more cruel than privations,—the

courage which renders them almost insensible to the loss of a fortune laboriously acquired, and instantly prompts to fresh exertions to make another. Courage of this kind is peculiarly necessary to the maintenance and prosperity of the American communities, and it is held by them in peculiar honor and estimation; to betray a want of it is to incur certain disgrace.

I have yet another characteristic point which may serve to place the idea of this chapter in stronger relief. In a democratic society like that of the United States, where fortunes are scanty and insecure, everybody works, and work opens a way to everything: this has changed the point of honor quite round, and has turned it against idleness. I have sometimes met in America with young men of wealth, personally disinclined to all laborious exertion, but who had been compelled to embrace a profession. Their disposition and their fortune allowed them to remain without employment: public opinion forbade it, too imperiously to be disobeyed. In the European countries, on the contrary, where aristocracy is still struggling with the flood which overwhelms it, I have often seen men, constantly spurred on by their wants and desires, remain in idleness, in order not to lose the esteem of their equals; and I have known them submit to ennui and privations rather than to work. No one can fail to perceive that these opposite obligations are two different rules of conduct, both nevertheless originating in the notion of honor.

What our forefathers designated as honor absolutely was in reality only one of its forms; they gave a generic name to what was only a species. Honor, therefore, is to be found in democratic as well as in aristocratic ages, but it will not be difficult to show that it assumes a different aspect in the former. Not only are its injunctions different, but we shall shortly see that they are less numerous, less precise, and that its dictates are less rigorously obeyed.

The position of a caste is always much more peculiar than that of a people. Nothing is so exceptional in the world as a small community invariably composed of the same families, (as was, for instance, the aristocracy of the

Middle Ages,) whose object is to concentrate and to retain, exclusively and hereditarily, education, wealth, and power amongst its own members. But the more exceptional the position of a community happens to be, the more numerous are its special wants, and the more extensive are its notions of honor corresponding to those wants.

The rules of honor will therefore always be less numerous amongst a people not divided into castes than amongst any other. If ever any nations are constituted in which it may even be difficult to find any peculiar classes of society, the notion of honor will be confined to a small number of precepts, which will be more and more in accordance with the moral laws adopted by the mass of mankind.

Thus the laws of honor will be less peculiar and less multifarious amongst a democratic people than in an aristocracy. They will also be more obscure; and this is a necessary consequence of what goes before; for as the distinguishing marks of honor are less numerous and less peculiar, it must often be difficult to distinguish them. To this other reasons may be added. Amongst the aristocratic nations of the Middle Ages, generation succeeded generation in vain; each family was like a never-dying, ever-stationary man, and the state of opinions was hardly more changeable than that of conditions. Every one then had the same objects always before his eyes, which he contemplated from the same point; his eyes gradually detected the smallest details, and his discernment could not fail to become in the end clear and accurate. Thus, not only had the men of feudal times very extraordinary opinions in matters of honor, but each of those opinions was present to their minds under a clear and precise form.

This can never be the case in America, where all men are in constant motion, and where society, transformed daily by its own operations, changes its opinions together with its wants. In such a country, men have glimpses of the rules of honor, but they seldom have time to fix attention upon them.

But even if society were motionless, it would still be difficult to determine the meaning which ought to be attached to the word honor. In the Middle Ages, as each class had its own honor, the same opinion was never received at the same time by a large number of men; and this rendered it possible to give it a determined and accurate form, which was the more easy, as all those by whom it was received, having a perfectly identical and most peculiar position, were naturally disposed to agree upon the points of a law which was made for themselves alone.

Thus the code of honor became a complete and detailed system, in which everything was anticipated and provided for beforehand, and a fixed and always palpable standard was applied to human actions. Amongst a democratic nation, like the Americans, in which ranks are confounded, and the whole of society forms one single mass, composed of elements which are all analogous though not entirely similar, it is impossible ever to agree beforehand on what shall or shall not be allowed by the laws of honor. . . .

12

The Middle Classes*

MICHEL CHEVALIER

Although Tocqueville offers a cogent explanation of problems of honor and self-esteem, he does not develop too clear a description of social stratification in America. He seems to assume that there was a broad, unitary, class system in the United States within which "fortunes are scanty and insecure, everybody works, and work opens the way to everything." Once again, the concreteness of Chevalier's *Society, Manners, and Politics in the United States* is a necessary complement to the abstractions of Tocqueville.

In his chapter entitled "The Middle Classes," Chevalier asserts that outside of the older states of the seaboard South, there are really only two classes in America: "the middle class and the democracy." The middle class consists of manufacturers, merchants, lawyers, and physicians; the democracy is composed of farmers and mechanics. If we are to accept Chevalier's testimony, then the only class struggle of any kind in America was between these two classes. On the whole, Chevalier seems to think that these two classes have similar domestic styles of life and "differ considerably only in respect of the sect to which they are attached and the pews they occupy." He does recognize the attempts of some "coteries" in American society to establish "certain fashionable distinctions," but he dismisses these aristocratic pretensions as "timid and often absurd protestations against the abuse of equality."

* From Michael Chevalier, *Society, Manners, and Politics in the United States,* John W. Ward, ed. (Garden City, New York, 1961), pp. 380–85, abridged.

American society is composed of elements quite different from European society in general, and French society in particular. On analyzing the latter, we find in the first place the shadow of an aristocracy, made up of the wrecks of the great families of the old order that have been saved from the revolutionary storm and the descendants of the Imperial nobility who seem to be already separated from their fathers by centuries.

Next below this is a numerous middle class (*bourgeoisie*) in two distinct parts: one, the active class, is engaged in commerce, manufactures, agriculture, and the liberal professions; the other, generally designated among us as idle, the *bourgeoisie oisive*, consists of men without active employment, landholders who derive an income of $500 or $1,500 from their estates by rents or by sharing the produce with the cultivator without attempting to increase it, and the small body of holders of public stock.

These two divisions of the middle class differ essentially from each other, the one laboring, the other only consuming and enjoying what they have. The one increases its means and consequently is able to keep itself above the waves and maintain, if not to raise, its level; the other, as M. Laffitte has said, transported by time into one stage of society after another, in each of which large additions are made to the general wealth, finds itself growing relatively poorer and must decrease in numbers. They differ no less in their origin; one belongs essentially to the commons; the other has some pretensions to nobility, being the offspring, or at least the heir and successor, of the country gentry. During the Restoration they differed also in their political views; one took the left side, the other preferred the right. At present, the former accepts the new dynasty without reluctance; the latter, more difficult to be satisfied in regard to the preservation of order and ready to take alarm at every violation of old established privileges, still preserves a secret preference for the legitimate line. In respect to religious sentiments, one is skeptical and prone to believe that the Voltairean philosophy and the theories broached by the Opposition during fifteen years are the _ne plus ultra_ of the human understanding; the other, shaken in its faith, still keeps alive the sacred fire of religious feeling, rejects the disorganizing doctrines of the eighteenth century, and holds in scorn the lucubrations of the liberal publicists of the Restoration. One piques itself on its adherence to the positive, the material; the other concerns itself about the great conservative principles of society, but refuses to recognize the new interests which must be allowed to share in the privileges of those of the past.

These two sections of the middle class are not wholly and sharply separated from each other; they run into and across each other. A large proportion partakes somewhat of both characters and joins one side or the other, according to times and circumstances. Yet, although often confounded in the same individual, the two interests are, nevertheless, substantially distinct from each other. The base of the pyramid is occupied by peasants and workers subdivided into two sections: one which has property, the other which has not yet reached that point but aspires after it with eagerness. On one side, we have mechanics and small proprietors; on the other, laborers. Today it is universally recognized that the middle class rules in France. The aristocracy is driven from power or stands aloof. The mechanics and small proprietors hardly yet begin to raise their heads. The laborers are nothing.

In the Northern States of the American Union, society is much less complex in its composition than in France. Exclusive of the colored caste, there are here only two classes: the middle class and the democracy. Of the two conflicting interests, one only, labor, has a public existence here. The middle class consists of manufacturers, merchants, lawyers, physicians. A small number of cultivators and persons devoted to letters or the fine arts is to be added to these.

The democracy is composed of the farmers and mechanics. In general, the cultivator is the owner of the soil;

in the West, this rule is without exception. Great land-holders do not exist, at least as a class, in the North and the Northwest. There is strictly speaking no proletariat; although there are day laborers and, both in the cities and country, many workmen without capital, yet these are in fact apprentices, for the most part foreigners, who in turn become proprietors and master-workmen and not infrequently rich manufacturers, wealthy speculators.

Between these two classes there is, however, no line of demarcation, for the attempts of some coteries to establish certain fashionable distinctions do not deserve notice, or at least have only a negative value as timid and often absurd protestations against the abuse of equality. The two classes have the same domestic habits, lead the same life, and differ considerably only in respect of the sect to which they are attached and the pews they occupy. One can get a sufficiently exact notion of the relations between these two classes by comparing them in France with the wealthy *bourgeoisie* and the wrecks of the aristocracy.

Political influence is at present entirely in the hands of the American democracy, just as with us it is monopolized by the middle classes. The latter have no chance of getting possession of power in the United States except temporarily, or by means of accidental divisions in the democratic ranks when they may rally to their standard a portion of the farmers and mechanics, as happened in 1834 after General Jackson's attack on the Bank. So in France it will be impossible for the aristocracy to raise, not its own banner (for it has none), but that of the legitimate line, unless the folly of the government should excite new troubles and inspire the middle class, who now support it heartily, with fears for the public security.

In the Southern States, the existence of slavery produces a state of society quite different from the North; half the population there consists of the proletariat in the strictest sense, that is of slaves. Slavery necessarily requires great landed property, which is aristocracy in fact. Great estates still continue to be held in the South despite the custom of equal partition, which has very much narrowed them.

Between these two extremes in the South, an intermediate class has sprung up consisting, like our middle class, of working men and men of leisure, the new interest and the old interest. Commerce, manufactures, and the liberal professions, on one side; on the other, the landholders, corresponding to our moderate country landholders, living on their estates by the sweat of their slaves, having no taste for work, not prepared for it by education, and even taking little oversight of the daily business of the plantation; men who would be incapable of applying themselves to any occupation if slavery were abolished, just as our proprietors would be unable to get a living if they were to be deprived of their estates.

It is plain that the equal partition of estates must have tended to increase the number of this class of men of leisure; it is numerous in the old Southern States, Virginia, the Carolinas, and Georgia, and also in Louisiana; the check which these States at first experienced in their career, while the North was advancing without a stop, and the contemporaneous increase of this class are two correlative facts which account for each other. But we do not find this class in the new States of the South. The new generation there, devoured as in the North with the passion of making money, has become as industrious as the Yankees. The cultivation of cotton offers a wide field of activity; in Alabama and Mississippi, cotton lands are sold at a very low price. The internal slave trade furnishes hands in abundance which are easily procured on credit when one has friends, but no patrimony. The sons of the old Southern States, instead of vegetating on a fragment of the paternal estate with a handful of Negroes, sell off their property at home, extend their means by aid of a loan which they are sure of being able to repay promptly, and go to the Southwest to establish a cotton plantation, a sort of agricultural factory, in which they are obliged to exercise more or less of the activity and to feel more or less of the hopes and fears of a manufacturer.

Thus the part of the middle class which works little or not at all is disappearing in the United States. In the

Western States, which are the true New World, it no longer exists at all, North or South; you meet with no one there who is not engaged in agriculture, commerce, manufactures, the liberal professions, or the Church. The United States, then, differ from us in having no aristocracy, no idle middle class, no class of mere laborers, at the least in the North. But a distinction should be made in regard to the absence of these three classes; for while it may be admitted that the last two are becoming absolutely extinct, it would be more correct to say that the first has not yet begun to exist.

Civilization in its passage from one continent to the other has, then, got rid of two classes. This twofold disappearance is, however, only a single phenomenon or, at most, two phases of a single fact, the industrial progress of mankind. It seems to me inevitable that in this matter the Old World should follow the example of the New; it moves toward the same goal under the influence of causes of its own, irresistibly driven onward by what is commonly called the force of events, that is, by the decree of Providence. . . .

13

The Higher Circles and the Lower Circles

The following illustration in *Graham's Lady's and Gentleman's Magazine* has a considerable cutting edge to its satire. The editorial comment which accompanied this engraving in wood included the following statement: "Among the *higher* class the *mode* is rather shadowy, the form being cared for more than the substance. . . . Among the *lower* class substance is a more material matter." This is certainly a view that suggests the growing egalitarian sentiments of the Jacksonian generation.

THE HIGHER CIRCLES AND THE LOWER CIRCLES.

From "The Higher Circles and Lower Circles"—a Satirical View, from *Graham's Lady's and Gentleman's Magazine* (1844), XXIV, 296.

14

The Artificial Inequality of Wealth*

WILLIAM M. GOUGE

William Gouge, a Philadelphia editor and political economist, was one of the leading theorists in the Jacksonian party. He did much to formulate the Jacksonian indictment of the banking and currency system of the United States in his treatise published in 1833 under the title, *A Short History of Paper Money and Banking in the United States.* The book was an instant success and went through several editions in the years of controversy over the Bank of the United States between 1833 and 1837. It was serialized in the New York *Evening Post* and the Washington *Globe*—both leading Democratic newspapers. In 1835, Gouge was summoned to Washington to a post in the Treasury Department where he helped to formulate some of the later phases of the Jackson administration's financial policy.

It is clear from the selection below that Gouge is operating with an ideology of conflict. He sees a struggle of classes in American society that is based on a division between "the hard-working members of society"—the honest capitalist, the honest farmer, and the honest mechanic—and the men who have "made commerce a game of hap-hazard" and who have grown rich by means of the *artificial* advantages provided in the chartered privileges of the banking system of the United States.

Gouge's vision of the good society is apparently based upon a conception of a simpler and more stable social

* From William M. Gouge, A *Short History of Paper Money and Banking in the United States* (New York, 1835), pp. 30–33, abridged.

order in which "some little wealth, at least enough for daily subsistence, is necessary for the enjoyment of life and the pursuit of happiness" and in which, whatever wealth there is, comes as a result of "industry, economy, enterprise, and prudence." One wonders whether Gouge and other Jacksonians like him have really come to terms with the new forces of industrialism and the new national market being created by the transportation revolution. The new forces of industry and transport required new types of business organization and larger amounts of capital. Can we assume, then, that Gouge's willingness to rely on natural laws and on the force of individual character to control the distribution of wealth was an intelligent way to prepare the Jacksonian generation to deal with the new economic realities?

[OF THE REMOTE CONSEQUENCES OF THE SYSTEM]

Our view of the extent to which paper-money Banking affects our social condition, will be very imperfect, if we confine it to the *direct* operations of the system. These are, as it were, but the first links of a long extended chain. Each effect becomes in its turn a cause: and the remote consequences are of more importance than the immediate. To prove this, a few plain truths will suffice.

If two men start in life at the same time, and the one gets, at the commencement, but a small advantage over the other, and retains the advantage for twenty or thirty years, their fortunes will, at the end of that period, be very unequal.

If a man at the age of twenty-one years is deprived of one hundred dollars which he had honestly earned, and honestly saved, the injury done to this man must be estimated by the advantage he would have derived from the use of his little property during the rest of his life. The want of it may prevent his turning his faculties to the best account. The loss may dispirit his future exertion.

If a man is, at any period of his life, deprived of a property, large or small, accumulated for him by the honest industry and economy of his ancestors, the wrong done to him is of the same character as that which he sustains when he is unjustly deprived of property which was the fruits of his own industry. It is the dictate of nature that parents shall leave their wealth to their children, and the law of the land, in this case, only confirms the dictate of nature.

It is not easy to set bounds to the effects of a single act of injustice. If you deprive a man of his property, you may thereby deprive him of the means of properly educating his children, and thus affect the moral and intellectual character of his descendants for several generations.

Such being the consequences of single acts, we may learn from them to estimate the effects of those political and commercial institutions which operate unequally. They lay the foundation of an *artificial* inequality of wealth: and whenever this is done, the wealth of the few goes on increasing the ratio of compound interest, while the reflex operations of the very causes to which the few owe their wealth, keep the rest of the community in poverty.

Where the distribution of wealth is left to natural and just laws, and the natural connexion of cause and effect is not violated, the tendency of "money to beget money," or rather of wealth to produce wealth, is not an evil. A man has as strong a natural right to the profits which are yielded by the capital which was formed by his labor, as he has to the immediate product of his labor. To deny this, would be to deny him a right to the whole product of his labor. The claims of the honest capitalist and of the honest laborer are equally sacred, and rest, in fact, on the same foundation. Nor is it the law of nature that the idle and improvident shall suffer temporary inconvenience only. By neglecting to form a capital for themselves, they render their future labor less productive than it otherwise might be: and finally make themselves dependent on others for the means of both subsistence and employment.

But unequal political and commercial institutions invest the operation of the natural and just causes of wealth and poverty—take much of the capital of a country from those whose industry produced it, and whose economy saved it, and give it to those who neither work nor save. The natural reward of industry then goes to the idle, and the natural punishment of idleness falls on the industrious.

Inasmuch as personal, political, commercial, and accidental causes, operate sometimes in conjunction and sometimes in opposition, it is difficult to say, in individual cases, in how great a degree wealth or poverty is owing to one cause or to another. Harsh judgments of rich and poor, taking them individually, are to be avoided. But it is notorious that, as regards different *classes* in different countries, wealth and poverty are the consequences of the positive institutions of those countries. Peculiar political privileges are commonly the ground of the distinction; but peculiar commercial privileges have the same effect; and when the foundation of the artificial inequality of fortune is once laid, (it matters not whether it be by feudal institutions or money corporations,) all the subsequent operations of society tend to increase the difference in the condition of different classes of the community.

One consequence of unequal institutions is increasing the demand for luxuries, and diminishing the effective demand for necessaries and comforts. Many being qualified to be producers of necessaries, and few to be producers of luxuries, the reward of the many is reduced, and that of the few raised to an enormous height. The inventor of some new means of gratification for the rich is sure to receive his recompense, though thousands of able-bodied men may be starving around him.

This may be illustrated by a case drawn from England, where the favorite opera-singer receives her thousands per annum, while the able-bodied agricultural laborer is forced to draw on the parish-rates for subsistence.

Something similar to it may be found in our own country, where the second-rate singers, dancers, and players of Europe, accumulate fortunes in a few years, while multitudes of humble but useful women in all our large cities, struggle hard for the means of a bare subsistence.

Now there is no cause of complaint in people's lavishing their thousands on favorite singers and dancers, if those thousands have been honestly earned and fairly got. But if they owe their thousands to political or commercial institutions, operating specially to their advantage, those political and commercial institutions are not of the kind most conducive to social happiness.

Through all the operations of business, the effects of an unequal distribution of wealth may be distinctly traced. The rich have the means of rewarding most liberally the professional characters whom they employ, and the tradesmen with whom they deal. An aristocracy in one department of society, introduces an aristocracy into all.

These effects are, it is true, most obvious in countries where the causes of an artificial inequality of wealth are of a permanent character, and interwoven with political organization: but they can be discovered in our own country. The inequality of reward our lawyers and physicians receive, is caused but in part by inequality of talent. It is owing in part to the inequality of the means of those who employ them: and in part to the disposition the many have to prefer the lawyer or the physician who is patronized by the rich and fashionable. They feel that their own education disqualifies them for forming a proper estimate of professional talent, and they take the judgment of those who they suppose must, from their superior wealth, have better means of information.

It is, however, among the hard-working members of society, that the ultimate effects of such causes are most observable.

The condition of a multitude of poor women in our large cities, has lately attracted the attention of the benevolent. It appears from the statements that have been published, that they can, by working ten or twelve hours every day, earn no more than from seventy-five cents to a dollar a week. Half of this sum goes for house rent and fuel, leaving them from thirty-seven and a half cents to fifty cents a week for food and clothing for themselves and children. Some thousands are said to be in this situation in Philadelphia alone.

Various proposals have been made to better their condition: some futile, others absolutely pernicious. The laws of supply and demand are too powerful to yield to sermons and essays. The low rate of the wages of these poor women, is the effect of general causes—causes which affect, in one way or another, every branch of business. In the great game we have been playing, much of the wealth of the country has passed into a few hands. Many men dying, have left nothing to their widows and children; and others who still live, cannot support their families, except by the additional industry of their wives. The work of a seamstress can be done by a woman in her own house, in the intervals she can spare from attention to her children. In this way the number of seamstresses has been increased.

On the other hand, many families who would gladly employ these poor women, are compelled by their own straitened circumstances, to do this kind of work themselves. In this way the demand for seamstresses is diminished.

Private benevolence may improve the condition of individuals of this class; but the class itself can be benefited by such causes only as will diminish the number of seamstresses or increase the demand for their labor. The cause that will improve the condition of one of the industrious classes of society, will improve the condition of all. When an end shall be put to unfair speculation, then, and not till then, will honest industry have its just reward.

[EFFECTS ON MORAL CHARACTER]

The practices of trade seem, in most countries, to fix the standard of commercial honesty. In the Hanse Towns and Holland, while they were rising to wealth, this standard was very high. Soldiers were not more careful to preserve their honor without stain, than merchants were to maintain their credit without blemish.

The practices of trade in the United States, have debased the standard of commercial honesty. Without clearly distinguishing the causes that have made commerce a game of hap-hazard, men have come to perceive clearly the nature of the effect. They see wealth passing continually out of the hands of those whose labor produced it, or whose economy saved it, into the hands of those who neither work nor save. They do not clearly perceive *how* the transfer takes place; but they are certain of the fact. In the general scramble they think themselves entitled to some portion of the spoil, and if they cannot obtain it by fair means, they take it by foul.

Hence we find men without scruple, incurring debts which they have no prospect of paying.

Hence we find them, when on the very verge of bankruptcy, embarrassing their friends by prevailing on them to endorse notes and sign custom-house bonds.

Instances not unfrequently occur of men who have failed once or twice, afterwards accumulating great wealth. How few of these honorably discharge their old debts by paying twenty shillings in the pound!

How many evade the just demands of their creditors, by privately transferring their property.

It is impossible, in the present condition of society, to pass laws which will punish dishonest insolvents, and not oppress the honest and unfortunate.

Neither can public opinion distinguish between them. The dishonest share the sympathy which should be given exclusively to their unfortunate neighbors; and the honest are forced to bear a part of the indignation which should fall entirely on the fraudulent.

The standard of commercial honesty can never be raised very high, while trade is conducted on present principles.

"It is hard," says Dr. Franklin, "for an empty bag to stand upright." The straits to which many men are reduced, cause them to be guilty of actions which they would regard with as much horror as their neighbors, if they were as prosperous as their neighbors.

We may be very severe in our censure of such men, but

what else ought we to expect, when laws and circumstances give to some men so great advantages in the great game in which the fortunes of the whole community are at issue— what else ought we to expect, but that those to whom the law gives no such advantage, should exert to the utmost such faculties as remain to them in the struggle for riches, and not be very particular whether the means they use are such as the law sanctions or the law condemns.

Let those who are in possession of property which has been acquired according to the strict letter of the law, be thankful that they have not been led into such temptations as those on whom the positive institutions of society have had an unfavorable influence.

But Banking has a more extensive effect on the moral character of the community, through the distribution of wealth which is the result of its various direct and remote operations. Moralists in all ages, have inveighed against luxury. To it they attribute the corruption of morals, and the downfall of nations. The word luxury is equivocal. What is regarded as a luxury in one stage of society, is, in another, considered as a comfort, and in a still more advanced stage, as a necessary. The desire of enjoyment is the great stimulus to social improvement. If men were content with bare necessaries, no people would, in the arts and sciences, and in whatever else renders life desirable, be in advance of the lowest caste of the Hindoos, or the unhappy peasantry of the most unhappy country of Europe.

But whatever moralists have said against luxury, is true when applied to that *artificial* unequality of fortune which is produced by *positive* institutions of unjust character. Its necessary effect is to corrupt one part of the community, and debase the other.

The bare prospect of inheriting great wealth, damps the energies of a young man. It is well if this is the only evil it produces. "An idle man's brain," says John Bunyan, "is the devil's workshop." Few men can have much leisure, and not be injured by it. To get rid of the *ennui* of existence, young men of wealth resort to the gambling-table, the race-ground, and other haunts of dissipation.

They cannot have these low means of gratification without debasing those less favored by fortune.

The children of the poor suffer as much in one way, as the children of the rich suffer in another. The whole energies of the father and mother are exhausted in providing bread for themselves and their family. They cannot attend properly to the formation of the moral character of their offspring—the most important branch of education. They can ill spare the means to pay for suitable intellectual instruction. Their necessities compel them to put their children to employments unsuited to their age and strength. The foundation is thus laid of diseases which shorten and embitter life.

Instances occur of men, by the force of their innate powers, overcoming the advantages of excess or defect of wealth; but it is true, as a general maxim, that in early life, and in every period of life, too much or too little wealth, is injurious to the character of the individual, and when it extends through a community, it is injurious to the character of that community.

In the general intercourse of society, this artificial inequality of wealth produces baneful effects. In the United States, the pride of wealth has more force than in any other country, because there is here no other pride to divide the human heart. Some of our good republicans do, indeed, boast of a descent from European nobility; but when they produce their coats of arms, and their geneological trees, they are laughed at. The question is propounded, if their noble ancestors left them any *money*. Genius confers on its possessor a very doubtful advantage. Virtue, with us, as in the days of the Roman poet, is viler than seaweed, unless it has a splendid retinue. Talent is estimated only as a means of increasing riches. Wealth alone can give permanent distinction, for he who is at the top of the political ladder to-day, may be at the bottom to-morrow.

One mischief this state of things produces is, that men are brought to regard wealth as the *only* means of happiness. Hence they sacrifice honor, conscience, health, friends, every thing to obtain it.

The other effects of artificial inequality of wealth, have been treated of at large, by moralists, from Solomon and Socrates downwards. To their works and to the modern treatises on crime and pauperism, we refer the reader. The last mentioned treatises are, for the most part, only illustrations of the ultimate effects of positive institutions, which operate unequally on different members of the community.

[EFFECTS ON HAPPINESS]

The inferences the intelligent reader must have drawn from what has already been stated, preclude the necessity of much detail in this part of our inquiry.

Wealth is, if independently considered, but one among fifty of the causes of happiness; and poverty, viewed in the same light, as but one among fifty of the causes of misery. The poorest young man, having health of body and peace of mind, and enjoying the play of the social sympathies, in the affections of wife, children and friends, is happier than the richest old man, bowed down by sickness, oppressed with anxiety for the future, or by remorse for the past, having nobody to love and beloved by nobody.

But though we may, by mental abstraction, consider wealth independently, or poverty independently, neither the one nor the other is absolutely independent in its operation. There is no cause in either the physical or the moral world, but what works in conjunction with other causes. Health of body and peace of mind, with the just play of the social affections, may give happiness, independently of wealth; but in extreme poverty, it is difficult to preserve either health of body or peace of mind, and the play of the social affections becomes then a source of misery.

Some little wealth, at least enough for daily subsistence, is necessary for the enjoyment of life and the pursuit of happiness; and hence it is, that the right to property is as important as the right to life and right to liberty. "You take my life when you do take the means by which I live."

The majority of men are of such temperament, that something more than the means of subsistence for the bare twenty-four hours, is necessary for their happiness. They must also have a prospect of enjoying the like means of subsistence in future days. But this is a prospect which, with the reflecting part of the poor, is frequently overcast with clouds and gloom. Few journeymen mechanics are able to make adequate provision for sickness and old age. The wages of a laborer will support him and his family while he enjoys health and while employment is steady; but in case of long-continued sickness he must look for relief from the hand of public or of private charity. If he casts his eyes on his wife and children, his dying hours are embittered with thoughts of the misery which may be their portion. Corroding care is the inmate of the poor man's breast. It is so heart-withering, that it may be made a question, whether the condition of some slaves in the Southern States is much worse than that of many citizens of the other States. The want of liberty is a great drawback on happiness; but the slave is free from care. He knows that when he grows old, or becomes infirm, his master is bound to provide for his wants.

There would be less objection to that artificial inequality of wealth which is the result of unjust positive institutions, if it increased the happiness of one class of society in the same proportion that it diminishes the happiness of another class. But increase of wealth beyond what is necessary to gratify the rational desires of a man, does not increase his happiness. If it gives birth to irrational desires, the gratification of them must produce misery. Even when inordinate wealth does not give birth to irrational desires, it is attended with an increase of care, and this is a foe to happiness.

With some men, the love of wealth seems to be a blind passion. The magpie, in hiding silver spoons in its nest, appears to act with as much reflection as they do, in piling money-bag on money-bag. They have no object in view beyond accumulation. But with most men, the desire of great wealth appears subordinate to the love of great power and distinction. This is the end, that the means. They love fine houses, splendid equipages, and large possessions, less for any physical gratification they impart, than for the distinction they confer, and the power they bestow. It is with some, as much an object of ambition to be ranked with the richest men, as it is with others to be ranked with the greatest warriors, poets, or philosophers.

The love of that kind of distinction which mere wealth confers, is not a feeling to be highly commended; but it is hardly to be reprobated, when it is constitutional, and when it is under the government of proper moral principle. In this case, it is a simple stimulus to vigorous industry and watchful economy. With some men, the love of ease is the ruling passion, with others the love of pleasure, and with others the love of science. If the love of riches were not, with many men, stronger than any of the other loves we have mentioned, there might not be enough wealth accumulated to serve the general purpose of society. They may claim the liberty of gratifying their particular passion in a reasonable way; but it is a passion which derives less gratification from the actual possession of a large store, than from the constant increase of a small one. The man whose wealth increases gradually from one hundred dollars to one thousand, thence to five thousand, thence to ten thousand, and thence to fifty thousand, has more satisfaction in the process than he who suddenly becomes possessed of one hundred thousand dollars. As to the distinction which mere wealth confers, it would be obtained in a state of society in which the distribution of wealth was left to natural laws, as certainly as in a state in which positive institutions operate to the advantage of the few, and to the disadvantage of the many. If the riches of men were made to depend entirely on their industry, economy, enterprise, and prudence, the possession of one hundred thousand dollars would confer as much distinction as the possession of five hundred thousand dollars confers at present. Those worth "a plum," would then rank among the "first men" on 'change; those who are worth "five plums" can rank no higher now. . . .

15

Resolutions on the Social, Civil, and Intellectual Condition of the Laboring Classes*

THE NATIONAL TRADES' UNION

Coinciding with the advent of Andrew Jackson to the presidency, was the appearance of workingmen's parties in larger eastern cities like Philadelphia, New York, and Boston. These workingmen's parties were short-lived, and it is doubtful whether they ever represented a distinctively working-class movement. They were never able to attract large numbers of votes in the working-class wards of cities like Philadelphia and Boston, and many of their leaders were middle-class intellectuals like Theodore Sedgewick, Samuel Clesson Allen, and William Gouge—or social visionaries like Robert Dale Owen, Fanny Wright, and Thomas Skidmore.

In the middle thirties, something like a genuine trade union movement came into existence in the United States. For several years, there had been a rapid growth of local trade unions and city trades' assemblies in eastern cities, and even in western cities like Pittsburgh, Cincinnati, and Louisville. These organizations were primarily concerned with improving wages and working conditions. In 1834, many of these local organizations were associated in the National Trades' Union—the first organization of American wage-earners on a national scale. It was estimated that 26,000 members in the eastern cities of the United States were represented by delegates to the first general convention.

The following selection from the proceedings of the first convention of the National Trades' Union offers

* From *The Man* (New York), August 30, 1834, II, 357.

some indication of the goals and values of these laboring men in the Jacksonian decade. They identify themselves as "producers" entitled to full equality of rights in the American democratic society. Can we not say that these resolutions reveal an intense anxiety about status? The workingmen at the National Trades' Union convention are concerned not only with the "unequal and unjustifiable distribution of the produce of labor," but also express their fears that the practices of employers are undermining the moral independence of workingmen, putting them in the status of "a humiliating, servile dependency, incompatible with the inherent natural equality of men."

[TRADES' UNION NATIONAL CONVENTION]

FIFTH AND LAST DAY

The Vice President took the chair. The minutes of the last meeting were read and accepted. . . .

Mr. Farrel, from the committee on resolutions, made the following report, which was accepted, and all the resolutions unanimously adopted.

The Committee to whom was referred the duty of drafting resolutions expressive of the views of the National Trades' Union Convention on the social, civil, and intellectual condition of the laboring classes, beg leave to report,

That whereas all the actions and pursuits of man have for their object the possession of happiness, that this object is attained in proportion to the ratio of the intelligence and virtue of man individually and collectively must be apparent to the most superficial observer;

And whereas society is conducive to happiness, it being good for man to associate with his fellow man, moral justice of necessity becomes the keystone to the arch of the social compact, and the permanence and value of all social institutions must be apportionate to their utility and their degree of assimilation with the principle of moral justice;

And whereas the social, civil, and intellectual condition of the laboring classes of these United States, and the like classes in all countries, exhibit the most unequal and unjustifiable distribution of the produce of labor, thus operating to produce a humiliating, servile dependency, incompatible with the inherent natural equality of man,

And whereas each and every man is by nature compelled to consume the produce of labor in the supply to his necessary wants, moral justice would exact from every individual, when not incapacitated by natural imbecility or accident, a fair and full equivalent to society for that which he consumes, and also that he should contribute his due portion of labor towards the contingencies of society, for the protection and security he derives therefrom;

And whereas the accumulation of the wealth of society in the hands of a few individuals (which has been abstracted from the producers thereof by means of the erroneous customs, usages, and laws of society) is subversive of the rights of man, seeing that wealth or property only can be justly acquired in three ways, viz. 1st, by producing, 2d, by exchanging labor for labor in equal quantities, and 3d, by donation; it therefore becomes a duty imperative on every productive laborer, who values the liberties of his country, the welfare of the human family, and his own social happiness, to keep the evils that exist in society steadily in view, that knowing them, he may the more effectually direct his energies to destroy the causes from whence they arise, and by a well concerted union with his fellow laborers, concoct and carry out into practice such measures as will secure, at least to the present generation, the gratitude of their descendants, for their having barked the tree of Corruption, and nourished that of *Liberty* and *Equality*, without which life itself is a burden to its possessor;

Therefore, be it

Resolved, That this Convention, deeply impressed with the conviction, that the primary causes of all the evils and difficulties with which the laboring classes are environed, can be traced to the want of a correct knowledge of their own value as producers, and the just estimate of their resources, would recommend, that such of the working classes of these United States as have not already formed themselves into societies for the protection of their industry, do so forthwith, that they may by these means be enabled effectively to make common cause with their oppressed brethren, and the more speedily disseminate such knowledge as may be most conducive to their interests in their respective trades and arts, as well as their general interests as productive laborers.

Resolved, That this Convention view the systems of Education now in operation in these United States as destructive of that Equality which is predicated in the Declaration of Independence, because of their exclusive character in giving instruction to the wealthy few at the expense of the industrious many, fostering, by means of Colleges, Universities, Military or Naval Academies, &c., a professional Monopoly of Knowledge, thereby drawing a line of demarcation between the producers of all the wealth, and the other portions of society which subsist upon the fruits of the Working Man's industry.

Resolved, That this Convention do recommend to the various Trades' Unions, that they take into their serious consideration the importance of an Equal, Universal Republican system of Education, and that they take such measures thereon as may to them be deemed advisable.

Resolved, That this Convention deprecate the system now practised in the disposal of the Public Lands, because of its violating the inherent rights of the citizen, seeing that the whole of the unseated lands belong unto the people, and should not be disposed of to the prejudice of any class of society each and every citizen having a just claim to an equitable portion thereof, a location upon which being the only just title thereunto.

Resolved, That this Convention would the more especially reprobate the *sale* of the Public Lands, because of its injurious tendency as it affects the interests and independence of the laboring classes, inasmuch as it debars them from the occupation of any portion of the same, unless provided with an amount of capital which the greater portion of them, who would avail themselves of this aid to arrive at personal independence, cannot hope to attain, owing to the many encroachments made upon them through the reduction in the wages of labor consequent upon its surplus quantity in the market, which surplus would be drained off, and a demand for the produce of mechanical labor increased, if these public lands were left open to actual settlers.

Resolved, That this committee view with serious alarm the deplorable condition of the male and female children employed in the cotton and woollen manufactories in this country, and the many privations they are subjected to, arising from the early age they are put to work in factories and the enormous length of time allotted for a day's labor. This subject is earnestly recommended to the attention of the various Unions of our country, and it is to be hoped they will forward memorials to the legislatures of their respective states, embodying therein the outlines of such a plan as may be approved by them, and it is also suggested that lawful security should be exacted from the proprietors of manufactories, for the education of every child employed by them therein.

Resolved, That the laws existing in portions of our country, under which Trades' Unions among mechanics for the maintenance of their rights, and the correction of abuses, are declared illegal Combinations, are a manifest violation of the Constitution of these United States, and an infringement of the lawful rights of every citizen:—and this Convention do hereby urge upon the serious consideration of every laboring man the absolute necessity of their repeal.

Resolved, That as productive labor is the only legitimate source of wealth, and as the productive laborers have been deprived of the advantages of their labor by bad legislation, it behooves this portion of the community to regain and maintain, by correct legislation, what they have lost by inattention to their own best interests.

Resolved, That hereafter it should be the first as well as the last duty of every laborer, to inform himself on the subject of his equal rights and labor to promote the good of the whole community, rather than to confer privileges on a favored few.

Signed on behalf of the Committee.
JOHN FARREL, Ch'n.

16

On Social Station*

JAMES FENIMORE COOPER

After his return to Jacksonian America, Cooper found it impossible to express himself only in fables and romances. He had things to say to his countrymen and he needed the didactic advantages of the essay form to say them. *A Letter To His Countrymen* (1834) was a first attempt to analyze political principles and social institutions, but *The American Democrat* published in 1838 contains the fullest statement of Cooper's social theory. "The work," he admitted in the Introduction, "is written more in the spirit of censure than of praise, for its aim is correction. . . ."

The chief abuse in American democracy is to be found in the extremes of the majority and the tyranny of opinion. "Public opinion," Cooper wrote, in a chapter by that title, "is the lever by which all things are moved in a democracy." And, in America, this lever is controlled by a dishonest press and political demagogues. Hence the chapter "On Station" is central to Cooper's conception of a corrective social principle. It contains his claim for the recognition of the special qualifications of the gentleman of talent and refinement for political and social leadership in a democracy. At a later point in *The American Democrat*, he declared: "They who do not see and feel the importance of possessing a class of such men in a community, to give it tone, a high and far-sighted policy, and lofty views in general, can know little of history. . . ."

Cooper's idea of the gentleman was received by many of his contemporaries as the reactionary notion of the

* From James Fenimore Cooper, *The American Democrat* (Cooperstown, 1838), pp. 77–83, unabridged.

son of a wealthy Federalist squire. After all, the Jacksonian generation believed that common sense and natural wisdom were more important for leadership than talent and learning. It was no less a person than Andrew Jackson who said in his first message to Congress—"In a country where offices are created solely for the benefit of the people, no man has any more intrinsic right to official station than another." Yet, we can assume that there were many of Cooper's contemporaries who shared Cooper's views and we may also wonder whether there was not considerable merit in Cooper's claim that talent, independence, knowledge, and decorum are indispensable qualities for democratic leadership.

Station may be divided into that which is political, or publick, and that which is social, or private. In monarchies and aristocracies the two are found united, since the higher classes, as a matter of course, monopolize all the offices of consideration; but, in democracies, there is not, nor is it proper that there should be, any intimate connexion between them.

Political, or publick station, is that which is derived from office, and in a democracy, must embrace men of very different degrees of leisure, refinement, habits and knowledge. This is characteristick of the institutions, which, under a popular government, confer on political station more power than rank, since the latter is expressly avoided in this system.

Social station is that which one possesses in the ordinary associations, and is dependent on birth, education, personal qualities, property, tastes, habits, and, in some instances, on caprice, or fashion. Although the latter undeniably is sometimes admitted to control social station, it generally depends, however, on the other considerations named.

Social station, in the main, is a consequence of property. So long as there is civilization there must be the rights of property, and so long as there are the rights of property, their obvious consequences must follow. All that democracies legitimately attempt is to prevent the advantages which accompany social station from accumulating rights that do not properly belong to the condition, which is effected by pronouncing that it shall have no factitious political aids.

They who have reasoned ignorantly, or who have aimed at effecting their personal ends by flattering the popular feeling, have boldly affirmed that "one man is as good as another;" a maxim that is true in neither nature, revealed morals, nor political theory.

That one man is not as good as another in natural qualities, is proved on the testimony of our senses. One man is stronger than another; he is handsomer, taller, swifter, wiser, or braver, than all his fellows. In short, the physical and moral qualities are unequally distributed, and, as a necessary consequence, in none of them, can one man be justly said to be as good as another. Perhaps no two human beings can be found so precisely equal in every thing, that one shall not be pronounced the superior of the other; which, of course, establishes the fact that there is no natural equality.

The advocates of exclusive political privileges reason on this circumstance by assuming, that as nature has made differences between men, those institutions which create political orders, are no more than carrying out the great designs of providence. The error of their argument is in supposing it a confirmation of the designs of nature to attempt to supplant her, for, while the latter has rendered men unequal, it is not from male to male, according to the order of primogeniture, as is usually established by human ordinances. In order not to interfere with the inequality of nature, her laws must be left to their own operations, which is just what is done in democracies, after a proper attention has been paid to the peace of society, by protecting the weak against the strong.

That one man is not deemed as good as another in the grand moral system of providence, is revealed to us in Holy Writ, by the scheme of future rewards and punishments, as well as by the whole history of those whom God has favored in this world, for their piety, or punished for their rebellion. As compared with each other, we are throughout the whole sacred history made to see, that, in a moral sense, one man is not as good as another. The evil doer is punished, while they who are distinguished for their qualities and acts, are intended to be preferred.

The absolute moral and physical equality that are inferred by the maxim, that "one man is as good as another," would at once do away with the elections, since a lottery would be both simpler, easier and cheaper than the present mode of selecting representatives. Men, in such a case, would draw lots for office, as they are now drawn for juries. Choice supposes a preference, and preference inequality of merit, or of fitness.

We are then to discard all visionary theories on this head, and look at things as they are. All that the most popular institutions attempt, is to prohibit that one *race* of men shall be made better than another by law, from father to son, which would be defeating the intentions of providence, creating a superiority that exists in neither physical nor moral nature, and substituting a political scheme for the will of God and the force of things.

As a principle, one man is as good as another in rights. Such is the extent of the most liberal institutions of this country, and this provision is not general. The slave is not as good as his owner, even in rights. But in those states where slavery does not exist all men have essentially the same rights, an equality, which, so far from establishing that "one man is as good as another," in a social sense, is the very means of producing the inequality of condition that actually exists. By possessing the same rights to exercise their respective faculties, the active and frugal become more wealthy than the idle and dissolute; the wise and gifted more trusted than the silly and ignorant; the polished and refined more respected and sought, than the rude and vulgar.

In most countries, birth is a principal source of social distinction, society being divided into castes, the noble having an hereditary claim to be the superior of the plebeian. This is an unwise and an arbitrary distinction that has led to most of the social diseases of the old world, and from which America is happily exempt. But great care must be had in construing the principles which have led to this great change, for America is the first important country of modern times, in which such positive distinctions have been destroyed.

Still some legal differences, and more social advantages, are produced by birth, even in America. The child inherits the property, and a portion of the consideration of the parent. Without the first of these privileges, men would not exert themselves to acquire more property than would suffice for their own personal necessities, parental affection being one of the most powerful incentives to industry. Without such an inducement, then, it would follow that civilization would become stationary, or, it would recede; the incentives of individuality and of the affections, being absolutely necessary to impel men to endure the labor and privations that alone can advance it.

The hereditary consideration of the child, so long as it is kept within due bounds, by being confined to a natural sentiment, is also productive of good, since no more active inducement to great and glorious deeds can offer, than the deeply seated interest that man takes in his posterity. All that reason and justice require is effected, by setting bounds to such advantages, in denying hereditary claims to trusts and power; but evil would be the day, and ominous the symptom, when a people shall deny that any portion of the consideration of the ancestor is due to the descendant.

It is as vain to think of altogether setting aside sentiment and the affections, in regulating human affairs, as to imagine it possible to raise a nature, known to be erring and weak, to the level of perfection.

The Deity, in that terrible warning delivered from the mount, where he declares that he "will visit the sins of the fathers upon the children, unto the third and fourth generation," does no more than utter one of those sublime moral truths, which, in conformity with his divine providence, pervade nature. It is merely an announcement of a principle that cannot safely be separated from justice, and one that is closely connected with all the purest motives and highest aspirations of man.

There would be a manifest injustice in visiting the offence of the criminal on his nearest of kin, by making the innocent man participate in the disgrace of a guilty relative, as is notoriously done most, by those most disposed to rail at reflected renown, and not to allow of the same participation in the glory. Both depend upon a sentiment deeper than human laws, and have been established for purposes so evidently useful as to require no explanation. All that is demanded of us, is to have a care that this sentiment do not degenerate to a prejudice, and that, in the one case, we do not visit the innocent too severely, or, in the other, exalt the unworthy beyond the bounds of prudence.

It is a natural consequence of the rights of property and of the sentiment named, that birth should produce some advantages, in a social sense, even in the most democratical of the American communities. The son imbibes a portion of the intelligence, refinement and habits of the father, and he shares in his associations. These must be enumerated as the legitimate advantages of birth, and without invading the private arrangements of families and individuals, and establishing a perfect community of education, they are unavoidable. Men of the same habits, the same degree of cultivation and refinement, the same opinions, naturally associate together, in every class of life. The day laborer will not mingle with the slave; the skilful mechanic feels his superiority over the mere laborer, claims higher wages and has a pride in his craft; the man in trade justly fancies that his habits elevate him above the mechanic, so far as social position is concerned, and the man of refinement, with his education, tastes and sentiments, is superior to all. Idle declamation on these points, does not impair the force of things, and life is a series of facts. These inequalities of condition, of manners, of mental cultivation must exist, unless it be intended to reduce all to a common level of ignorance and vulgarity, which would be virtually to return to a condition of barbarism.

The result of these undeniable facts, is the inequalities of social station, in America, as elsewhere, though it is an inequality that exists without any more arbitrary distinctions than are indispensably connected with the maintenance of civilization. In a social sense, there are orders here, as in all other countries, but the classes run into each other more easily, the lines of separation are less strongly drawn, and their shadows are more intimately blended.

This social inequality of America is an unavoidable result of the institutions, though nowhere proclaimed in them, the different constitutions maintaining a profound silence on the subject, they who framed them probably knowing that it is as much a consequence of civilized society, as breathing is a vital function of animal life.

See page 185 for description of Plates 9–12.

[9] Making Shirts for a Shilling; or, Misery and Magnificence.

[10] *Riot at Hoboken.*

[11] The Jerking Exercise.

[12] *Southern Ideas of Liberty*. Photograph by courtesy of The New-York Historical Society, New York City.

17

Envy and Debt: Two Stories*

MCGUFFEY'S READERS

The standard fare of education in the schools of the United States in the early nineteenth century included books known as "Readers." These were graded collections of stories, poetry, essays, and orations which were designed to provide materials for the improvement of reading, spelling, and rhetoric-composition. But the reading selections obviously were also selected to encourage the development of certain desirable traits of character and to discourage the formation of bad habits. Hence, the Readers are important social documents; they help us to understand something about the basic values being taught to the hundreds of thousands of children who attended school in the Jacksonian generation.

Among the more popular Readers in the Jacksonian decade were those prepared by William Holmes McGuffey. McGuffey was a leading educator of the day, who taught at Miami University in Ohio, served as president of Cincinnati College and of Ohio University, and finally, in 1845, accepted the chair of moral philosophy at the University of Virginia. He was an active promoter of the public school movement in Ohio and Virginia and a famed lecturer on educational, moral, and religious topics. His First and Second Readers were published in 1836, and other graded Readers designed for upper grades and the secondary schools appeared in

* From McGuffey's *Newly Revised Eclectic Second Reader* (New York and Cincinnati, 1848), pp. 39–40, unabridged; and McGuffey's *Rhetorical Guide, Containing Elegant Extracts in Prose and Poetry—For High Schools and Academies* (New York and Cincinnati, 1853), pp. 128–30, unabridged.

quick succession. It is estimated that more than a hundred million copies of McGuffey's Readers were sold in the nineteenth century.

The two selections that follow are taken from opposite ends of the graded series of McGuffey's Readers —*The Second Reader* and *The Rhetorical Guide* for high schools and academies. Both selections have to do with considerations of class and status. One is the story of a poor boy who does not envy the rich but who is building his future on the firm foundation of industry, diligence, piety, and punctuality. The other is an ironical essay on debt which disparages the public sympathy for debtors and suggests that it is the creditor who deserves the compassion and praise of men. The second selection, in particular, suggests that wealth and business success have been mistreated too often in the public discourse of the Jacksonian generation. Both selections seem to betray the defensiveness of middle-class Americans in the age of the common man.

[The Poor Boy]

1. The good boy whose parents are poor, rises very early in the morning; and, all day long, does as much as he can, to help his father and mother.

2. When he goes to school he walks quickly, and does not lose time on the road. "My parents," says he, "are very good, to save some of their money, in order that I may learn to read and write; but they can not give much, nor can they spare me long: therefore I must learn as fast as I can; if any body has time to lose, I am sure I have not."

3. "I should be very sorry when I am a man, not to know how to read in the Bible, and other good books; and when I leave my parents, not to be able to read their letters, and to write them word where I am, and how I do."

4. "I must also learn accounts; for when I grow up I shall have many things to reckon, about my work, and what I buy: I shall perhaps have bills to make out, as my father has; and perhaps I shall be employed in a store."

5. When he has finished his lessons, he does not stay to play, but runs home; he wants to see his father and mother, and to help them.

6. He often sees naughty boys in the streets, who fight, and steal, and do many bad things; and he hears them swear, and call names, and tell lies; but he does not like to be with them, for fear they should make him as bad as they are; and lest any body who sees him with them, should think that he too is naughty.

7. When he is at home, he is very industrious. He takes care of the little children, weeds his father's garden, and hoes, and rakes it, and sows seed in it.

8. Sometimes he goes with his father to work; then he is very glad; and though he is but a little fellow, he works very hard, almost like a man.

9. When he comes home to dinner, he says, "How hungry I am! and how good this bread is, and this bacon! Indeed, I think every thing we have is very good. I am glad I can work: I hope that I shall soon be able to earn all my clothes, and my food too."

10. When he sees little boys and girls riding on pretty horses, or in coaches, or walking with ladies and gentlemen, and having on very fine clothes, he does not envy them, nor wish to be like them.

11. He says, "I have often been told, and I have read, that it is God who makes some poor, and others rich; that the rich have many troubles which we know nothing of; and that the poor, if they are but good, may be very happy: indeed, I think that when I am good, nobody can be happier than I am."

[Ironical Eulogy on Debt]

1. Debt is of the very highest antiquity. The first debt in the history of man is the debt of nature, and the first instinct is to put off the payment of it to the last moment. Many persons, it will be observed, following the natural procedure, would die before they would pay their debts.

2. Society is composed of two classes, debtors and creditors. The creditor class has been erroneously supposed the more enviable. Never was there a greater misconception; and the hold it yet maintains upon opinion, is a remarkable example of the obstinacy of error, notwithstanding the plainest lessons of experience. The debtor has the sympathies of mankind. He is seldom spoken of but with expressions of tenderness and compassion—"the poor debtor!"—and "the unfortunate debtor!" On the other hand, "harsh" and "hard-hearted" are the epithets allotted to the creditor. Who ever heard the "poor creditor," the "unfortunate creditor" spoken of? No, the creditor never becomes the object of pity, until he passes into the debtor class. A creditor may be ruined by the poor debtor, but it is not until he becomes unable to pay his own debts, that he begins to be compassionated.

3. A debtor is a man of mark. Many eyes are fixed upon him; many have interest in his well-being: his movements are of concern: he can not disappear unheeded; his name is in many mouths; his name is upon many books; he is a man of note—of *promissory* note; he fills the speculation of many minds; men conjecture about him, wonder about him, wonder and conjecture whether he *will pay*. He is a man of consequence, for many are running after him. His door is thronged with duns. He is inquired after every hour of the day. *Judges* hear of him and know him. Every meal he swallows, every coat he puts upon his back, every dollar he borrows, appears before the country in some formal document. Compare *his* notoriety with the obscure lot of the creditor, of the man who has nothing but *claims* on the world; a landlord, or fund-holder, or some *such* disagreeable, hard character.

4. The man who *pays* his way is *unknown* in his neighborhood. You ask the milk-man at his door, and he can not tell his name. You ask the butcher where Mr. Payall lives, and he tells you that he knows no such name, for it is not in his books. You shall ask the baker, and he will tell you that there is no such person in the neighborhood. People that have his *money* fast in their pockets, have no

thought of his *person* or *appellation*. His *house* only is known. No. 31 is good pay. No. 31 is ready money. Not a scrap of paper is ever made out for No. 31. It is an *anonymous* house; its owner pays his way to obscurity. No one knows anything about him, or heeds his movements. If a carriage be seen at his door, the neighborhood is not full of concern lest he be going to run away. If a package be moved from his house, a score of boys are not employed to watch whether it be carried to the pawnbroker. Mr. Payall fills no place in the public mind; no one has any hopes or fears about him.

5. The creditor always figures in the fancy as a sour, single man, with grizzled hair, a scowling countenance, and a peremptory air, who lives in a dark apartment, with musty deeds about him, and an iron safe, as impenetrable as his heart, grabbing together what he does not enjoy, and what there is no one about him to enjoy. The debtor, on the other hand, is always pictured with a wife and six fair-haired daughters, bound together in affection and misery, full of sensibility, and suffering without a fault. The creditor, it is never doubted, thrives without a merit. He has no wife and children to pity. No one ever thinks it desirable that *he* should have the means of living. He is a brute for insisting that he must receive, in order to pay. It is not in the imagination of man to *conceive* that his creditor has demands upon him which must be satisfied, and that he must do to others as others must do to him. A creditor is a personification of exaction. He is supposed to be always taking in, and never giving out.

6. People idly fancy, that the possession of riches is desirable. What blindness! Spend and regale. Save a shilling and you lay it by for a thief. The *prudent men* are the men that live beyond their means. Happen what may, *they* are safe. *They* have taken time by the forelock. *They* have anticipated·fortune. "The wealthy fool, with gold in store," has only denied himself so much enjoyment, which another will seize at his expense. Look at these people in a *panic*. See who are the fools *then*. You know them by their long faces. You may say, as one of them goes by, in

an agony of apprehension, "There is a stupid fellow who fancied himself rich, because he had fifty thousand dollars in bank." The history of the last ten years has taught the moral, "spend, and regale." Whatever is laid up beyond the *present hour*, is put in jeopardy. There is no certainty but in instant enjoyment. Look at school-boys sharing a plum-cake. The knowing ones eat, as for a race; but a *stupid* fellow *saves his* portion; just nibbles a bit, and "keeps the rest for another time." Most provident blockhead! The others, when they have gobbled up *their* shares, set upon *him*, plunder him, and thresh him for crying out.

7. Before the terms "depreciation," "suspension," and "going into liquidation," were heard, there might have been some reason in the practice of "laying up;" but *now* it denotes the darkest blindness. The *prudent men* of the present time, are the men in debt. The tendency being to sacrifice creditors to debtors, and the debtor party acquiring daily new strength, every one is in haste to get into the favored class. In any case, the *debtor* is safe. He has put his enjoyments *behind* him; they are safe; no turns of fortune can disturb them. The substance he has eaten up, is irrecoverable. The future can not trouble his past. He has nothing to apprehend. He has anticipated more than fortune would ever have granted him. He has *tricked* fortune; and his creditors—bah! who feels for creditors? What *are* creditors? Landlords; a pitiless and unpitiable tribe; all griping extortioners! What would become of the world of debtors, if it did not steal a march upon this rapacious class?

18

The Honest School Boy Rewarded

Charles W. Sanders was one of the leading educational reformers in the Jacksonian era. After seventeen years of country school teaching in New York State, he moved to the metropolis and plunged into the writing and compilation of readers and spellers for elementary schools. Between 1838 and 1860, he turned out an amazing succession of forty titles of primers, spellers, graded readers, charts and cards for teaching, and school singing books. It is estimated that thirteen million Sanders' Readers were sold between 1838 and 1860.

Sanders sought to reform the reading books of his own time by means of the careful grading of the literary selections, the simplicity and moral interest of the contents, and the use of pictures. Thus, his readers were designed for American children in the age of the common man. The following illustration from his Second Reader adorns a moral tale in which an honest school boy receives a reward for returning a lost pocketbook. The moral lesson is driven home to the readers of this little story with the concluding words: "Thus this honest boy gained, not only the promised reward, but what is far better, *a good name.*" In this way, honesty and a good personal reputation are presented as important ingredients for personal success.

THE HONEST SCHOOL BOY REWARDED.

From Charles W. Sanders, *The School Reader*, Second Book (New York, 1853), p. 44.

19

The Necessity of Education
in a Republican Government*

HORACE MANN

The name of Horace Mann is inextricably linked with
the battle for free public schools which was part of the
restless striving after social reform in the Jacksonian
period. He became interested in educational reforms
while serving in the Massachusetts Senate and he gave
important aid to the passage of a bill to establish a State
Board of Education. To the surprise of many of his
friends, he gave up a promising career in law and politics
to become the first Secretary of the new Board of Education in 1837.

The main job of the Secretary was to arouse public
support for the improvement of the common schools,
and Mann swept like a whirlwind through the State
of Massachusetts, lecturing, publishing his views in the
press, and issuing a series of remarkable reports on education. In the twelve years that he held this office, Mann
won much of his battle: the school fund was doubled,
new schoolhouses were built, salaries of teachers were
increased, the school term was lengthened, normal
schools were established, and teaching methods were
improved. His fame was so great that he was called upon
to lecture on behalf of educational reform in every
section of the United States.

The selection that follows is taken from a lecture
which Mann gave at the end of his first year as Secretary
of the Board of Education on the necessity of education
in a republican society. The striking thing about the

* From *The Life and Works of Horace Mann*, Mrs. Mary
Mann, ed. (Cambridge, Mass., 1867), II, 149–88, abridged.

lecture is its unrelieved tone of dread. According to Mann, the free institutions of a republican society like that of America "wake up unexampled energies," "multiply temptations," "quicken the activity and enlarge the sphere of the appetites and passions." Only by the cultivation of morality and intelligence in "the docile and teachable years of childhood" can we control the "terrible propensities" released in a social system based on equal rights and open social competition.

There is much that is puzzling in Mann's conception of society and of education. He seems at times to be defending middle-class values; in other places in his lecture he seems to be inveighing against the excessive striving after material gain; in still others, he denigrates the pursuit of office and power by men who lack the qualities of talent and excellence. Somehow, he seems to be exhibiting a syndrome with all of the reciprocating anxieties of the age of the common man.

. . . It is a truism, that free institutions multiply human energies. A chained body cannot do much harm; a chained mind can do as little. In a despotic government, the human faculties are benumbed and paralyzed; in a Republic, they glow with an intense life, and burst forth with uncontrollable impetuosity. In the former, they are circumscribed and straitened in their range of action; in the latter, they have "ample room and verge enough," and may rise to glory or plunge into ruin. Amidst universal ignorance, there cannot be such wrong notions about right, as there may be in a community partially enlightened; and false conclusions which have been reasoned out are infinitely worse than blind impulses.

To demonstrate the necessity of education in our government, I shall not attempt to derive my proofs from the history of other Republics. Such arguments are becoming stale. Besides, there are so many points of difference between our own political institutions, and those of any other government calling itself free, which has ever existed, that the objector perpetually eludes or denies the force of our reasoning, by showing some want of analogy between the cases presented.

I propose, therefore, on this occasion, not to adduce, as proofs, what has been true only in past times; but what is true at the present time, and must always continue to be true. I shall rely, not on precedents, but on the nature of things; and draw my arguments less from history than from humanity.

Now it is undeniable that, with the possession of certain higher faculties,—common to all mankind,—whose proper cultivation will bear us upward to hitherto undiscovered regions of prosperity and glory, we possess, also, certain lower faculties or propensities;—equally common;—whose improper indulgence leads, inevitably, to tribulation, and anguish, and ruin. The propensities to which I refer seem indispensable to our temporal existence, and, if restricted within proper limits, they are promotive of our enjoyment; but, beyond those limits, they work dishonor and infatuation, madness and despair. As servants, they are indispensable; as masters, they torture as well as tyrannize. Now despotic and arbitrary governments have dwarfed and crippled the powers of doing evil as much as the powers of doing good; but a republican government, from the very fact of its freedom, unreins their speed, and lets loose their strength. It is justly alleged against despotisms, that they fetter, mutilate, almost extinguish the noblest powers of the human soul; but there is a *per contra* to this, for which we have not given them credit;—they circumscribe the ability to do the greatest evil, as well as to do the greatest good.

My proposition, therefore, is simply this:—If republican institutions do wake up unexampled energies in the whole mass of a people, and give them implements of unexampled power wherewith to work out their will, then these same institutions ought also to confer upon that people unexampled wisdom and rectitude. If these institutions give greater scope and impulse to the lower order of faculties belonging to the human mind, then they must also give more authoritative control and more skilful guidance to the higher ones. If they multiply temptations, they must fortify against them. If they quicken the activity and enlarge the sphere of the appetites and passions, they must, at least in an equal ratio, establish the authority and extend the jurisdiction of reason and conscience. In a word, we must not add to the impulsive, without also adding to the regulating forces.

If we maintain institutions, which bring us within the action of new and unheard-of powers, without taking any corresponding measures for the government of those powers, we shall perish by the very instruments prepared for our happiness.

The truth has been so often asserted, that there is no security for a republic but in morality and intelligence, that a repetition of it seems hardly in good taste. But all permanent blessings being founded on permanent truths, a continued observance of the truth is the condition of a continued enjoyment of the blessing. I know we are often admonished that, without intelligence and virtue, as a chart and a compass, to direct us in our untried political voyage, we shall perish in the first storm; but I venture to add that, without these qualities, we shall not wait for a storm,—we cannot weather a calm. If the sea is as smooth as glass we shall founder, for we are in a stone boat. Unless these qualities pervade the general head and the general heart, not only will republican institutions vanish from amongst us, but the words *prosperity* and *happiness* will become obsolete. And all this may be affirmed, not from historical examples merely, but from the very constitution of our nature. We are created and brought into life with a set of innate, organic dispositions or propensities, which a free government rouses and invigorates, and which, if not bridled and tamed, by our actually seeing the eternal laws of justice, as plainly as we can see the sun in the heavens, —and by our actually feeling the sovereign sentiment of duty, as plainly as we feel the earth beneath our feet,— will hurry us forward into regions populous with every form of evil. . . .

Let us now turn for a moment to see what means and

stimulants our institutions have provided for the use of the mighty powers and passions they have unloosed. No apparatus so skilful was ever before devised. Instead of the slow and cumbrous machinery of former times, we have provided that which is quick-working and far-reaching, and which may be used for the destruction as easily as for the welfare of its possessors. Our institutions furnish as great facilities for wicked men, in all departments of wickedness, as phosphorus and lucifer matches furnish to the incendiary. What chemistry has done, in these preparations, over the old art of rubbing two sticks together, for the wretch who would fire your dwelling, our social partnerships have done for flagitious and unprincipled men. Through the right,—almost universal,—of suffrage, we have established a community of power; and no proposition is more plain and self-evident, than that nothing but mere popular inclination lies between a community of power and a community in every thing else. And though, in the long-run, and when other things are equal, a righteous cause always has a decisive advantage over an evil one, yet, in the first onset between right and wrong, bad men possess one advantage over the good. They have double resources,—two armories. The arts of guilt are as welcome to them as the practices of justice. They can use poisoned weapons as well as those approved by the usages of war.

Again; has it been sufficiently considered, that all which has been said,—and truly said,—of the excellence of our institutions, if administered by an upright people, must be reversed and read backwards, if administered by a corrupt one? I am aware that some will be ready to say, "We have been unwise and infatuated to confide all the constituents of our social and political welfare to such irresponsible keeping." But let me ask of such,—of what avail is their lamentation? The irresistible movement in the diffusion of power is still progressive, not retrograde. Every year puts more of social strength into the hands of physical strength. The arithmetic of numbers is more and more excluding all estimate of moral forces, in the administration of government. And this, whether for good or for evil, will continue to be. Human beings cannot be re-manded to the dungeons of imbecility, if they are to those of ignorance. The sun can as easily be turned backwards in its course, as one particle of that power, which has been conferred upon the millions, can be again monopolized by the few. To discuss the question, therefore, whether our institutions are not too free, is, for all practical purposes, as vain as it would be to discuss the question whether, on the whole, it was a wise arrangement on the part of Divine Providence, that the American continent should ever have been created, or that Columbus should have discovered it. And let me ask, further, have those who believe our institutions to be too free, and who, therefore, would go back to less liberal ones,—have they settled the question, how far back they will go? Will they go back to the dark ages, and recall an eclipse which lasted centuries long? or will they ascend a little higher for their models,—to a time when our ancestors wore undressed skins, and burrowed in holes of the earth? or will they strike at once for the institutions of Egypt, where, though the monkey was a god, there was still a sufficient distance between him and his human worshipper? But all such discussions are vain. The oak will as soon go back into the acorn, or the bird into its shell, as we return to the monarchical or aristocratic forms of by-gone ages.

Nor let it be forgotten, in contemplating our condition, that the human passions, as unfolded and invigorated by our institutions, are not only possessed of all the prerogatives, and equipped with all the implements of sovereignty; but that they are forever roused and spurred to the most vehement efforts. It is a law of the passions, that they exert strength in proportion to the causes which excite them,—a law which holds true in cases of sanity, as well as in the terrible strength of insanity. And with what endless excitements are the passions of men here plied! With us, the Press is such a clarion, that it proclaims all the great movements of this great country, with a voice that sweeps over its whole surface, and comes back to us in echoes from its extremest borders. From the Atlantic to the Pacific, from the Lakes to the Gulf, men cheer, inflame, exasperate each other, as though they were neighbors in the same street. What the ear of Dionysius was to him, making report of every word uttered by friend or foe, our institutions have made this land to every citizen. It is a vast sounding gallery; and from horizon to horizon every shout of triumph and every cry of alarm are gathered up and rung in every man's dwelling. All objects which stimulate the passions of men are made to pass before the eyes of all, as in a circling panorama. In very truth we are all hung upon the same electrical wire, and if the ignorant and vicious get possession of the apparatus, the intelligent and the virtuous must take such shocks as the stupid or profligate experimenters may choose to administer.

Mark how the excitements which our institutions supply have wrought upon the love of gain and the love of place. Vast speculations,—such as in other countries would require not only royal sanctions and charters, but the equipment of fleets, and princely outfits of gold and arms, —are here rushed into, on flash paper, by clerks and apprentices, not out of their time. What party can affirm that it is exempt from members who prize office, rather than the excellence that deserves it? *Where* can I be,—not *what* can I be,—is the question suggested to aspirants for fame. How many have their eyes fixed upon posts of honor and emolument which but one only can fill! While few will be satisfied with occupying less than their portion of space in the public eye, thousands have marked out some great compartment of the sky for the blazonry of their names. And hence it is, that, wherever there is a signal of gain, or of power, the vultures of cupidity and of ambition darken the air. Young men launch into this tumultuous life, years earlier than has ever been witnessed elsewhere. They seek to win those prizes without delay, which, according to Nature's ordinances and appointments, are the rewards of a life of labor. Hence they find no time for studying the eternal principles of justice, veracity, equality, benevolence, and for applying them to the complicated affairs of men. What cares a young adventurer for the immutable laws of trade, when he has purchased a ticket in some lottery of speculation, from which he expects to draw a fortune? Out of such an unbridled, unchastened love of gain, whether it traffics in townships of land or in two-penny toys, do we not know beforehand, there will come infinite falsehoods, knavery and bankruptcy? Let this state of things continue, and he will be a happy man who dares to say of any article of food or of apparel, which he eats or wears, that it has not, at some period of its preparation, or in some of its transfers, been contaminated by fraud. And what a state of society would it argue, in other respects, if the people at large should ever become indifferent to the question, whether fraud be, or be not, inwoven into the texture, and kneaded into the substance of what they daily consume,—whether what they eat or drink or wear be not an embodiment of the spirit of lies! . . .

Again, then, I ask, with unmitigated anxiety, what institutions we now possess, that can furnish defence or barrier against the action of those propensities, which each generation brings into the world as a part of its being, and which our institutions foster and stimulate into unparalleled activity and vigor? Can any Christian man believe, that God has so constituted and so governs the human race, that it is always and necessarily to be suicidal of its earthly welfare? No! the thought is impious. The same Almighty Power which implants in our nature the germs of these terrible propensities, has endowed us also with reason and conscience and a sense of responsibility to Him; and, in his providence, he has opened a way by which these nobler faculties can be elevated into dominion and supremacy over the appetites and passions. But if this is ever done, it must be mainly done during the docile and teachable years of childhood. I repeat it, my friends, *if this is ever done, it must be mainly done during the docile and teachable years of childhood*. Wretched, incorrigible, demoniac, as any human being may ever have become, there was a time when he took the first step in error and in crime; when, for the first time, he just nodded to his fall, on the brink of ruin. Then, ere he was irrecoverably lost, ere he plunged into the abyss of infamy and guilt, he might have been recalled, as it were by the waving of the hand. Fathers, mothers, patriots, Christians! it is this very hour of peril through which our children are now passing. They know it not, but we know it; and where the knowledge is, there rests the responsibility. Society is responsible; —not society considered as an abstraction, but society as it consists of living members, which members we are. Clergymen are responsible;—all men who have enjoyed the opportunities of a higher education in colleges and universities are responsible, for they can convert their means, whether of time or of talent, into instruments for elevating the masses of the people. The conductors of the public press are responsible, for they have daily access to the public ear, and can infuse just notions of this high duty into the public mind. Legislators and rulers are responsible. In our country, and in our times, no man is worthy the honored name of a statesman, who does not include the highest practicable education of the people in all his plans of administration. He may have eloquence, he may have a knowledge of all history, diplomacy, jurisprudence; and by these he might claim, in other countries, the elevated rank of a statesman; but, unless he speaks, plans, labors, at all times and in all places, for the culture and edification of the whole people, he is not, he cannot be, an American statesman. . . .

20

Fighting and Throwing Stones

The other side of the moral plots that were so insistently presented to the children of the common schools in the Jacksonian generation is emphasized in the following illustration from Rensselaer Bentley's *Pictorial Spelling Book*. Life is pictured as a continual conflict between good and evil, and the main battleground is the conscience of the individual. Thus, fighting and throwing stones is held up as an example of bad conduct. The lesson that follows the illustration emphasizes the necessity of obedience and prudent behavior. In the words of the text, "These are all bad boys: their conduct is not only shameful, but they should be shunned by all good children. . . . When at school, obey your teacher. Always speak the truth; and never do anything to injure others." Such internalized moral controls would provide the check to the social violence that, in the imagination of many of the educational reformers of the Jacksonian era, always seemed to be seething beneath the crust of the democratic social order.

FIGHTING AND THROWING STONES.

From Rensselaer Bentley, *The Pictorial Spelling Book* (New York, 1854), p. 85.

21

"There seemed to be a general union of ministerial influence against us."*

CHARLES GRANDISON FINNEY

One of the important manifestations of social ferment in Jacksonian America was the heightened activity of evangelical Protestantism. Religious revivalism had been endemic in America since the Great Awakening of the eighteenth century, but in the 1830s and 1840s a truly amazing crop of new prophets, revelations, and sects appeared in America. Bewildering varieties of Presbyterians and Baptists split away from older denominational structures, and millennialism, spiritualism, and Mormonism added new forms to the religious zeal of the times. Moreover, the religious intensity of the Jacksonian era found further outlets in the numerous humanitarian and social reform movements. Anti-Masonry, the temperance crusade, prison reform, and the anti-slavery movement were all infused with the enormous energies of religious evangelism.

Charles Grandison Finney was one of the greatest evangelistic preachers of the Jacksonian generation. He was practicing law in western New York in 1821 when he was led to an experience of religious conversion by a Presbyterian preacher. Hence, at the age of twenty-nine, this successful lawyer, who had been known in his county as an accomplished horseman, marksman, and sailor, entered the ministry and began to preach with such a fervor of conviction that his ministry took on the color of emotional revivals. Calls for his services

* From Charles G. Finney, *Memoirs of Rev. Charles G. Finney* (New York, 1876), pp. 87–91, 332–33, 343–44, 352, abridged.

everywhere brought him into his lifelong career as a traveling revivalist. In 1835, he was appointed to the faculty of Oberlin College, a newly founded educational institution in Ohio which quickly became known as a center of reformist ideas in religion and in associated humanitarian movements.

Finney had an abiding contempt for the methods of teaching and preaching which were characteristic of the religious establishment of the major Protestant denominations. He advocated a form of religious populism and used what he called "the language of common life" in the pulpit. The chapter from Finney's autobiography reveals the continued atmosphere of conflict that existed between orthodox ministers and the new revivalistic preachers. Can we not assume that this conflict revealed an undercurrent of anxiety about status as well as a disagreement over methods of teaching and preaching? After all, clergymen of "the standing order" had held leadership and a clearly defined social position in previous generations. Now, they were plunged into a hectic social competition, lost in a throng of new religious and moral prophets seeking to lead a restless people.

. . . The more experience I had, the more I saw the results of my method of preaching, the more I conversed with all classes, high and low, educated and uneducated, the more was I confirmed in the fact that God had led me, had taught me, had given me right conceptions in regard to the best manner of winning souls. I say that God taught me; and I know it must have been so; for surely I never had obtained these notions from man. And I have often thought that I could say with perfect truth, as Paul said, that I was not taught the Gospel by man, but by the Spirit of Christ himself. And I was taught it by the Spirit of the Lord in a manner so clear and forcible, that no argument of my ministerial brethren, with which I was plied so often and so long, had the least weight with me.

I mention this as a matter of duty. For I am still solemnly impressed with the conviction, that the schools are to a great extent spoiling the ministers. Ministers in these days have great facilities for obtaining information on all theological questions; and are vastly more learned, so far as theological, historical, and Biblical learning is concerned, than they perhaps ever have been in any age of the world. Yet with all their learning, they do not know how to use it. They are, after all, to a great extent, like David in Saul's armor. A man can never learn to preach except by preaching.

But one great thing above all others ministers need, and that is singleness of eye. If they have a reputation to secure and to nurse, they will do but little good. Many years ago a beloved pastor of my acquaintance, left home for his health, and employed a young man, just from the seminary, to fill his pulpit while he was absent. This young man wrote and preached as splendid sermons as he could. The pastor's wife finally ventured to say to him, "You are preaching over the heads of our people. They do not understand your language or your illustrations. You bring too much of your learning into the pulpit." He replied, "I am a young man. I am cultivating a style. I am aiming to prepare myself for occupying a pulpit and surrounding myself with a cultivated congregation. I cannot descend to your people. I must cultivate an elevated style." I have had my thought and my eye upon this man ever since. I am not aware that he is yet dead; but I have never seen his name connected with any revival, amidst all the great revivals that we have had, from year to year, since that time: and I never expect to, unless his views are radically changed, and unless he addresses the people from an entirely different stand-point, and from entirely different motives. . . .

It was very common, as I learned, among ministers in my earlier years of preaching, to agree among themselves that if I were to succeed in the ministry, it would bring the schools into disrepute; and men would come to think it hardly worth while to support them with their funds, if a man could be accepted as a successful preacher without them. Now I never had a thought of undervaluing the education furnished by colleges or theological seminaries; though I did think, and think now, that in certain respects they are greatly mistaken in their modes of training their students. They do not encourage them to talk to the people, and accustom themselves to extemporaneous addresses to the people in the surrounding country, while pursuing their studies. Men can not learn to preach by study without practice. The students should be encouraged to exercise, and prove, and improve, their gifts and calling of God, by going out into any places open to them, and holding Christ up to the people in earnest talks. They must thus learn to preach. Instead of this, the students are required to write what they call sermons, and present them for criticism; to preach, that is, read them to the class and the professor. Thus they play preaching. No man can preach in this manner. These so-called sermons will of course, under the criticism they receive, degenerate into literary essays. The people have no respect for such sermons, as sermons. This reading of elegant literary essays, is not to them preaching. It is gratifying to literary taste, but not spiritually edifying. It does not meet the wants of the soul. It is not calculated to win souls to Christ. The students are taught to cultivate a fine, elevated style of writing. As for real eloquence, that gushing, impressive, and persuasive oratory, that naturally flows from an educated man whose soul is on fire with his subject, and who is free to pour out his heart to a waiting and earnest people, they have none of it.

A reflecting mind will feel as if it were infinitely out of place to present in the pulpit to immortal souls, hanging upon the verge of everlasting death, such specimens of learning and rhetoric. They know that men do not do so on any subject where they are really in earnest. The captain of a fire company, when a city is on fire, does not read to his company an essay, or exhibit a fine specimen of rhetoric, when he shouts to them and directs their movements. It is a question of urgency, and he intends that every word shall be understood. He is entirely in earnest with them; and they feel that criticism would be out of place in regard to the language he uses.

So it always is when men are entirely in earnest. Their language is in point, direct and simple. Their sentences are short, cogent, powerful. The appeal is made directly for action; and hence all such discourses take effect. This is the reason why, formerly, the ignorant Methodist preachers, and the earnest Baptist preachers produced so much more effect than our most learned theologians and divines. They do so now. The impassioned utterance of a common exhorter will often move a congregation far beyond anything that those splendid exhibitions of rhetoric can effect. Great sermons lead the people to praise the preacher. Good preaching leads the people to praise the Saviour. . . .

Soon after I returned to New York, I commenced my labors in the Tabernacle. The Spirit of the Lord was poured out upon us, and we had a precious revival, as long as I continued to be pastor of that church. While in New York, I had many applications from young men, to take them as students in theology. I, however, had too much on my hands, to undertake such a work. But the brethren who built the Tabernacle had this in view; and prepared a room under the choir, which we expected to use for prayer-meetings, but more especially for a theological lecture-room. The number of applications had been so large, that I had made up my mind to deliver a course of theological lectures in that room each year, and let such students as chose, attend them gratuitously.

But about this time, and before I had opened my lectures in New York, the breaking up at Lane Seminary took place, on account of the prohibition by the trustees, of the discussion of the question of slavery among the students. When this occurred, Mr. Arthur Tappan proposed to me, that if I would go to some point in Ohio, and take rooms where I could gather those young men, and give them my views in theology, and prepare them for the work of preaching throughout the West, he would be at the entire expense of the undertaking. He was very earnest in this proposal. But I did not know how to leave New York; and I did not see how I could accomplish the wishes of Mr. Tappan, although I strongly sympathized with him in regard to helping those young men. They were most of them converts in those great revivals, in which I had taken more or less part.

While this subject was under consideration, I think, in January, 1835, Rev. John Jay Shipherd, of Oberlin, and Rev. Asa Mahan, of Cincinnati, arrived in New York, to persuade me to go to Oberlin, as professor of theology. Mr. Mahan had been one of the trustees of Lane Seminary—the only one, I think, that had resisted the prohibition of free discussion. Mr. Shipherd had founded a colony, and organized a school at Oberlin, about a year before this time, and had obtained a charter broad enough for a university. Mr. Mahan had never been in Oberlin. The trees had been removed from the college square, some dwelling-houses and one college building had been erected, and about a hundred pupils had been gathered, in the preparatory or academic department of the institution.

The proposal they laid before me was, to come on, and take those students that had left Lane Seminary, and teach them theology. These students had themselves proposed to go to Oberlin, in case I would accept the call. This proposal met the views of Arthur and Lewis Tappan, and many of the friends of the slave, who sympathized with Mr. Tappan, in his wish to have those young men instructed, and brought into the ministry. We had several consultations on the subject. The brethren in New York who were interested in the question, offered, if I would go and spend half of each year in Oberlin, to endow the institution, so far as the professorships were concerned, and to do it immediately. . . .

I came to Oberlin, and saw that there was nothing to prevent the building up of a college, on the principles that seemed to me not only to lie at the foundation of all success in establishing a college here at the West, but on principles of reform, such as I knew were dear to the hearts of those who had undertaken the support and building up of Oberlin College. The brethren that were here on the ground, were heartily in favor of building up a school on radical principles of reform. . . .

After a year or two, the cry of antinomian perfectionism was heard, and this charge brought against us. Letters were written, and ecclesiastical bodies were visited, and much pains taken to represent our views here as entirely heretical. Such representations were made to ecclesiastical bodies, throughout the length and breadth of the land, as to lead many of them to pass resolutions, warning the churches against the influence of Oberlin theology. There seemed to be a general union of ministerial influence against us. We understood very well here what had set this on foot, and by what means all this excitement was raised. But we said nothing. We had no controversy with those brethren that, we were aware, were taking pains to raise such a powerful public sentiment against us. . . .

The ministers, far and near, carried their opposition to a great extreme. At that time a convention was called to meet at Cleveland, to consider the subject of Western education, and the support of Western colleges. The call had been so worded that we went out from Oberlin, expecting to take part in the proceedings of the convention. When we arrived there, we found Dr. Beecher on the ground; and soon saw that a course of proceedings was on foot, to shut out Oberlin brethren, and those that sympathized with Oberlin, from the convention. I was therefore not allowed a seat in the convention as a member; yet I attended several of its sessions. I recollect hearing it distinctly said, by one of the ministers from the neighborhood, who was there, that he regarded Oberlin doctrines and influence as worse than those of Roman Catholicism. . . .

Before I return to my revival record, in order to give some idea of the relation of things, I must dwell a little more upon the progress of the anti-slavery, or abolition movement, not only at Oberlin, but elsewhere, as connected with my own labors. I have spoken of the state of public feeling on this subject, all around us, and have mentioned that even the legislature of the state, at that time democratic, endeavored to find some pretext for repealing our charter, because of our anti-slavery sentiments and action. It was at first reported on every side of us, that we intended to encourage marriage between colored and white students, and even to compel them to intermarry; and that our object was to introduce a universal system of miscegenation. A little fact will illustrate the feeling that existed among many people in the neighborhood. I had occasion to ride out a few miles, soon after we came, and called upon a farmer on some errand. He looked very sullen and suspicious, when he found who I was, and from whence I came; and intimated to me that he did not want to have anything to do with the people of Oberlin; that our object was to introduce amalgamation of the races, and compel the white and colored students to intermarry; that we also intended to bring about the union of church and state, and that our ideas and projects were altogether revolutionary and abominable. He was quite in earnest about this. But the thing was so ridiculous, that I knew that if I attempted a serious answer, I should laugh him in the face. . . .

22

"There is and always has been . . . a conflict between labor and capital."*

JOHN C. CALHOUN

John C. Calhoun is known to every American school-boy as a champion of State rights and the author of constitutional doctrines designed to protect the minority rights of the South. Unquestionably, he is one of the political giants of the Jacksonian era and at the beginning of the Jackson administration he even had high hopes that his position as Vice President of the United States would be a steppingstone to the presidency.

At a very early point in the Jackson administration, Calhoun became and remained an implacable foe of Andrew Jackson. The two men were involved in bitter personal quarrels within Jackson's cabinet and Calhoun was outraged by Jackson's support of a protective tariff law in 1832. Moreover, Calhoun played a leading role in South Carolina's attempted nullification of the tariff laws of 1828 and 1832, and President Jackson's obvious willingness to use force against South Carolina only served to increase the enmity between the two leaders. Indeed, Calhoun's defense of minority rights in his works of political theory—*The Disquisition on Government* and the *Discourses on the Constitution and the Government of the United States*—stemmed from his reaction against the majoritarian principles of the Jacksonian Democrats as they were applied in the nullification controversy.

But Calhoun is more than a spokesman for the

* From *The Works of John C. Calhoun*, Richard Crallé, ed. (New York, 1853), II, 626–33, abridged.

abstract doctrines of State rights and the concurrent majority. He became, in the Jacksonian decade, an important barometer of Southern fears for the future. He was among the first to respond to the attacks of the new and militant abolitionist movement in the North; he sought to restrict the reception of abolitionist positions in the Senate and to limit the circulation of abolitionist literature in the federal postal system throughout the Southern states. The following selection exhibits very clearly the fears that existed among the slaveholders for the security of the class and caste system that had developed in the race relations of the South. Moreover, the speech contains one of the first articulations by Calhoun of a theory of progress through exploitation: that, throughout the history of mankind, the progress of civilization had rested upon the exploitation of a laboring class by a master class.

. . . The peculiar institution of the South—that, on the maintenance of which the very existence of the slaveholding States depends, is pronounced to be sinful and odious, in the sight of God and man; and this with a systematic design of rendering us hateful in the eyes of the world—with a view to a general crusade against us and our institutions. This, too, in the legislative halls of the Union; created by these confederated States, for the better protection of their peace, their safety, and their respective institutions;—and yet, we, the representatives of twelve of these sovereign States against whom this deadly war is waged, are expected to sit here in silence, hearing ourselves and our constituents day after day denounced, without uttering a word; for if we but open our lips, the charge of agitation is resounded on all sides, and we are held up as seeking to aggravate the evil which we resist. Every reflecting mind must see in all this a state of things deeply and dangerously diseased. . . .

As widely as this incendiary spirit has spread, it has not yet infected this body, or the great mass of the intelligent and business portion of the North; but unless it be speedily stopped, it will spread and work upwards till it brings the two great sections of the Union into deadly conflict. This is not a new impression with me. Several years since, in a discussion with one of the Senators from Massachusetts (Mr. Webster), before this fell spirit had showed itself, I then predicted that the doctrine of the proclamation and the Force Bill,—that this Government had a right, in the last resort, to determine the extent of its own powers, and enforce its decision at the point of the bayonet, which was so warmly maintained by that Senator, would at no distant day arouse the dormant spirit of abolitionism. I told him that the doctrine was tantamount to the assumption of unlimited power on the part of the Government, and that such would be the impression on the public mind in a large portion of the Union. The consequence would be inevitable. A large portion of the Northern States believed slavery to be a sin, and would consider it as an obligation of conscience to abolish it if they should feel themselves in any degree responsible for its continuance, —and that this doctrine would necessarily lead to the belief of such responsibility. I then predicted that it would commence as it has with this fanatical portion of society, and that they would begin their operations on the ignorant, the weak, the young, and the thoughtless,—and gradually extend upwards till they would become strong enough to obtain political control, when he and others holding the highest stations in society, would, however reluctant, be compelled to yield to their doctrines, or be driven into obscurity. But four years have since elapsed, and all this is already in a course of regular fulfilment.

Standing at the point of time at which we have now arrived, it will not be more difficult to trace the course of future events now than it was then. They who imagine that the spirit now abroad in the North, will die away of itself without a shock or convulsion, have formed a very inadequate conception of its real character; it will continue to rise and spread, unless prompt and efficient measures to stay its progress be adopted. Already it has taken possession of the pulpit, of the schools, and, to a considerable extent, of the press; those great instruments by which the mind of the rising generation will be formed.

However sound the great body of the non-slaveholding States are at present, in the course of a few years they will be succeeded by those who will have been taught to hate the people and institutions of nearly one-half of this Union, with a hatred more deadly than one hostile nation ever entertained towards another. It is easy to see the end. By the necessary course of events, if left to themselves, we must become, finally, two people. It is impossible under the deadly hatred which must spring up between the two great sections, if the present causes are permitted to operate unchecked, that we should continue under the same political system. The conflicting elements would burst the Union asunder, powerful as are the links which hold it together. Abolition and the Union cannot co-exist. As the friend of the Union I openly proclaim it,—and the sooner it is known the better. The former may now be controlled, but in a short time it will be beyond the power of man to arrest the course of events. We of the South will not, cannot surrender our institutions. To maintain the existing relations between the two races, inhabiting that section of the Union, is indispensable to the peace and happiness of both. It cannot be subverted without drenching the country in blood, and extirpating one or the other of the races. Be it good or bad, it has grown up with our society and institutions, and is so interwoven with them, that to destroy it would be to destroy us as a people. But let me not be understood as admitting, even by implication, that the existing relations between the two races in the slaveholding States is an evil:—far otherwise; I hold it to be a good, as it has thus far proved itself to be to both, and will continue to prove so if not disturbed by the fell spirit of abolition. I appeal to facts. Never before has the black race of Central Africa, from the dawn of history to the present day, attained a condition so civilized and so improved, not only physically, but morally and intellectually. It came among us in a low, degraded, and savage condition, and in the course of a few generations it has grown up under the fostering care of our institutions, reviled as they have been, to its present comparatively civilized condition. This, with the rapid increase of numbers, is conclusive proof of the general happiness of the race, in spite of all the exaggerated tales to the contrary.

In the mean time, the white or European race has not degenerated. It has kept pace with its brethren in other sections of the Union where slavery does not exist. It is odious to make comparison; but I appeal to all sides whether the South is not equal in virtue, intelligence, patriotism, courage, disinterestedness, and all the high qualities which adorn our nature. I ask whether we have not contributed our full share of talents and political wisdom in forming and sustaining this political fabric; and whether we have not constantly inclined most strongly to the side of liberty, and been the first to see and first to resist the encroachments of power. In one thing only are we inferior—the arts of gain; we acknowledge that we are less wealthy than the Northern section of this Union, but I trace this mainly to the fiscal action of this Government, which has extracted much from, and spent little among us. Had it been the reverse,—if the exaction had been from the other section, and the expenditure with us, this point of superiority would not be against us now, as it was not at the formation of this Government.

But I take higher ground. I hold that in the present state of civilization, where two races of different origin, and distinguished by color, and other physical differences, as well as intellectual, are brought together, the relation now existing in the slaveholding States between the two, is, instead of an evil, a good—a positive good. I feel myself called upon to speak freely upon the subject where the honor and interests of those I represent are involved. I hold then, that there never has yet existed a wealthy and civilized society in which one portion of the community did not, in point of fact, live on the labor of the other. Broad and general as is this assertion, it is fully borne out by history. This is not the proper occasion, but if it were, it would not be difficult to trace the various devices by which the wealth of all civilized communities has been so unequally divided, and to show by what means so small a share has been allotted to those by whose labor it was produced, and so large a share given to the non-producing classes. The devices are almost innumerable, from the brute force and gross superstition of ancient times, to the subtle and artful fiscal contrivances of modern. I might well challenge a comparison between them and the more direct, simple, and patriarchal mode by which the labor of the African race is, among us, commanded by the European. I may say with truth, that in few countries so much is left to the share of the laborer, and so little exacted from him, or where there is more kind attention paid to him in sickness or infirmities of age. Compare his condition with the tenants of the poor houses in the more civilized portions of Europe—look at the sick, and the old and infirm slave, on one hand, in the midst of his family and friends, under the kind super-intending care of his master and mistress, and compare it with the forlorn and wretched condition of the pauper in the poor house. But I will not dwell on this aspect of the question; I turn to the political; and here I fearlessly assert that the existing relation between the two races in the South, against which these blind fanatics are waging war, forms the most solid and durable foundation on which to rear free and stable political institutions. It is useless to disguise the fact. There is and always has been in an advanced stage of wealth and civilization, a conflict between labor and capital. The condition of society in the South exempts us from the disorders and dangers resulting from this conflict; and which explains why it is that the political condition of the slaveholding States has been so much more stable and quiet than that of the North. The advantages of the former, in this respect, will become more and more manifest if left undisturbed by interference from without, as the country advances in wealth and numbers. We have, in fact, but just entered that condition of society where the strength and durability of our political institutions are to be tested; and I venture nothing in predicting that the experience of the next generation will fully test how vastly more favorable our condition of society is to that of other sections for free and stable institutions, provided we are not disturbed by the interference of others, or shall have sufficient intelligence and spirit to resist promptly and successfully such interference. It rests with ourselves to meet and repel them. I look not for aid to this Government, or to the other States; not but there are kind feelings towards us on the part of the great body of the non-slaveholding States; but as kind as their feelings may be, we may rest assured that no political party in those States will risk their ascendency for our safety. If we do not defend ourselves none will defend us; if we yield we will be more and more pressed as we recede; and if we submit we will be trampled under foot. Be assured that emancipation itself would not satisfy these fanatics:—that gained, the next step would be to raise the negroes to a social and political equality with the whites; and that being effected, we would soon find the present condition of the two races reversed. They and their northern allies would be the masters, and we the slaves; the condition of the white race in the British West India Islands, bad as it is, would be happiness to ours. There the mother country is interested in sustaining the supremacy of the European race. It is true that the authority of the former master is destroyed, but the African will there still be a slave, not to individuals but to the community,— forced to labor, not by the authority of the overseer, but by the bayonet of the soldiery and the rod of the civil magistrate. . . .

23

New England Reformers*

RALPH WALDO EMERSON

In this lecture, delivered in Boston in 1844, Emerson
develops one of the more memorable contemporary com-
mentaries on the multitude of reform movements that
seemed to spring up everywhere during the Jacksonian
era. He recognized that this insatiable urge to social reform expressed a fundamental attitude toward America
and its possibilities.

The essay below not only develops an arresting image
of the reforms of the day but in it we find an interesting
exhibit of Emerson's own uncertainties. While he seems
to approve of the protest against existing evils and to
admire the keen scrutiny of traditional institutions, his
distrust of the narrow self-righteousness of reformers
is also evident. His ambivalence toward the established
institutions deserves our close attention. How are we to
interpret his claim that "it is handsomer to remain in
the establishment better than the establishment, and
conduct that in the best manner, than to make a sally
against evil by some single improvement"? Or what
shall we say about his attitude toward the "laws of
property" when he asks, "Can we not play the game of
life with these counters as well as with those; in the
institution of property, as well as out of it"?

Whoever has had opportunity of acquaintance with society in New England, during the last twenty-five years,
with those middle and with those leading sections that

* From *The Prose Works of Ralph Waldo Emerson* (Boston,
1870), I, 549–55, abridged.

may constitute any just representation of the character and aim of the community, will have been struck with the great activity of thought and experimenting. His attention must be commanded by the signs that the Church, or religious party, is falling from the church nominal, and is appearing in temperance and non-resistance societies, in movements of abolitionists and of socialists, and in very significant assemblies, called Sabbath and Bible Conventions,—composed of ultraists, of seekers, of all the soul of the soldiery of dissent, and meeting to call in question the authority of the Sabbath, of the priesthood, and of the church. In these movements, nothing was more remarkable than the discontent they begot in the movers. The spirit of protest and of detachment drove the members of these Conventions to bear testimony against the church, and immediately afterward, to declare their discontent with these Conventions, their independence of their colleagues, and their impatience of the methods whereby they were working. They defied each other, like a congress of kings, each of whom had a realm to rule, and a way of his own that made concert unprofitable. What a fertility of projects for the salvation of the world! One apostle thought all men should go to farming; and another, that no man should buy or sell; that the use of money was the cardinal evil; another, that the mischief was in our diet, that we eat and drink damnation. These made unleavened bread, and were foes to the death to fermentation. It was in vain urged by the housewife, that God made yeast, as well as dough, and loves fermentation just as dearly as he loves vegetation; that fermentation develops the saccharine element in the grain, and makes it more palatable and more digestible. No; they wish the pure wheat, and will die but it shall not ferment. Stop, dear nature, these incessant advances of thine; let us scotch these ever-rolling wheels! Others attacked the system of agriculture, the use of animal manures in farming; and the tyranny of man over brute nature; these abuses polluted his faces. The ox must be taken from the plough, and the horse from the cart, the hundred acres of the farm must be spaded, and the man must walk wherever boats and locomotives will not carry him. Even the insect world was to be defended,—and had been too long neglected, and a society for the protection of ground-worms, slugs, and mosquitoes was to be incorporated without delay. With these appeared the adepts of hominopathy, of hydropathy, of mesmerism, of phrenology, and the wonderful theories of the Christian miracles! Others assailed particular vocations, as that of the lawyer, that of the merchant, of the manufacturer, of the clergyman, of the scholar. Others attacked the institution of marriage, as the fountain of social evils. Others devoted themselves to the worrying of churches and meetings for public worship; and the fertile forms of antinomianism among the elder puritans seemed to have their match in the plenty of the new harvest of reform.

With this din of opinion and debate, there was a keener scrutiny of institutions and domestic life than any we had known, there was sincere protesting against existing evils, and there were changes of employment dictated by conscience. No doubt, there was plentiful vaporing, and cases of backsliding might occur. But in each of these movements emerges a good result, a tendency to the adoption of simpler methods and an assertion of the sufficiency of the private man. Thus it was directly in the spirit and genius of the age, what happened in one instance, when a church censured and threatened to excommunicate one of its members, on account of the somewhat hostile part to the church, which his conscience led him to take in the antislavery business; the threatened individual immediately excommunicated the church in a public and formal process. This has been several times repeated; it was excellent when it was done the first time, but, of course, loses all value when it is copied. Every project in the history of reform, no matter how violent and surprising, is good, when it is the dictate of a man's genius and constitution, but very dull and suspicious when adopted from another. It is right and beautiful in any man to say, 'I will take this coat, or this book, or this measure of corn of yours,'—in whom we see the act to be original, and to flow from the whole spirit and faith of him; for then that taking will have a giving as free and divine: but we are very easily disposed to resist the same generosity of speech, when we miss originality and truth to character in it.

There was in all the practical activities of New England, for the last quarter of a century, a gradual withdrawal of tender consciences from the social organizations. There is observable throughout, the contest between mechanical and spiritual methods, but with a steady tendency of the thoughtful and virtuous to a deeper belief and reliance on spiritual facts.

In politics, for example, it is easy to see the progress of dissent. The country is full of rebellion; the country is full of kings. Hands off! let there be no control and no inter-ference in the administration of the affairs of this kingdom of me. Hence the growth of the doctrine and of the party of Free Trade, and the willingness to try that experiment, in the face of what appear incontestable facts. I confess, the motto of the Globe newspaper is so attractive to me, that I can seldom find much appetite to read what is be-low it in its columns, "The world is governed too much." So the country is frequently affording solitary examples of resistance to the government, solitary nullifiers, who throw themselves on their reserved rights; nay, who have reserved all their rights; who reply to the assessor, and to the clerk of court, that they do not know the State; and embarrass the courts of law, by non-juring, and the com-mander-in-chief of the militia, by non-resistance.

The same disposition to scrutiny and dissent appeared in civil, festive, neighborly, and domestic society. A rest-less, prying, conscientious criticism broke out in unex-pected quarters. Who gave me the money with which I bought my coat? Why should professional labor and that of the counting-house be paid so disproportionately to the labor of the porter and woodsawyer? This whole business of Trade gives me to pause and think, as it constitutes false relations between men; inasmuch as I am prone to count myself relieved of any responsibility to behave well and nobly to that person whom I pay with money; whereas if I had not that commodity, I should be put on my good behavior in all companies, and man would be a benefactor to man, as being himself his only certificate that he had a right to those aids and services which each asked of the other. Am I not too protected a person? is there not a wide disparity between the lot of me and the lot of thee, my poor brother, my poor sister? Am I not defrauded of my best culture in the loss of those gymnastics which manual labor and the emergencies of poverty constitute; I find nothing healthful or exalting in the smooth conventions of society; I do not like the close air of saloons. I begin to suspect myself to be a prisoner, though treated with all this courtesy and luxury. I pay a destructive tax in my conformity.

The same insatiable criticism may be traced in the efforts for the reform of Education. The popular education has been taxed with a want of truth and nature. It was complained that an education to things was not given. We are students of words: we are shut up in schools, and colleges, and recitation-rooms, for ten or fifteen years, and come out at last with a bag of wind, a memory of words, and do not know a thing. We cannot use our hands, or our legs, or our eyes, or our arms. We do not know an edible root in the woods, we cannot tell our course by the stars, nor the hour of the day by the sun. It is well if we can swim and skate. We are afraid of a horse, of a cow, of a dog, of a snake, of a spider. The Roman rule was to teach a boy nothing that he could not learn standing. The old English rule was, 'All summer in the field, and all winter in the study.' And it seems as if a man should learn to plant, or to fish, or to hunt, that he might secure his subsistence at all events, and not be painful to his friends and fellow-men. The lessons of science should be experimental also. The sight of the planet through a telescope is worth all the course on astronomy; the shock of the electric spark in the elbow outvalues all the theories; the taste of the nitrous oxide, the firing of an artificial volcano, are better than volumes of chemistry.

One of the traits of the new spirit is the inquisition it fixed on our scholastic devotion to the dead languages. The ancient languages, with great beauty of structure, contain wonderful remains of genius, which draw, and always will draw, certain likeminded men,—Greek men, and Roman men, in all countries, to their study; but by a wonderful drowsiness of usage, they had exacted the study of *all* men. Once (say two centuries ago), Latin and Greek had a relation to all the science and culture there was in Europe, and the Mathematics had a momentary importance at some era of activity in physical science. These things became sterotyped as *education*, as the manner of men is. But the Good Spirit never cared for the colleges, and though all men and boys were now drilled in Latin, Greek, and Mathematics, it had quite left these shells high and dry on the beach, and was now creating and feeding other matters at other ends of the world. But in a hundred high schools and colleges, this warfare against common sense still goes on. Four, or six, or ten years, the pupil is parsing Greek and Latin, and as soon as he leaves the University, as it is ludicrously styled, he shuts those books for the last time. Some thousands of young men are graduated at our colleges in this country every year, and the persons who, at forty years, still read Greek, can all be counted on your hand. I never met with ten. Four or five persons I have seen who read Plato.

But is not this absurd, that the whole liberal talent of this country should be directed in its best years on studies which lead to nothing? What was the consequence? Some intelligent persons said or thought: 'Is that Greek and Latin some spell to conjure with, and not words of reason? If the physician, the lawyer, the divine, never use it to come at their ends, I need never learn it to come at mine. Conjuring is gone out of fashion, and I will omit this conjugating, and go straight to affairs.' So they jumped the Greek and Latin, and read law, medicine, or sermons, without it. To the astonishment of all, the self-made men took even ground at once with the oldest of the regular graduates, and in a few months the most conservative circles of Boston and New York had quite forgotten who of their gownsmen was college-bred, and who was not.

One tendency appears alike in the philosophical speculation, and in the rudest democratical movements, through all the petulance and all the puerility, the wish, namely, to cast aside the superfluous, and arrive at short methods, urged, as I suppose, by an intuition that the human spirit is equal to all emergencies alone, and that man is more often injured than helped by the means he uses.

I conceive this gradual casting off of material aids, and the indication of growing trust in the private, self-supplied powers of the individual, to be the affirmative principle of the recent philosophy; and that it is feeling its own profound truth, and is reaching forward at this very hour to the happiest conclusions. I readily concede that in this, as in every period of intellectual activity, there has been a noise of denial and protest; much was to be resisted, much was to be got rid of by those who were reared in the old, before they could begin to affirm and to construct. Many a reformer perishes in his removal of rubbish,—and that makes the offensiveness of the claim. They are partial; they are not equal to the work they pretend. They lose their way; in the assault on the kingdom of darkness, they expend all their energy on some accidental evil, and lose their sanity and power of benefit. It is of little moment that one or two, or twenty errors of our social system be corrected, but of much that the man be in his senses.

The criticism and attack on institutions which we have witnessed has made one thing plain, that society gains nothing whilst a man, not himself renovated, attempts to renovate things around him: he has become tediously good in some particular, but negligent or narrow in the rest; and hypocrisy and vanity are often the disgusting result.

It is handsomer to remain in the establishment better than the establishment, and conduct that in the best manner, than to make a sally against evil by some single improvement, without supporting it by a total regeneration. Do not be so vain of your one objection. Do you think there is only one? Alas! my good friend, there is no part of

society or of life better than any other part. All our things
are right and wrong together. The wave of evil washes all
our institutions alike. Do you complain of our Marriage?
Our marriage is no worse than our education, our diet, our
trade, our social customs. Do you complain of the laws of
Property? It is a pedantry to give such importance to them.
Can we not play the game of life with these counters as
well as with those; in the institution of property, as well
as out of it. Let into it the new and renewing principle of
love, and property will be universality. No one gives the
impression of superiority to the institution, which he must
give who will reform it. It makes no difference what you
say; you must make me feel that you are aloof from it; by
your natural and supernatural advantages, do easily see to
the end of it,—do see how man can do without it. Now all
men are on one side. No man deserves to be heard against
property. Only Love, only an idea, is against property, as
we hold it.

I cannot afford to be irritable and captious, nor to waste
all my time in attacks. If I should go out of church whenever I hear a false sentiment, I could never stay there five
minutes. But why come out? the street is as false as the
church, and when I get to my house, or to my manners, or
to my speech, I have not got away from the lie. When we
see an eager assailant of one of these wrongs, a special
reformer, we feel like asking him, What right have you,
sir, to your one virtue? Is virtue piecemeal? This is a jewel
amidst the rags of a beggar.

In another way the right will be vindicated. In the midst
of abuses, in the heart of cities, in the aisles of false
churches, alike in one place and in another,—wherever,
namely, a just and heroic soul finds itself, there it will do
what is next at hand, and by the new quality of character
it shall put forth, it shall abrogate that old condition, law
or school in which it stands, before the law of its own
mind. . . .

24

Symptoms of Revolution*

MICHEL CHEVALIER

One of the more interesting reflections of Michel Chevalier in his *Society, Manners, and Politics in the United States* comes in a chapter entitled "Symptoms of Revolution." In these pages, he describes the increasing tendency in America to riots, disorders, and various forms of mob action. These manifestations of social disorder are significant, not only because of their "general prevalence" and "frequent repetition," but also because they find so few voices to condemn them. Chevalier remarks, at one point, that "It seems as if no political principle existed in the United States but the pleasure of the passions. . . ."

Perhaps, we might wish to say, from our point of historical perspective, that the riots and disorders were symptomatic of the powerful tensions created by the uncertainties of status, the unhinging of old institutional arrangements, and the derangement of old values and sentiments. Indeed, Chevalier recognizes that the crisis of the Jacksonian decade had some of these psychic and social dimensions when he points out that the relations established in the early days of the Republic were "unfitted to the new state of things"—"In the North, the removal of all restrictions on the right of suffrage without the creation of any counterpoise has destroyed the equilibrium. In the South, the old foundation . . . on which the South has attempted to raise the superstructure of a new social order in the nineteenth century, shakes and threatens to bury the thoughtless builders under the

* From Michael Chevalier, *Society, Manners, and Politics in the United States,* John W. Ward, ed. (Garden City, New York, 1961), pp. 371–80, abridged.

ruins of their half-finished work. In the West, a population sprung from the soil under the influence of circumstances unparalleled in the history of the world already
affects a superiority, or rather lays claim to dominion,
over the North and South."

Two years ago Mr. Clay began a speech in the Senate
with these words, which have become celebrated on this
side of the Atlantic: "We are in the midst of a revolution."
It was at the time when, by an act of authority before
unheard of in American history, General Jackson had just
settled the bank question which his friends in Congress
and even his own ministers had refused to decide. These
words have often been repeated by others. More recently,
since the scenes of murder, outrage, and destruction which
have been exhibited through the United States, both in
the slaveholding States and in those in which slavery does
not exist, in the country as well as in the towns, at Boston,
the republican city *par excellence*, as well as at Baltimore,
where the bloody excesses during the War of 1812 with
England earned it the title of the *Mob Town*, good citizens
have repeated with grief: "We are in the midst of a revolution."

It must be granted to the honor of the English race that
it is, more deeply than any other, imbued with a feeling of
reverence for the law. Until lately, Americans have shown
themselves in this respect, as well as in others, to be
double-distilled Englishmen. There are nations who only
conceive of law in a living form, that is, only so far as it is
personified in a man. They know how to obey a leader but
they cannot learn to respect a lifeless letter. With them the
glory and prosperity of a state depend little on the character of the laws, but much on the character of the men
who are charged with interpreting them. In their view, the
empire rises and falls by turns, according as the sovereign,
whatever may be his title, is a superior man or an ordinary
personage. Such appears to be, in general, the character of
the Asiatics. The Englishman is formed in a different

mold; he willingly bows to the authority of a text but he stoops to man with reluctance. He does not require that obedience to law should be inculcated by the voice of man, he obeys it without an effort and by instinct. In a word, the Englishman has in himself the principle of self-government. This fact accounts for the success of his political system in the United States, where the native character of the English race is fully developed.

Unfortunately, reverence for the laws seems to be disappearing among Americans. These people, eminently practical in everything else, have allowed themselves to be pushed into the excess of theory in politics and have here taken up abstract logic in spite of everything; they have shrunk from none of the consequences of popular sovereignty, at least while those consequences were flattering to their pride; as if there were a single principle in the world, not excepting Christian charity itself, which could be carried to its extreme logical consequences without resulting in absolute absurdity. They have, therefore, been driven in the United States to deny that there is any principle true in and by itself and to assert that the will of the people is always and necessarily just; the infallibility of the people in everything and at all times has, in fact, become received doctrine, and thus a door has been opened to the tyranny of a turbulent minority which always calls itself the people.

The appearance of this miscalled *popular justice*, administered by the hands of a few desperate or furious men who call themselves the successors of the Boston Tea Party of 1773, is a great calamity in the bosom of a country where there is no other guarantee of the public peace than a reverence for law and where the legislator, taking for granted the prevalence of order, has made no provisions against disorder. This popular justice has the greater condemnation of being for the most part grossly unjust. Most of the men who have been hanged or flogged or tortured in twenty other atrocious ways in the South as Abolitionists, that is, as guilty of instigating the slaves to rise against their masters, were according to all appearances merely guilty of having expressed their abhorrence of slavery with too little caution. It is even doubtful whether the pretended plots for which whites and blacks have been summarily executed really existed. At least no proof of their reality which would be admitted by a court of justice has yet been brought forward. During the outrages last month at Baltimore which lasted four days, this self-styled justice was most stupidly unjust. The mob gave out that it wished to punish those knaves who had shamefully abused the credulity of the poor in the affair of the Bank of Maryland. It is a matter of public notoriety that the bankruptcy of the bank was fraudulent; that just before it stopped payment it had offered a high rate of interest on deposits of any amount in order to attract to its counter the savings of the laboring classes; but it was also a matter of notoriety that the criminal acts of the bank were wholly the work of one Evan Poultney, who alone was, in fact, the bank. Instead of going to take vengeance for the ruin of the artisan, the widow, and the orphan on the author of it, the mob went to call to account the bankruptcy commissioners appointed by the court. It was not till the third day that it thought to make a visit to Poultney, who, without being at all disconcerted, began to cry out that he was a sinner, that he had been guilty of wronging his neighbor. He beat his breast in sign of repentance and in a puritanical slang accused himself more loudly than the rioters had done. Blinded, like Orgon, by so much sanctity, they excused themselves to Tartuffe, carefully swept the hall and the marble doorsteps which they had soiled, and hastened to sack the house of the mayor because a small detachment of militia, spontaneously assembled, had fired upon them in self-defense after having stood patient for some time under a shower of stones.

These disorders are alarming from their general prevalence and frequent repetition and, more so, because their importance is little realized. They meet with few voices to condemn them, but they find many to excuse them. One of the defects of democracy is that it is forgetful of the past and careless of the future. A riot which in France would put a stop to business prevents no one here from going to the Exchange, speculating, turning over a dollar and making money. On meeting in the morning, each one asks and tells the news; here a Negro has been hanged, there a white man has been flogged; at Philadelphia, ten houses have been demolished; at Buffalo, at Utica, some people of color have been scourged. Then they go on to the price of cotton and coffee, the arrivals of flour, lumber, and tobacco, and become absorbed in calculations the rest of the day. I am surprised to see how dead the word *equality* falls when a good citizen pronounces it; the reign of law seems to be at an end; we have fallen under that of expediency. Farewell to justice, farewell to the great principles of 1776 and 1789! All hail to the interest of the moment, interpreted by nobody knows who, for the success of some petty intrigue of politics or business!

Five men, five white men, have been hanged at Vicksburg in Mississippi without even the form of a trial; they were gamblers, you are told, the scourge of the country. The *most respectable* citizens of Vicksburg assisted in their execution. But, one asks, the law which guarantees to all your fellow citizens trial by a jury of peers; but that old Saxon justice of which you boast! What is become of them? The answer—no court would have been able to rid us of them; morality and religion condemn them, and the moral and religious decree, for want of others, we have executed; it was necessary. *Expediency!* In Virginia, travelers from Northern States, on the slightest pretense, for some tavern gossip or some conversation in the coach, have been dragged before the self-styled *Committees of Vigilance*, then beaten, tarred, and feathered. Others, whose crime consisted in inadvertently having in their pocket some papers which the slaveholder has been pleased to pronounce Abolitionist writings, have been seized by these fanatics and hanged as emissaries of insurrection. What is become of that article of the Constitution which secures to the citizens of each State the protection of the laws in every other State? If we were to insist on these points, we would endanger our union with the South. *Expediency!*

Merchants of New York! The planters of one of the parishes of Louisiana have set a price on the head of one of your number because, as they say, he is an Abolitionist, an amalgamator. Will not your national sensibility, so lively in regard to France, be touched by this act of audacity? Our commerce with the South constitutes half the prosperity of New York. *Expediency!* Men of New England! Citizens of the cradle of American liberty! Sons of the pilgrims, self-exiled first to Holland and then to the sandy shores of Massachusetts rather than bow their opinions to the will of the Stuarts! You, so proud of your liberties, how can you abandon the dearest of all, the liberty of the press, to the hands of a postmaster? Always the same reply: *Expediency!*

It seems as if no political principle existed in the United States but the pleasure of the passions, as if law had no force when it jarred with interest. When a State feels itself injured by a tariff, it declares the law null and void, arms its militia, buys powder, and throws down the glove to Congress. When another State, Ohio, is dissatisfied with the boundary line assigned to it, it declares war against Michigan, its neighbor, in order to extend its frontiers by force. When the fanatics of Massachusetts, in their savage intolerance, feel offended by the presence of a Catholic convent in which the Sisters devote themselves to the work of educating young girls without distinction of sect, they plunder it and set it on fire; and the sacred edifice is burned in sight of a city of 70,000 without a drop of water thrown upon the flames and without it being possible to find a jury that would convict the authors of the cowardly outrage. When a governor of Georgia comes into collision with an upright magistrate who interposes his authority between the rapacity of the whites and the poor Indian whom they are impatient to rob, he denounces the just judge to the legislature and urges the passing of a law that will make him a State criminal. And, I repeat it, the worst and most fatal symptom of the times is that the perpetration of these outrages, however frequent they become, excites no sensation. The destruction of the churches and schoolhouses of the blacks in New York was looked upon as a show, and the passing merchants of the city paused to take a moment's relaxation from the sight; the fall of the building was greeted with loud cheers. In Baltimore, a numerous crowd applauded the work of demolition without inquiring whose house was pulled down, and the women, in the excitement of the moment, waved their handkerchiefs in the air. . . .

. . . The American system no longer works well. In the North, the removal of all restrictions on the right of suffrage without the creation of any counterpoise has destroyed the equilibrium. In the South, the old foundation borrowed from pre-Christian times, on which the South has attempted to raise the superstructure of a new social order in the nineteenth century, shakes and threatens to bury the thoughtless builders under the ruins of their half-finished work. In the West, a population sprung from the soil under the influence of circumstances unparalleled in the history of the world already affects a superiority, or rather lays claim to dominion, over the North and South. Everywhere, the relations established by the old federal compact are unfitted to the new state of things. The dissolution of the Union, the mere thought of which would have caused a shudder of horror ten years ago, which was numbered among those acts of infamy that are not to be named—the dissolution of the Union has been demanded and no thunder fell upon the head of the perpetrator of the sacrilege. At present it is a common topic of conversation. The dissolution of the Union, if it should take place, would be the most complete of all revolutions.

What will be the character of this revolution which one feels approaching? To what institutions will it give birth? Who must perish in the day of account? Who will rise on the storm? Who will resist the action of ages? I have not the gift of prophecy and I shall not try to pierce the mystery of the destinies of the New World. But I have a firm faith that a people with the energy and intelligence which the Americans possess, a people which like it has the genius of industry, which combines perseverance with the resources of ingenuity, which is essentially regular in its habits and orderly in its disposition, which is deeply imbued with religious habits even when a lively faith is wanting, such a people cannot be born yesterday to vanish tomorrow. The American people, in spite of its original defects, in spite of the numerous voids which a hasty growth and a superficial education have left in its ideas, feelings, and customs, is still a great and powerful people. For such nations, the most violent storms are wholesome trials which strengthen, solemn warnings which teach, elevate, and purify.

25

Social Ferment

(See Plates 9–12 following page 134.)

The drawings and engravings that embellished the popular magazines of the Jacksonian era offer us many fascinating glimpses of the social ferment being stirred up as Americans tried to adjust themselves to new forms of labor, new groups of immigrants, and new ideas of religious and social reconstruction. Plates 9–12 reveal some key aspects of these potent social forces.

PLATE 9. *Making Shirts for a Shilling; or, Misery and Magnificence.* From *Godey's Lady's Book* (1853), XLVII, 528.

Despite their fondness for sentimental moralizing, the editors of *Godey's Lady's Book* were not blind to some of the social evils in the Jacksonian generation. This illustration accompanied a melodramatic tale which exposed the hypocrisy of men of business who exploit poor and helpless seamstresses and, at the same time, hold up their heads in society with an "unblushing front" because they "subscribe largely to missions, attend church regularly, and are looked upon as very good, benevolent, and pious citizens."

PLATE 10. *Riot at Hoboken.* From *Gleason's Pictorial Drawing Room Companion* (1851), I, 140.

The riot at Hoboken pictured in the illustration from *Gleason's Pictorial* magazine was part of the familiar pattern of social violence in America that Michel Chevalier noted in his commentary on American society. This particular riot occurred when a group of Germans who were enjoying a musical and social celebration on the Cricket Ground were attacked by a group of rowdies from New York known as the "Short

Boys." According to the printed account of this riot, similar battles had taken place before in various neighborhoods of New York. The size of the fighting mob gives us some indication of the magnitude of the social tensions that were generated by the growing number of immigrant groups in the cities of Jacksonian America.

PLATE 11. *The Jerking Exercise.* From S. G. Goodrich, *Recollections of a Lifetime* (New York, 1856), I, 202.
Samuel G. Goodrich was undoubtedly the most successful author of juvenile books in the Jacksonian generation. He was known to countless children by his pen name of Peter Parley. Beginning with the *Tales of Peter Parley About America* (1827), more than a hundred other Peter Parley books followed in the next thirty years dealing with biography, history, geography, poetry, and fiction. All told, about seven million copies of Peter Parley's books were sold in the author's lifetime. The remarkable drawing of the "jerking exercise" illustrated Goodrich's recollections of religious revivals that he had seen frequently in his lifetime. From this engraving we can get some idea of the great emotional intensity of the religious revivals of the Jacksonian generation.

PLATE 12. *Southern Ideas of Liberty.*
This is one of the earliest anti-slavery cartoons of the Jacksonian period. Presumably done in 1835, this satirical drawing reminds us that the abolitionists were frequently victims of violence in the Jacksonian generation. The drawing depicts a man with donkey's ears seated on a bale of cotton with a copy of the Constitution under his feet. In the background a man hangs from the gallows; in the foreground another is being manhandled by a crowd. The printed legend that appeared with this cartoon is as follows: "Sentence passed upon one for supporting that clause of our Declaration viz, All men are born free and equal. 'Strip him to the skin! Give him a coat of tar and feathers!! Hang him by the neck, between Heaven and Earth!!! As a Beacon to warn the Northern fanatics of their danger!!!!'"

PART III

The New Uses of Power

26

A Veto, a Proclamation, and a Protest*

ANDREW JACKSON

The emerging changes in technology and economic organization in the Jacksonian generation produced important alterations in the conformation of social power. Accompanying these dislocations were important innovations in the uses of power within the established institutions of government. On the one hand, pressures were developing that threatened to shift the centers of decision making from the local sources of power in the states toward the authority of the national government. Internal improvements, banking and credit facilities, and tariff protection raised political questions that had to be negotiated and settled in the agencies of the national government. At the same time, there was a notable transfer of decision-making power from the Congress and from the federal judiciary to the presidency. President Jackson used the veto power with much greater frequency than his predecessors and he used it to set his interpretations of the people's will against that of Congress. In addition, he made bold to set his interpretation of the Constitution against that of the Supreme Court.

The selections which follow are from three of the more important state papers prepared by Andrew Jackson. The first is taken from his Veto Message concerning the bill to recharter the Bank of the United States. From this executive document we are able to get an idea of Jackson's mode of constitutional interpretation, of his conception of the structure of economic power in Ameri-

* From James D. Richardson, A Compilation of the Messages and Papers of the Presidents, 1789–1897 (Washington, D.C., 1896), II, 576–91, 640–50; III, 69–93, abridged.

can society, and of his vision of appropriate social purposes for America. The second is taken from the
Proclamation issued at the time of South Carolina's
attempted nullification of the federal tariff laws. In
this document we get a further view of Jackson's
thinking about the constitutional powers of the federal
government as well as some significant evidence of his
commitment to the symbols of nationalism. The third
selection is taken from Jackson's famous Protest against
the Senate resolution of censure regarding the removal
of the Bank deposit, and, in it, we can find a full statement of Jackson's conception of the presidency.

Can we not say that these changes in the uses of
power contributed as much as the derangement of values
and the uncertainties of status to increase the tensions
of politics in the Jacksonian era? Indeed, the political
battles of the Jacksonian administration always operated
close to the point of explosion. There is a constant piling
up of political crises beginning with the Maysville
Road veto, and continuing through the Cabinet crisis,
the Bank veto, the Nullification crisis, the removal of
the Bank deposits, the Senate resolution of censure and
Jackson's Protest, and, finally, the controversial Specie
Circular. Moreover, the stresses within the American
political system continued after Jackson left the presidency, even though most of his successors lacked his
qualities of leadership. Thereafter, there were very few
years of quiet or complacency in American politics
until the ultimate resort to violence in the Civil War.

[Veto Message]

To the Senate:

The bill "to modify and continue" the act entitled "An
act to incorporate the subscribers to the Bank of the
United States" was presented to me on the 4th July instant. Having considered it with that solemn regard to the
principles of the Constitution which the day was calculated to inspire, and come to the conclusion that it ought

not to become a law, I herewith return it to the Senate, in which it originated, with my objections.

A bank of the United States is in many respects convenient for the Government and useful to the people. Entertaining this opinion, and deeply impressed with the belief that some of the powers and privileges possessed by the existing bank are unauthorized by the Constitution, subversive of the rights of the States, and dangerous to the liberties of the people, I felt it my duty at an early period of my Administration to call the attention of Congress to the practicability of organizing an institution combining all its advantages and obviating these objections. I sincerely regret that in the act before me I can perceive none of those modifications of the bank charter which are necessary, in my opinion, to make it compatible with justice, with sound policy, or with the Constitution of our country. . . .

It is maintained by the advocates of the bank that its constitutionality in all its features ought to be considered as settled by precedent and by the decision of the Supreme Court. To this conclusion I can not assent. Mere precedent is a dangerous source of authority, and should not be regarded as deciding questions of constitutional power except where the acquiescence of the people and the States can be considered as well settled. So far from this being the case on this subject, an argument against the bank might be based on precedent. One Congress, in 1791, decided in favor of a bank; another, in 1811, decided against it. One Congress, in 1815, decided against a bank; another, in 1816, decided in its favor. Prior to the present Congress, therefore, the precedents drawn from that source were equal. If we resort to the States, the expressions of legislative, judicial, and executive opinions against the bank have been probably to those in its favor as 4 to 1. There is nothing in precedent, therefore, which, if its authority were admitted, ought to weigh in favor of the act before me.

If the opinion of the Supreme Court covered the whole ground of this act, it ought not to control the coordinate authorities of this Government. The Congress, the Executive, and the Court must each for itself be guided by its own opinion of the Constitution. Each public officer who takes an oath to support the Constitution swears that he will support it as he understands it, and not as it is understood by others. It is as much the duty of the House of Representatives, of the Senate, and of the President to decide upon the constitutionality of any bill or resolution which may be presented to them for passage or approval as it is of the supreme judges when it may be brought before them for judicial decision. The opinion of the judges has no more authority over Congress than the opinion of Congress has over the judges, and on that point the President is independent of both. The authority of the Supreme Court must not, therefore, be permitted to control the Congress or the Executive when acting in their legislative capacities, but to have only such influence as the force of their reasoning may deserve.

But in the case relied upon the Supreme Court have not decided that all the features of this corporation are compatible with the Constitution. It is true that the court have said that the law incorporating the bank is a constitutional exercise of power by Congress; but taking into view the whole opinion of the court and the reasoning by which they have come to that conclusion, I understand them to have decided that inasmuch as a bank is an appropriate means for carrying into effect the enumerated powers of the General Government, therefore the law incorporating it is in accordance with that provision of the Constitution which declares that Congress shall have power "to make all laws which shall be necessary and proper for carrying those powers into execution." Having satisfied themselves that the word *"necessary"* in the constitution means *"needful," "requisite," "essential," "conducive to,"* and that *"a bank"* is a convenient, a useful, and essential instrument in the prosecution of the Government's "fiscal operations," they conclude that to "use one must be within the discretion of Congress" and that "the act to incorporate the Bank of the United States is a law made in pursuance of the Constitution;" "but," say they, "*where the law is not prohibited and is really calculated to effect any of the objects intrusted to the Government, to undertake here to inquire into the degree of its necessity would be to pass the line which circumscribes the judicial department and to tread on legislative ground.*"

The principle here affirmed is that the "degree of its necessity," involving all the details of a banking institution, is a question exclusively for legislative consideration. A bank is constitutional, but it is the province of the Legislature to determine whether this or that particular power, privilege, or exemption is "necessary and proper" to enable the bank to discharge its duties to the Government, and from their decision there is no appeal to the courts of justice. Under the decision of the Supreme Court, therefore, it is the exclusive province of Congress and the President to decide whether the particular features of this act are *necessary* and *proper* in order to enable the bank to perform conveniently and efficiently the public duties assigned to it as a fiscal agent, and therefore constitutional, or *unnecessary* and *improper*, and therefore unconstitutional. . . .

It is maintained by some that the bank is a means of executing the constitutional power "to coin money and regulate the value thereof." Congress have established a mint to coin money and passed laws to regulate the value thereof. The money so coined, with its value so regulated, and such foreign coins as Congress may adopt are the only currency known to the Constitution. But if they have other power to regulate the currency, it was conferred to be exercised by themselves, and not to be transferred to a corporation. If the bank be established for that purpose, with a charter unalterable without its consent, Congress have parted with their power for a term of years, during which the Constitution is a dead letter. It is neither necessary nor proper to transfer its legislative power to such a bank, and therefore unconstitutional.

By its silence, considered in connection with the decision of the Supreme Court in the case of McCulloch against the State of Maryland, this act takes from the States the power to tax a portion of the banking business carried on within their limits, in subversion of one of the strongest barriers which secured them against Federal encroachments. Banking, like farming, manufacturing, or any other occupation or profession, is *a business*, the right to follow which is not originally derived from the laws. Every citizen and every company of citizens in all of our States possessed the right until the State legislatures deemed it good policy to prohibit private banking by law. If the prohibitory State laws were now repealed, every citizen would again possess the right. The State banks are a qualified restoration of the right which has been taken away by the laws against banking, guarded by such provisions and limitations as in the opinion of the State legislatures the public interest requires. These corporations, unless there be an exemption in their charter, are, like private bankers and banking companies, subject to State taxation. The manner in which these taxes shall be laid depends wholly on legislative discretion. It may be upon the bank, upon the stock, upon the profits, or in any other mode which the sovereign power shall will.

Upon the formation of the Constitution the States guarded their taxing power with peculiar jealousy. They surrendered it only as it regards imports and exports. In relation to every other object within their jurisdiction, whether persons, property, business, or professions, it was secured in as ample a manner as it was before possessed. All persons, though United States officers, are liable to a poll tax by the States within which they reside. The lands of the United States are liable to the usual land tax, except in the new States, from whom agreements that they will not tax unsold lands are exacted when they are admitted into the Union. Horses, wagons, any beasts or vehicles, tools, or property belonging to private citizens, though employed in the service of the United States, are subject to State taxation. Every private business, whether carried on by an officer of the General Government or not, whether it be mixed with public concerns or not, even if it be carried on by the Government of the United States itself, separately or in partnership, falls within the scope of the taxing power of the State. Nothing comes more fully within it than banks and the business of banking, by whomsoever instituted and carried on. Over this whole subject-matter it is just as absolute, unlimited, and uncontrollable as if the Constitution had never been adopted, because in the formation of that instrument it was reserved without qualification.

The principle is conceded that the States can not rightfully tax the operations of the General Government. They can not tax the money of the Government deposited in the State banks, nor the agency of those banks in remitting it; but will any man maintain that their mere selection to perform this public service for the General Government would exempt the State banks and their ordinary business from State taxation? Had the United States, instead of establishing a bank at Philadelphia, employed a private banker to keep and transmit their funds, would it have deprived Pennsylvania of the right to tax his bank and his usual banking operations? It will not be pretended. Upon what principle, then, are the banking establishments of the Bank of the United States and their usual banking operations to be exempted from taxation? It is not their public agency or the deposits of the Government which the States claim a right to tax, but their banks and their banking powers, instituted and exercised within State jurisdiction for their private emolument—those powers and privileges for which they pay a bonus, and which the States tax in their own banks. The exercise of these powers within a State, no matter by whom or under what authority, whether by private citizens in their original right, by corporate bodies created by the States, by foreigners or the agents of foreign governments located within their limits, forms a legitimate object of State taxation. From this and like sources, from the persons, property, and business that are found residing, located, or carried on under their jurisdiction, must the States, since the surrender of their right to raise a revenue from imports and exports, draw all the money necessary for the support of their governments and the maintenance of their independence. There is no more appropriate subject of taxation than banks, banking, and bank stocks, and none to which the States ought more pertinaciously to cling.

It can not be *necessary* to the character of the bank as a fiscal agent of the Government that its private business should be exempted from that taxation to which all the State banks are liable, nor can I conceive it *"proper"* that the substantive and most essential powers reserved by the States shall be thus attacked and annihilated as a means of executing the powers delegated to the General Government. It may be safely assumed that none of those sages who had an agency in forming or adopting our Constitution ever imagined that any portion of the taxing power of the States not prohibited to them nor delegated to Congress was to be swept away and annihilated as a means of executing certain powers delegated to Congress.

If our power over means is so absolute that the Supreme Court will not call in question the constitutionality of an act of Congress the subject of which "is not prohibited, and is really calculated to effect any of the objects intrusted to the Government," although, as in the case before me, it takes away powers expressly granted to Congress and rights scrupulously reserved to the States, it becomes us to proceed in our legislation with the utmost caution. Though not directly, our own powers and the rights of the States may be indirectly legislated away in the use of means to execute substantive powers. We may not enact that Congress shall not have the power of exclusive legislation over the District of Columbia, but we may pledge the faith of the United States that as a means of executing other powers it shall not be exercised for twenty years or forever. We may not pass an act prohibiting the States to tax the banking business carried on within their limits, but we may, as a means of executing our powers over other objects, place that business in the hands of our agents and then declare it exempt from State taxation in their hands. Thus may our own powers and the rights of the States, which we can not directly curtail or invade, be frittered away and extinguished in the use of means employed by us to execute other powers. That a bank of the United States, competent to all the duties which may be required by the Government, might be so organized as not to infringe on our own delegated powers or the reserved rights of the States I do not entertain a doubt. Had the Executive been called upon to furnish the project of such an institution, the duty would have been cheerfully performed. In the absence of such a call it was obviously proper that he should confine himself to pointing out those prominent features in the act presented which in his opinion make it incompatible with the Constitution and sound policy. A general discussion will now take place, eliciting new light and settling important principles; and a new Congress, elected in the midst of such discussion, and furnishing an equal representation of the people according to the last census, will bear to the Capitol the verdict of public opinion, and, I doubt not, bring this important question to a satisfactory result.

Under such circumstances the bank comes forward and asks a renewal of its charter for a term of fifteen years upon conditions which not only operate as a gratuity to the stockholders of many millions of dollars, but will sanction any abuses and legalize any encroachments.

Suspicions are entertained and charges are made of gross abuse and violation of its charter. An investigation unwillingly conceded and so restricted in time as necessarily to make it incomplete and unsatisfactory discloses enough to excite suspicion and alarm. In the practices of the principal bank partially unveiled, in the absence of important witnesses, and in numerous charges confidently made and as yet wholly uninvestigated there was enough to induce a majority of the committee of investigation—a committee which was selected from the most able and honorable members of the House of Representatives—to recommend a suspension of further action upon the bill and a prosecution of the inquiry. As the charter had yet four years to run, and as a renewal now was not necessary to the successful prosecution of its business, it was to have been expected that the bank itself, conscious of its purity and proud of its character, would have withdrawn its application for the present, and demanded the severest scrutiny into all its transactions. In their declining to do so there seems to be an additional reason why the functionaries of the Government should proceed with less haste and more caution in the renewal of their monopoly.

The bank is professedly established as an agent of the executive branch of the Government, and its constitutionality is maintained on that ground. Neither upon the propriety of present action nor upon the provisions of this act was the Executive consulted. It has had no opportunity to say that it neither needs nor wants an agent clothed with such powers and favored by such exemptions. There is nothing in its legitimate functions which makes it necessary or proper. Whatever interest or influence, whether public or private, has given birth to this act, it can not be found either in the wishes or necessities of the executive department, by which present action is deemed premature, and the powers conferred upon its agent not only unnecessary, but dangerous to the Government and country.

It is to be regretted that the rich and powerful too often bend the acts of government to their selfish purposes. Distinctions in society will always exist under every just government. Equality of talents, of education, or of wealth can not be produced by human institutions. In the full enjoyment of the gifts of Heaven and the fruits of superior industry, economy, and virtue, every man is equally entitled to protection by law; but when the laws undertake to add to these natural and just advantages artificial distinctions, to grant titles, gratuities, and exclusive privileges, to make the rich richer and the potent more powerful, the humble members of society—the farmers, mechanics, and laborers—who have neither the time nor the means of securing like favors to themselves, have a right to complain of the injustice of their Government. There are no necessary evils in government. Its evils exist only in its abuses. If it would confine itself to equal protection, and, as Heaven does its rains, shower its favors alike on the high and the low, the rich and the poor, it would be an unqualified blessing. In the act before me there seems to be a wide and unnecessary departure from these just principles.

Nor is our Government to be maintained or our Union preserved by invasions of the rights and powers of the several States. In thus attempting to make our General Government strong we make it weak. Its true strength consists in leaving individuals and States as much as possible to themselves—in making itself felt, not in its power, but in its beneficence; not in its control, but in its protection; not in binding the States more closely to the center, but leaving each to move unobstructed in its proper orbit.

Experience should teach us wisdom. Most of the difficulties our Government now encounters and most of the dangers which impend over our Union have sprung from an abandonment of the legitimate objects of Government by our national legislation, and the adoption of such principles as are embodied in this act. Many of our rich men have not been content with equal protection and equal benefits, but have besought us to make them richer by act of Congress. By attempting to gratify their desires we have in the results of our legislation arrayed section against section, interest against interest, and man against man, in a fearful commotion which threatens to shake the foundations of our Union. It is time to pause in our career to review our principles, and if possible revive that devoted patriotism and spirit of compromise which distinguished the sages of the Revolution and the fathers of our Union. If we can not at once, in justice to interests vested under improvident legislation, make our Government what it ought to be, we can at least take a stand against all new grants of monopolies and exclusive privileges, against any prostitution of our Government to the advancement of the few at the expense of the many, and in favor of compromise and gradual reform in our code of laws and system of political economy. . . .

[PROCLAMATION]

. . . To preserve this bond of our political existence from destruction, to maintain inviolate this state of national honor and prosperity, and to justify the confidence my fellow-citizens have reposed in me, I, Andrew Jackson, President of the United States, have thought proper to issue this my proclamation, stating my views of the Constitution and laws applicable to the measures adopted by the convention of South Carolina and to the reasons they have put forth to sustain them, declaring the course which duty will require me to pursue, and, appealing to the understanding and patriotism of the people, warn them of the consequences that must inevitably result from an observance of the dictates of the convention.

Strict duty would require of me nothing more than the exercise of those powers with which I am now or may hereafter be invested for preserving the peace of the Union and for the execution of the laws; but the imposing aspect which opposition has assumed in this case, by clothing itself with State authority, and the deep interest which the people of the United States must all feel in preventing a resort to stronger measures while there is a hope that anything will be yielded to reasoning and remonstrance, perhaps demand, and will certainly justify, a full exposition to South Carolina and the nation of the views I entertain of this important question, as well as a distinct enunciation of the course which my sense of duty will require me to pursue. . . .

The people of the United States formed the Constitution, acting through the State legislatures in making the compact, to meet and discuss its provisions, and acting in separate conventions when they ratified those provisions; but the terms used in its construction show it to be a Government in which the people of all the States, collectively, are represented. We are *one people* in the choice of President and Vice-President. Here the States have no other agency than to direct the mode in which the votes shall be given. The candidates having the majority of all the votes are chosen. The electors of a majority of States may have given their votes for one candidate, and yet another may be chosen. The people, then, and not the States, are represented in the executive branch.

In the House of Representatives there is this difference, that the people of one State do not, as in the case of President and Vice-President, all vote for the same officers. The people of all the States do not vote for all the members, each State electing only its own representatives. But this creates no material distinction. When chosen, they are all representatives of the United States, not representatives of the particular State from which they come. They are paid by the United States, not by the State; nor are they accountable to it for any act done in the performance of their legislative functions; and however they may in practice, as it is their duty to do, consult and prefer the interests of their particular constituents when they come in conflict with any other partial or local interest, yet it is their first and highest duty, as representatives of the United States, to promote the general good.

The Constitution of the United States, then, forms a *government*, not a league; and whether it be formed by compact between the States or in any other manner, its character is the same. It is a Government in which all the people are represented, which operates directly on the people individually, not upon the States; they retained all the power they did not grant. But each State, having expressly parted with so many powers as to constitute, jointly with the other States, a single nation, can not, from that period, possess any right to secede, because such secession does not break a league, but destroys the unity of a nation; and any injury to that unity is not only a breach which would result from the contravention of a compact, but it is an offense against the whole Union. To say that any State may at pleasure secede from the Union is to say that the United States are not a nation, because it would be a solecism to contend that any part of a nation might dissolve its connection with the other parts, to their injury or ruin, without committing any offense. Secession, like any other revolutionary act, may be morally justified by the extremity of oppression; but to call it a constitutional right is confounding the meaning of terms, and can only be done through gross error or to deceive those who are willing to assert a right, but would pause before they made a revolution or incur the penalties consequent on a failure. . . .

The States severally have not retained their entire sovereignty. It has been shown that in becoming parts of a nation, not members of a league, they surrendered many of their essential parts of sovereignty. The right to make treaties, declare war, levy taxes, exercise exclusive judicial and legislative powers, were all of them functions of sovereign power. The States, then, for all these important purposes were no longer sovereign. The allegiance of their citizens was transferred, in the first instance, to the Government of the United States; they became American citizens and owed obedience to the Constitution of the United States and to laws made in conformity with the powers it vested in Congress. This last position has not been and can not be denied. How, then, can that State be said to be sovereign and independent whose citizens owe obedience to laws not made by it and whose magistrates are sworn to disregard those laws when they come in conflict with those passed by another? What shows conclusively that the States can not be said to have reserved an undivided sovereignty is that they expressly ceded the right to punish treason—not treason against their separate power, but treason against the United States. Treason is an offense against *sovereignty*, and sovereignty must reside with the power to punish it. But the reserved rights of the States are not less sacred because they have, for their common interest, made the General Government the depository of these powers. The unity of our political character (as has been shown for another purpose) commenced with its very existence. Under the royal Government we had no separate character; our opposition to its oppressions began as *united colonies*. We were the *United States* under the Confederation, and the name was perpetuated and the Union rendered more perfect by the Federal Constitution. In none of these stages did we consider ourselves in any other light than as forming one nation. Treaties and alliances were made in the name of all. Troops were raised for the joint defense. How, then, with all these proofs that under all changes of our position we had, for designated purposes and with defined powers, created national governments, how is it that the most perfect of those several modes of union should now be considered as a mere league that may be dissolved at pleasure? It is from an abuse of terms. Compact is used as synonymous with league, although the true term is not employed, because it would at once show the fallacy of the reasoning. It would not do to say that our Constitution was only a league, but it is labored to prove it a compact (which in one sense it is) and then to argue that as a league is a compact every compact between nations must of course be a league, and that from such an engagement every sovereign power has a right to recede. But it has been shown that in this sense the States are not sovereign, and that even if they were, and the national Constitution had been formed by compact, there would be no right in any one State to exonerate itself from its obligations.

So obvious are the reasons which forbid this secession that it is necessary only to allude to them. The Union was formed for the benefit of all. It was produced by mutual sacrifices of interests and opinions. Can those sacrifices be recalled? Can the States who magnanimously surrendered their title to the territories of the West recall the grant? Will the inhabitants of the inland States agree to pay the duties that may be imposed without their assent by those on the Atlantic or the Gulf for their own benefit? Shall there be a free port in one State and onerous duties in another? No one believes that any right exists in a single State to involve all the others in these and countless other evils contrary to engagements solemnly made. Everyone must see that the other States, in self-defense, must oppose it at all hazards. . . .

This, then, is the position in which we stand: A small majority of the citizens of one State in the Union have elected delegates to a State convention; that convention has ordained that all the revenue laws of the United States must be repealed, or that they are no longer a member of the Union. The governor of that State has recommended to the legislature the raising of an army to carry the secession into effect, and that he may be empowered to give clearances to vessels in the name of the State. No act of violent opposition to the laws has yet been committed, but such a state of things is hourly apprehended. And it is the intent of this instrument to *proclaim*, not only that the duty imposed on me by the Constitution "to take care that the laws be faithfully executed" shall be performed to the extent of the powers already vested in me by law, or of such others as the wisdom of Congress shall devise and intrust to me for that purpose, but to warn the citizens of South Carolina who have been deluded into an opposition to the laws of the danger they will incur by obedience to the illegal and disorganizing ordinance of the convention; to exhort those who have refused to support it to persevere in their determination to uphold the Constitution and laws of their country; and to point out to all the perilous situation into which the good people of that State have been led, and that the course they are urged to pursue is one of ruin and disgrace to the very State whose rights they affect to support.

Fellow-citizens of my native State, let me not only admonish you, as the First Magistrate of our common country, not to incur the penalty of its laws, but use the influence that a father would over his children whom he saw rushing to certain ruin. In that paternal language, with that paternal feeling, let me tell you, my countrymen, that you are deluded by men who are either deceived themselves or wish to deceive you. Mark under what pretenses you have been led on to the brink of insurrection and treason on which you stand. First, a diminution of the value of your staple commodity, lowered by overproduction in other quarters, and the consequent diminution in the value of your lands were the sole effect of the tariff laws. The effect of those laws was confessedly injurious, but the evil was greatly exaggerated by the unfounded theory you were taught to believe—that its burthens were in proportion to your exports, not to your consumption of imported articles. Your pride was roused by the assertion that a submission to those laws was a state of vassalage and that resistance to them was equal in patriotic merit to the opposition our fathers offered to the oppressive laws of Great Britain. You were told that this opposition might be peaceably, might be constitutionally, made; that you might enjoy all the advantages of the Union and bear none of its burthens. Eloquent appeals to your passions, to your State pride, to your native courage, to your sense of real injury, were used to prepare you for the period when the mask which concealed the hideous features of *disunion* should be taken off. It fell, and you were made to look with complacency on objects which not long since you would have regarded with horror. Look back to the arts which have brought you to this state; look forward to the consequences to which it must inevitably lead! Look back to what was first told you as an inducement to enter into this dangerous course. The great political truth was repeated to you that you had the revolutionary right of resisting all laws that were palpably unconstitutional and intolerably oppressive. It was added that the right to nullify a law rested on the same principle, but that it was a peaceable remedy. This character which was given to it made you receive with too much confidence the assertions that were made of the unconstitutionality of the law and its oppressive effects. Mark, my fellow-citizens, that by the admission of your leaders the unconstitutionality must be *palpable*, or it will not justify either resistance or nullification. What is the meaning of the word *palpable* in the sense in which it is here used? That which is apparent to everyone; that which no man of ordinary intellect will fail to perceive. Is the unconstitutionality of these laws of that description? Let those among your leaders who once approved and advocated the principle of protective duties answer the question; and let them choose whether they will be considered as incapable then of perceiving that which must have been apparent to every man of common understanding, or as imposing upon your confidence and endeavoring to mislead you now. In either case they are unsafe guides in the perilous path they urge you to tread. Ponder well on this circumstance, and you will know how to appreciate the exaggerated language they address to you. They are not champions of liberty, emulating the fame of our Revolutionary fathers, nor are you an oppressed people, contending, as they repeat to you, against worse than colonial vassalage. You are free members of a flourishing and happy Union. There is no settled design to oppress you. You have indeed felt the unequal operation of laws which may have been unwisely, not unconstitutionally, passed; but that inequality must necessarily be removed. At the very moment when you were madly urged on to the unfortunate course you have begun a change in public opinion had commenced. The nearly approaching payment of the public debt and the consequent necessity of a diminution of duties had already produced a considerable reduction, and that, too, on some articles of general consumption in your State. The importance of this change was underrated, and you were authoritatively told that no further alleviation of your burthens was to be expected at the very time when the condition of the country imperiously demanded such a modification of the duties as should reduce them to a just and equitable scale. But, as if apprehensive of the effect of this change in allaying your discontents, you were precipitated into the fearful state in which you now find yourselves.

I have urged you to look back to the means that were used to hurry you on to the position you have now assumed and forward to the consequences it will produce. Something more is necessary. Contemplate the condition of that country of which you still form an important part. Consider its Government, uniting in one bond of common interest and general protection so many different States, giving to all their inhabitants the proud title of *American citizen*, protecting their commerce, securing their literature and their arts, facilitating their intercommunication, defending their frontiers, and making their name respected in the remotest parts of the earth. Consider the extent of its territory, its increasing and happy population, its advance in arts which render life agreeable, and the sciences which elevate the mind! See education spreading the lights of religion, morality, and general information into every cottage in this wide extent of our Territories and States. Behold it as the asylum where the wretched and the oppressed find a refuge and support. Look on this picture of happiness and honor and say, *We too are citizens of America.* Carolina is one of these proud States; her arms have defended, her best blood has cemented, this happy Union. And then add, if you can, without horror and remorse, This happy Union we will dissolve; this picture of peace and prosperity we will deface; this free intercourse we will interrupt; these fertile fields we will deluge with blood; the protection of that glorious flag we renounce; the very name of Americans we discard. And for what, mistaken men? For what do you throw away these inestimable blessings? For what would you exchange your share in the advantages and honor of the Union? For the dream of a separate independence—a dream interrupted by bloody conflicts with your neighbors and a vile dependence on a foreign power. If your leaders could succeed in establishing a separation, what would be your situation? Are you united at home? Are you free from the apprehension of civil discord, with all its fearful consequences? Do our neighboring republics, every day suffering some new revolution or contending with some new insurrection, do they excite your envy? But the dictates of a high duty oblige me solemnly to announce that you can not succeed. The laws of the United States must be executed. I have no discretionary power on the subject; my duty is emphatically pronounced in the Constitution. Those who told you that you might peaceably prevent their execution deceived you; they could not have been deceived themselves. They know that a forcible opposition could alone prevent the execution of the laws, and they know that such opposition must be repelled. Their object is disunion. But be not deceived by names. Disunion by armed force is *treason*. Are you really ready to incur its guilt? If you are, on the heads of the instigators of the act be the dreadful consequences; on their heads be the dishonor, but on yours may fall the punishment. On your unhappy State will inevitably fall all the evils of the conflict you force upon the Government of your country. It can not accede to the mad project of disunion, of which you would be the first victims. Its First Magistrate can not, if he would, avoid the performance of his duty. The consequence must be fearful for you, distressing to your fellow-citizens here and to the friends of good government throughout the world. Its enemies have beheld our prosperity with a vexation they could not conceal; it was a standing refutation of their slavish doctrines, and they will point to our discord with the triumph of malignant joy. It is yet in your power to disappoint them. There is yet time to show that the descendants of the Pinckneys, the Sumpters, the Rutledges, and of the thousand other names which adorn the pages of your Revolutionary history will not abandon that Union to support which so many of them fought and bled and died. I adjure you, as you honor their memory, as you love the cause of freedom, to which they dedicated their lives, as you prize the peace of your country, the lives of its best citizens, and your own fair fame, to retrace your steps. Snatch from the archives of your State the disorganizing edict of its convention; bid its members to reassemble and promulgate the decided expressions of your will to remain in the path which alone can conduct you to safety, prosperity, and honor. Tell them that compared to disunion all other evils are light, because that brings with it an accumulation of all. Declare that you will never take the field unless the star-spangled banner of your country shall float over you; that you will not be stigmatized when dead, and dishonored and scorned while you live, as the authors of the first attack on the Constitution of your country. Its destroyers you can not be. You may disturb its peace, you may interrupt the course of its prosperity, you may cloud its reputation for stability; but its tranquillity will be restored, its prosperity will return, and the stain upon its national character will be transferred and remain an eternal blot on the memory of those who caused the disorder. . . .

[PROTEST]

To the Senate of the United States:

It appears by the published Journal of the Senate that on the 26th of December last a resolution was offered by a member of the Senate, which after a protracted debate was on the 28th day of March last modified by the mover and passed by the votes of twenty-six Senators out of forty-six who were present and voted, in the following words, viz:

Resolved, That the President, in the late Executive proceedings in relation to the public revenue, has assumed upon himself authority and power not conferred by the Constitution and laws, but in derogation of both.

Having had the honor, through the voluntary suffrages of the American people, to fill the office of President of the United States during the period which may be presumed to have been referred to in this resolution, it is sufficiently evident that the censure it inflicts was intended for myself. Without notice, unheard and untried, I thus find myself charged on the records of the Senate, and in a form hitherto unknown in our history, with the high crime of violating the laws and Constitution of my country. . . .

By the Constitution "the executive power is vested in a President of the United States." Among the duties imposed upon him, and which he is sworn to perform, is that of "taking care that the laws be faithfully executed."

Being thus made responsible for the entire action of the executive department, it was but reasonable that the power of appointing, overseeing, and controlling those who execute the laws—a power in its nature executive—should remain in his hands. It is therefore not only his right, but the Constitution makes it his duty, to "nominate and, by and with the advice and consent of the Senate, appoint" all "officers of the United States whose appointments are not in the Constitution otherwise provided for," with a proviso that the appointment of inferior officers may be vested in the President alone, in the courts of justice, or in the heads of Departments.

The executive power vested in the Senate is neither that of "nominating" nor "appointing." It is merely a check upon the Executive power of appointment. If individuals are proposed for appointment by the President by them deemed incompetent or unworthy, they may withhold their consent and the appointment can not be made. They check the action of the Executive, but can not in relation to those very subjects act themselves nor direct him. Selections are still made by the President, and the negative given to the Senate, without diminishing his responsibility, furnishes an additional guaranty to the country that the subordinate executive as well as the judicial offices shall be filled with worthy and competent men.

The whole executive power being vested in the President, who is responsible for its exercise, it is a necessary consequence that he should have a right to employ agents of his own choice to aid him in the performance of his duties, and to discharge them when he is no longer willing to be responsible for their acts. In strict accordance with this principle, the power of removal, which, like that of appointment, is an original executive power, is left unchecked by the Constitution in relation to all executive officers, for whose conduct the President is responsible, while it is taken from him in relation to judicial officers, for whose acts he is not responsible. In the Government from which many of the fundamental principles of our system are derived the head of the executive department originally had power to appoint and remove at will all officers, executive and judicial. It was to take the judges out of this general power of removal, and thus make them independent of the Executive, that the tenure of their offices was changed to good behavior. Nor is it conceivable why they are placed in our Constitution upon a tenure different from that of all other officers appointed by the Executive unless it be for the same purpose. . . .

The Congress of the United States have never passed an act imperatively directing that the public moneys shall be kept in any particular place or places. From the origin of the Government to the year 1816 the statute book was wholly silent on the subject. In 1789 a Treasurer was created, subordinate to the Secretary of the Treasury, and through him to the President. He was required to give bond safely to keep and faithfully to disburse the public moneys, without any direction as to the manner or places in which they should be kept. By reference to the practice of the Government it is found that from its first organization the Secretary of the Treasury, acting under the supervision of the President, designated the places in which the public moneys should be kept, and especially directed all transfers from place to place. This practice was continued, with the silent acquiescence of Congress, from 1789 down to 1816, and although many banks were selected and discharged, and although a portion of the moneys were first placed in the State banks, and then in the former Bank of the United States, and upon the dissolution of that were again transferred to the State banks, no legislation was thought necessary by Congress, and all the operations were originated and perfected by Executive authority. The Secretary of the Treasury, responsible to the President, and with his approbation, made contracts and arrangements in relation to the whole subject-matter, which was thus entirely committed to the direction of the President under his responsibilities to the American people and to those who were authorized to impeach and punish him for any breach of this important trust.

The act of 1816 establishing the Bank of the United States directed the deposits of public money to be made in that bank and its branches in places in which the said bank and branches thereof may be established, "unless the Secretary of the Treasury should otherwise order and direct," in which event he was required to give his reasons to Congress. This was but a continuation of his preexisting power as the head of an Executive Department to direct where the deposits should be made, with the superadded obligation of giving his reasons to Congress for making them elsewhere than in the Bank of the United States and its branches. It is not to be considered that this provision in any degree altered the relation between the Secretary of the Treasury and the President as the responsible head of the executive department, or released the latter from his constitutional obligation to "take care that the laws be faithfully executed." On the contrary, it increased his responsibilities by adding another to the long list of laws which it was his duty to carry into effect.

It would be an extraordinary result if because the person charged by law with a public duty is one of his Secretaries it were less the duty of the President to see that law faithfully executed than other laws enjoining duties upon subordinate officers or private citizens. If there be any difference, it would seem that the obligation is the stronger in relation to the former, because the neglect is in his presence and the remedy at hand.

It can not be doubted that it was the legal duty of the Secretary of the Treasury to order and direct the deposits of the public money to be made elsewhere than in the Bank of the United States *whenever sufficient reasons existed for making the change.* If in such a case he neglected or refused to act, he would neglect or refuse to execute the law. What would be the sworn duty of the President? Could he say that the Constitution did not bind him to see the law faithfully executed because it was one of his Secretaries and not himself upon whom the service was specially imposed? Might he not be asked whether there was any such limitation to his obligations prescribed in the

Constitution? Whether he is not equally bound to take care that the laws be faithfully executed, whether they impose duties on the highest officer of State or the lowest subordinate in any of the Departments? Might he not be told that it was for the sole purpose of causing all executive officers, from the highest to the lowest, faithfully to perform the services required of them by law that the people of the United States have made him their Chief Magistrate and the Constitution has clothed him with the entire executive power of this Government? The principles implied in these questions appear too plain to need elucidation.

But here also we have a cotemporaneous construction of the act which shows that it was not understood as in any way changing the relations between the President and Secretary of the Treasury, or as placing the latter out of Executive control even in relation to the deposits of the public money. Nor on that point are we left to any equivocal testimony. The documents of the Treasury Department show that the Secretary of the Treasury did apply to the President and obtained his approbation and sanction to the original transfer of the public deposits to the present Bank of the United States, and did carry the measure into effect in obedience to his decision. They also show that transfers of the public deposits from the branches of the Bank of the United States to State banks at Chillicothe, Cincinnati, and Louisville, in 1819, were made with the approbation of the President and by his authority. They show that upon all important questions appertaining to his Department, whether they related to the public deposits or other matters, it was the constant practice of the Secretary of the Treasury to obtain for his acts the approval and sanction of the President. These acts and the principles on which they were founded were known to all the departments of the Government, to Congress and the country, and until very recently appear never to have been called in question.

Thus was it settled by the Constitution, the laws, and the whole practice of the Government that the entire executive power is vested in the President of the United States; that as incident to that power the right of appointing and removing those officers who are to aid him in the execution of the laws, with such restrictions only as the Constitution prescribes, is vested in the President; that the Secretary of the Treasury is one of those officers; that the custody of the public property and money is an Executive function which, in relation to the money, has always been exercised through the Secretary of the Treasury and his subordinates; that in the performance of these duties he is subject to the supervision and control of the President, and in all important measures having relation to them consults the Chief Magistrate and obtains his approval and sanction; that the law establishing the bank did not, as it could not, change the relation between the President and the Secretary—did not release the former from his obligation to see the law faithfully executed nor the latter from the President's supervision and control; that afterwards and before the Secretary did in fact consult and obtain the sanction of the President to transfers and removals of the public deposits, and that all departments of the Government, and the nation itself, approved or acquiesced in these acts and principles as in strict conformity with our Constitution and laws. . . .

The dangerous tendency of the doctrine which denies to the President the power of supervising, directing, and controlling the Secretary of the Treasury in like manner with the other executive officers would soon be manifest in practice were the doctrine to be established. The President is the direct representative of the American people, but the Secretaries are not. If the Secretary of the Treasury be independent of the President in the execution of the laws, then is there no direct responsibility to the people in that important branch of this Government to which is committed the care of the national finances. And it is in the power of the Bank of the United States, or any other corporation, body of men, or individuals, if a Secretary

See page 285 for description of Plates 13–16.

[13] *The Downfall of Mother Bank.* By E. W. Clay (?). Photograph by courtesy of The New-York Historical Society, New York City.

[14] *King Andrew the First.* Artist unknown. Photograph by courtesy of The New-York Historical Society, New York City.

[15] *The Times.* By E. W. Clay. Photograph by courtesy of The New-York Historical Society, New York City.

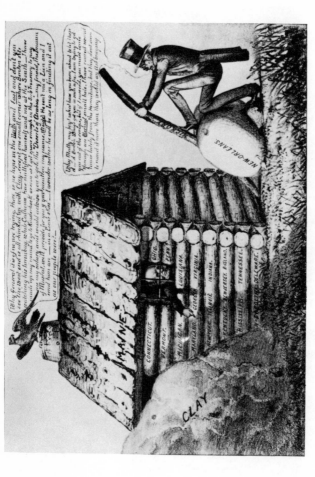

[16] *The New Era Whig Trap Sprung.* By Napoleon Sarony (?). Photograph by courtesy of The New-York Historical Society, New York City.

shall be found to accord with them in opinion or can be induced in practice to promote their views, to control through him the whole action of the Government (so far as it is exercised by his Department) in defiance of the Chief Magistrate elected by the people and responsible to them.

But the evil tendency of the particular doctrine adverted to, though sufficiently serious, would be as nothing in comparison with the pernicious consequences which would inevitably flow from the approbation and allowance by the people and the practice by the Senate of the unconstitutional power of arraigning and censuring the official conduct of the Executive in the manner recently pursued. Such proceedings are eminently calculated to unsettle the foundations of the Government, to disturb the harmonious action of its different departments, and to break down the checks and balances by which the wisdom of its framers sought to insure its stability and usefulness.

The honest differences of opinion which occasionally exist between the Senate and the President in regard to matters in which both are obliged to participate are sufficiently embarrassing; but if the course recently adopted by the Senate shall hereafter be frequently pursued, it is not only obvious that the harmony of the relations between the President and the Senate will be destroyed, but that other and graver effects will ultimately ensue. If the censures of the Senate be submitted to by the President, the confidence of the people in his ability and virtue and the character and usefulness of his Administration will soon be at an end, and the real power of the Government will fall into the hands of a body holding their offices for long terms, not elected by the people and not to them directly responsible. If, on the other hand, the illegal censures of the Senate should be resisted by the President, collisions and angry controversies might ensue, discreditable in their progress and in the end compelling the people to adopt the conclusion either that their chief Magistrate was unworthy of their respect or that the Senate was chargeable with calumny and injustice. Either of these results would impair public confidence in the perfection of the system and lead to serious alterations of its framework or to the practical abandonment of some of its provisions.

The influence of such proceedings on the other departments of the Government, and more especially on the States, could not fail to be extensively pernicious. When the judges in the last resort of official misconduct themselves overleap the bounds of their authority as prescribed by the Constitution, what general disregard of its provisions might not their example be expected to produce? And who does not perceive that such contempt of the Federal Constitution by one of its most important departments would hold out the strongest temptations to resistance on the part of the State sovereignties whenever they shall suppose their just rights to have been invaded? Thus all the independent departments of the Government, and the States which compose our confederated Union, instead of attending to their appropriate duties and leaving those who may offend to be reclaimed or punished in the manner pointed out in the Constitution, would fall to mutual crimination and recrimination and give to the people confusion and anarchy instead of order and law, until at length some form of aristocratic power would be established on the ruins of the Constitution or the States be broken into separate communities.

Far be it from me to charge or to insinuate that the present Senate of the United States intend in the most distant way to encourage such a result. It is not of their motives or designs, but only of the tendency of their acts, that it is my duty to speak. It is, if possible, to make Senators themselves sensible of the danger which lurks under the precedent set in their resolution, and at any rate to perform my duty as the responsible head of one of the coequal departments of the Government, that I have been compelled to point out the consequences to which the discussion and passage of the resolution may lead if the tendency of the measure be not checked in its inception. It is due to the high trust with which I have been charged, to those who may be called to succeed me in it, to the representatives of the people whose constitutional prerogative has been unlawfully assumed, to the people and to the States, and to the Constitution they have established that I should not permit its provisions to be broken down by such an attack on the executive department without at least some effort "to preserve, protect, and defend" them. With this view, and for the reasons which have been stated, I do hereby *solemnly protest* against the aforementioned proceedings of the Senate as unauthorized by the Constitution, contrary to its spirit and to several of its express provisions, subversive of that distribution of the powers of government which it has ordained and established, destructive of the checks and safeguards by which those powers were intended on the one hand to be controlled and on the other to be protected, and calculated by their immediate and collateral effects, by their character and tendency, to concentrate in the hands of a body not directly amenable to the people a degree of influence and power dangerous to their liberties and fatal to the Constitution of their choice.

The resolution of the Senate contains an imputation upon my private as well as upon my public character, and as it must stand forever on their journals, I can not close this substitute for that defense which I have not been allowed to present in the ordinary form without remarking that I have lived in vain if it be necessary to enter into a formal vindication of my character and purposes from such an imputation. In vain do I bear upon my person enduring memorials of that contest in which American liberty was purchased; in vain have I since periled property, fame, and life in defense of the rights and privileges so dearly bought; in vain am I now, without a personal aspiration or the hope of individual advantage, encountering responsibilities and dangers from which by mere inactivity in relation to a single point I might have been exempt, if any serious doubts can be entertained as to the purity of my purposes and motives. If I had been ambitious, I should have sought an alliance with that powerful institution which even now aspires to no divided empire. If I had been venal, I should have sold myself to its designs. Had I preferred personal comfort and official ease to the performance of my arduous duty, I should have ceased to molest it. In the history of conquerors and usurpers, never in the fire of youth nor in the vigor of manhood could I find an attraction to lure me from the path of duty, and now I shall scarcely find an inducement to commence their career of ambition when gray hairs and a decaying frame, instead of inviting to toil and battle, call me to the contemplation of other worlds, where conquerors cease to be honored and usurpers expiate their crimes. The only ambition I can feel is to acquit myself to Him to whom I must soon render an account of my stewardship, to serve my fellow-men, and live respected and honored in the history of my country. No; the ambition which leads me on is an anxious desire and a fixed determination to return to the people unimpaired the sacred trust they have confided to my charge; to heal the wounds of the Constitution and preserve it from further violation; to persuade my countrymen, so far as I may, that it is not in a splendid government supported by powerful monopolies and aristocratical establishments that they will find happiness or their liberties protection, but in a plain system, void of pomp, protecting all and granting favors to none, dispensing its blessings, like the dews of Heaven, unseen and unfelt save in the freshness and beauty they contribute to produce. It is such a government that the genius of our people requires; such an one only under which our States may remain for ages to come united, prosperous, and free. If the Almighty Being who has hitherto sustained and protected me will but vouchsafe to make my feeble powers instrumental to such a result, I shall anticipate with pleasure the place to be assigned me in the history of my country, and die contented with the belief that I have contributed in some small degree to increase the value and prolong the duration of American liberty.

To the end that the resolution of the Senate may not

be hereafter drawn into precedent with the authority of silent acquiescence on the part of the executive department, and to the end also that my motives and views in the Executive proceedings denounced in that resolution may be known to my fellow-citizens, to the world, and to all posterity, I respectfully request that this message and protest may be entered at length on the journals of the Senate.

27

Monopolies and Corporations*

WILLIAM LEGGETT

Even though the emerging changes in the economic order called for a strong national government, there was only a limited use of the possibilities of national power in matters of economic policy by the Jackson administration. To be sure, President Jackson had taken a forceful stand against the South Carolina nullifiers, but any really overweening centralization of power in the American federal system existed only in the overwrought imaginations of Southern fire-eaters. President Jackson and most of the leadership of the Democratic party not only respected the rights of the states under the Constitution, but also looked to the powers of the states for important assistance in effectuating their economic policies. After all, Jackson's war on the Bank of the United States struck at only a limited area of economic privileges; the overwhelming majority of banks and other corporations were chartered by the state legislatures. Hence, the more militant Jacksonians pressed vigorously for state legislation to reform the existing evils of corporate privilege.

William Leggett was an editorial writer for the influential New York *Evening Post* and he used this strategic position in a leading Democratic newspaper to carry on a ceaseless campaign against the system of special charters of incorporation. In New York, as in other states, every incorporated business received its charter from the legislature by a special act of incorporation. This method of incorporation encouraged various

* Theodore Sedgewick, Jr., *A Collection of the Political Writings of William Leggett* (New York, 1840), pp. 140–44, unabridged.

forms of special influence which worked to the advantage of those who already possessed wealth and economic power. In the two editorials that follow, Leggett is urging the Democratic governor and legislature of New York to enact a general law of incorporation with the privilege of limited liability so that any group of "humble men" might have the same opportunity for the advantages of incorporation as "the purse-proud men who now almost monopolize certain branches of business."

From our historical perspective, we are likely to wonder how any man could be so naïve as to suppose that a general act of incorporation would limit the possibilities of monopoly in the rapidly expanding market economy of America. On the other hand, it may be unhistorical for us to assume that Leggett or any other intelligent Jacksonian could have foreseen the possibilities of large aggregations of capital and large-scale business organizations coming into positions of dominance in a national market. After all, much of the marketing activities in the Jacksonian decade were still operating primarily in local markets, despite the developing transportation revolution. Outside of certain banking institutions all of the visible market power was still relatively small and limited. Nevertheless, it is clear that, even in their use of the powers of the state governments, the Jacksonians were not trying to invent new techniques of regulation. Their whole imaginative effort was directed to formulating laws that would create a self-regulating world within which the free competition of individuals and small joint-stock proprietorships could ensure economic justice and equality of opportunity.

[MONOPOLIES]

From the Evening Post, December 30, 1834.

This day week the Legislature will convene at Albany. Seldom has it happened that the meeting of that body has been looked forward to with so much general interest. The Message of Governor Marcy will probably be communicated to both Houses of the Legislature on the first day of the session, and we expect to be able to place it before our readers on the following Thursday. By the sentiments of that Message, will Governor Marcy be tried. They will either raise him in our estimation, and in the estimation of all who are animated by truly democratic principles, to a most enviable height, or sink him to the level of the gross herd of petty, selfish, short-sighted and low-minded politicians. The rare opportunity is presented to him now, by one single act, to inscribe his name among those of the greatest benefactors of mankind. If he should stand forth as the honest, bold, unequivocal asserter of the great principle of Equal Rights, and strenuously recommend to the Legislature to pursue such measures only as are consistent with that principle; if he should urge upon their attention the evil effects of the partial and unequal system of legislation which we have been pursuing for years; if he should illustrate the incompatibility of all acts of special incorporation with the fundamental principle of our Government, and show their tendency to build up a privileged order, and to concentrate all wealth and power in the hands of the few; if he should sternly oppose all further extension of exclusive or partial privileges, and earnestly recommend, instead, the adoption of a general law of joint stock partnerships, by which whatever of truly valuable is now effected by private incorporations might be done by voluntary associations of men, possessing no privileges above their fellow-citizens, and liable to the same free competition which the merchant, the mechanic, the labourer, and the farmer are, in their vocations—if he should take such a stand, his name would go down to posterity inseparably associated with that of the patriotic and democratic man, who, at the head of the National Government, has done so much to restore to the People their violated rights, and check the course of unequal, aristocratic legislation. If, on the contrary, Governor Marcy should listen to the suggestions of selfish interest or short-sighted policy; if, through timidity of character or subserviency to the views of unprincipled demagogues, who assume to be the "leaders" of the democracy, and claim a right to legislative rewards, he should recommend "a middle course," or should cloak his sentiments in ambiguities, or fetter them with qualifications that take from them all force and meaning; if he should either approve a continuance of the fatal course of legislation which has done so much to oppress the people, or express disapproval of it in such mincing, shuffling, evasive terms as to pass for nothing; if he should object to the incorporation of more banks, *except in places where more banks are asked for*, and should suggest the propriety of prohibiting the small note currency, *at some future and indefinite period*: if Governor Marcy, instead of realizing the expectations of the honest democracy of the state, should pursue such a trimming, paltry, time-serving course, most completely will he forfeit the high prize of fame which is now within his reach, most blindly will he turn aside from the proud destiny which it is in his power to achieve. We await his message with anxiety, but not without strong hopes.

[JOINT-STOCK PARTNERSHIP LAW]

From the Evening Post, December 30, 1834.

The charters of several incorporated companies in this city are about to expire, and we have several times been asked if this paper, in pursuance of the doctrines we profess, would feel called upon to oppose the renewal of those charters. To this our answer is most unequivocally in the affirmative. We shall oppose, with all our might and zeal, the granting or renewing of any special charter of incorporation whatever, no matter who may be the applicants, or what the objects of the association.

But at the same time, we wish it to be distinctly understood, that we do not desire to break up those incorporated associations the charters of which are about to expire. How so? You would refuse to re-charter them, and thus they would inevitably be broken up. Not at all; as we shall explain.

It is not against the objects effected by incorporated companies that we contend; but simply against the false principle, politically and politico-economically, of special grants and privileges. Instead of renewing the charters of Insurance Companies, or any other companies, about to expire, or granting charters to new applicants, we would recommend the passing of one general law of joint stock partnerships, allowing any number of persons to associate for any object, (with one single temporary exception, which we shall state in the proper place) permitting them to sue and be sued under their partnership name, to be secure from liability beyond the amount of capital invested, to conduct their business according to their own good pleasure, and, in short, to possess all the powers defined by the revised statutes as belonging to corporations. There is nothing not perfectly equitable in the principle which exempts men from liability to any greater amount than the capital actually invested in any business, provided proper notoriety be given of the extent and circumstances of that investment. If such a law were passed, the stockholders in an insurance company, or the stockholders in any other chartered company, when their corporate privileges were about to expire, would have merely to give the proper public notification of their intention to continue their business in the mode specified in the general joint-stock partnership law, and they might go on precisely the same as if their special privileges had been renewed. The only difference would be that these privileges would no longer be special, but would belong to the whole community, any number of which might associate together, form a new company for the same objects, give due notification to the public, and enter into free competition with pre-existing companies or partnerships; precisely as one man, or set of associated men, may now enter into mercantile business by the side of other merchants, import the same kinds of goods, dispose of them on the same terms, and compete with them in all the branches of their business.

There has been a great deal said about our ultraism and

Utopianism; and this is the extent of it. By a general law of joint-stock partnerships all the good effects of private incorporations would be secured, and all the evil ones avoided. The humblest citizens might associate together, and wield, through the agency of skilful and intelligent directors, chosen by themselves, a vast aggregate capital, composed of the little separate sums which they could afford to invest in such an enterprise, in competition with the capitals of the purse-proud men who now almost monopolize certain branches of business.

The exception to which we have alluded above, is the business of banking. Our views on this subject were fully stated yesterday. We would not have banking thrown open to the whole community, until the legislature had first taken measures to withdraw our paper money from circulation. As soon as society should be entirely freed, by these measures, from the habit of taking bank-notes as money, we would urge the repeal of the restraining law, and place banking on as broad a basis as any other business whatever.

28

The Decision of the Supreme Court in the Charles River Bridge Case*

ROGER B. TANEY

One of the more effective uses of executive power in the Jacksonian decade can be seen in President Jackson's reconstruction of the Supreme Court. During the long years that John Marshall served as Chief Justice, the Supreme Court had been an active expounder of the doctrines of constitutional nationalism and a stalwart defender of the rights of property against any attempts by state legislatures to impair the obligation of contracts. In his two terms as President, Andrew Jackson had the fortunate opportunity of appointing five justices to a court then composed of seven justices. Moreover, the death of John Marshall in 1835 removed the powerful and awesome influence of the old-time Federalist Chief Justice and gave the President a chance to appoint a man whose interpretation of the Constitution would be firmly grounded in the premises of the Jacksonian ideology. The appointment of Roger B. Taney as Chief Justice brought to the bench a man who had been a forceful leader in formulating and implementing some of the key policies associated with the Jacksonian war on the Bank of the United States.

Almost immediately, the Court moved toward a decision in a crucial case involving the contractual rights of a corporation. In the Charles River Bridge case of 1837, a significant opinion of the Court was read by the Chief Justice. Taney took the position that no rights were

* From Richard Peters, *Reports of Cases Argued and Adjudged in the Supreme Court of the United States, 1828–1842* (Philadelphia, 1828–43), XI, 536–53, abridged.

granted in any corporate charter except those explicitly conferred by the words of the charter. He denied the contention of the Charles River Bridge Company that a charter was a contract that could not be impaired explicitly or implicitly by any subsequent state actions —such as the chartering of a competing and neighboring bridge over the Charles River. Any ambiguity in the terms of a corporation charter, he argued, must be construed in favor of the rights of the whole community.

Although Taney's reasoning certainly revealed the drift of the Jacksonian majority on the Supreme Court toward a narrowing of the immunities of corporations and an enlargement of the possibilities for social legislation by the state governments, is it possible to assume that the Jacksonians intended any broad schemes of social legislation and economic regulation? The concluding section of Taney's decision does no more than to emphasize the importance of encouraging the greatest possible freedom of enterprise in order to bring into social utilization "the light of science" and "those improvements which are now adding to the wealth and prosperity." Is this not further evidence that the Jacksonians were simply using judicial power to preserve a self-regulating market in which the free competition of individuals and properly chartered corporations would ensure a fair chance in the pursuit of wealth and comfort?

Mr. Chief Justice TANEY delivered the opinion of the Court.

The questions involved in this case are of the gravest character, and the Court have given to them the most anxious and deliberate consideration. The value of the right claimed by the plaintiffs is large in amount; and many persons may no doubt be seriously affected in their pecuniary interests by any decision which the Court may pronounce; and the questions which have been raised as to the power of the several states, in relation to the corporations they have chartered, are pregnant with important consequences; not only to the individuals who are concerned in the corporate franchises, but to the communities in which they exist. The Court are fully sensible that it is their duty, in exercising the high powers conferred on them by the constitution of the United States, to deal with these great and extensive interests with the utmost caution; guarding, as far as they have the power to do so, the rights of property, and at the same time carefully abstaining from any encroachment on the rights reserved to the states.

It appears, from the record, that in the year 1650, the legislature of Massachusetts, granted to the president of Harvard college "the liberty and power," to dispose of the ferry from Charlestown to Boston, by lease or otherwise, in the behalf and for the behoof of the college: and that, under that grant, the college continued to hold and keep the ferry by its lessees or agents, and to receive the profits of it until 1785. In the last mentioned year, a petition was presented to the legislature, by Thomas Russell and others, stating the inconvenience of the transportation by ferries, over Charles river, and the public advantages that would result from a bridge; and praying to be incorporated for the purpose of erecting a bridge in the place where the ferry between Boston and Charlestown was then kept. Pursuant to this petition, the legislature, on the 9th of March, 1785, passed an act incorporating a company, by the name of "The Proprietors of the Charles River Bridge," for the purposes mentioned in the petition. Under this charter the company were empowered to erect a bridge, in "the place where the ferry was then kept;" certain tolls were granted, and the charter was limited to forty years, from the first opening of the bridge for passengers; and from the time the toll commenced, until the expiration of this term, the company were to pay two hundred pounds, annually, to Harvard college; and at the expiration of the forty years the bridge was to be the property of the commonwealth; "saving (as the law expresses it) to the said college or university, a reasonable annual compensation, for the annual income of the ferry, which they might have received had not the said bridge been erected."

The bridge was accordingly built, and was opened for

passengers on the 17th of June, 1786. In 1792, the charter was extended to seventy years, from the opening of the bridge; and at the expiration of that time it was to belong to the commonwealth. The corporation have regularly paid to the college the annual sum of two hundred pounds, and have performed all of the duties imposed on them by the terms of their charter.

In 1828, the legislature of Massachusetts incorporated a company by the name of "The Proprietors of the Warren Bridge," for the purpose of erecting another bridge over Charles river. This bridge is only sixteen rods, at its commencement, on the Charlestown side, from the commencement of the bridge of the plaintiffs; and they are about fifty rods apart at their termination on the Boston side. The travellers who pass over either bridge, proceed from Charlestown square, which receives the travel of many great public roads leading from the country; and the passengers and travellers who go to and from Boston, used to pass over the Charles River Bridge, from and through this square, before the erection of the Warren Bridge.

The Warren Bridge, by the terms of its charter, was to be surrendered to the state, as soon as the expenses of the proprietors in building and supporting it should be reimbursed; but this period was not, in any event, to exceed six years from the time the company commenced receiving toll.

When the original bill in this case was filed, the Warren Bridge had not been built; and the bill was filed after the passage of the law, in order to obtain an injunction to prevent its erection, and for general relief. The bill, among other things, charged as a ground for relief, that the act for the erection of the Warren Bridge impaired the obligation of the contract between the commonwealth and the proprietors of the Charles River Bridge; and was therefore repugnant to the constitution of the United States. Afterwards, a supplemental bill was filed, stating that the bridge had then been so far completed, that it had been opened for travel, and that divers persons had passed over, and thus avoided the payment of the toll, which would other-

wise have been received by the plaintiffs. The answer to
the supplemental bill admitted that the bridge had been
so far completed, that foot passengers could pass; but
denied that any persons but the workmen and the superin-
tendents had passed over with their consent. In this state of
the pleadings, the cause came on for hearing in the
supreme judicial court for the county of Suffolk, in the
commonwealth of Massachusetts, at November term, 1829;
and the court decided that the act incorporating the
Warren Bridge, did not impair the obligation of the
contract with the proprietors of the Charles River Bridge,
and dismissed the complainants' bill: and the case is
brought here by writ of error from that decision. It is,
however, proper to state, that it is understood that the
state court was equally divided upon the question; and
that the decree dismissing the bill upon the ground above
stated, was pronounced by a majority of the court, for the
purpose of enabling the complainants to bring the question for decision before this Court. . . .

Borrowing, as we have done, our system of jurisprudence
from the English law; and having adopted, in every other
case, civil and criminal, its rules for the construction of
statutes; is there any thing in our local situation, or in
the nature of our political institutions, which should lead
us to depart from the principle where corporations are
concerned? Are we to apply to acts of incorporation, a rule
of construction differing from that of the English law, and,
by implication, make the terms of a charter in one of the
states, more unfavourable to the public, than upon an act
of parliament, framed in the same words, would be
sanctioned in an English court? Can any good reason be
assigned for excepting this particular class of cases from
the operation of the general principle; and for introducing
a new and adverse rule of construction in favour of corporations, while we adopt and adhere to the rules of construction known to the English common law, in every
other case, without exception? We think not; and it would
present a singular spectacle, if, while the courts in England
are restraining, within the strictest limits, the spirit of

monopoly, and exclusive privileges in nature of monopolies, and confining corporations to the privileges plainly given to them in their charter; the courts of this country should be found enlarging these privileges by implications; and construing a statute more unfavourably to the public, and to the rights of the community, than would be done in a like case in an English court of justice.

But we are not now left to determine, for the first time, the rules by which public grants are to be construed in this country. The subject has already been considered in this Court; and the rule of construction, above stated, fully established. In the case of the United States v. Arredondo, 8 Pet. 738, the leading cases upon this subject are collected together by the learned judge who delivered the opinion of the Court; and the principle recognised, that in grants by the public, nothing passes by implication.

The rule is still more clearly and plainly stated in the case of Jackson v. Lamphire, in 3 Pet. 289. That was a grant of land by the state; and in speaking of this doctrine of implied covenants in grants by the state, the Court use the following language, which is strikingly applicable to the case at bar:—"The only contract made by the state, is the grant to John Cornelius, his heirs and assigns, of the land in question. The patent contains no covenant to do, or not to do any further act in relation to the land; and we do not feel ourselves at liberty, in this case, to create one by implication. The state has not, by this act, impaired the force of the grant; it does not profess or attempt to take the land from the assigns of Cornelius, and give it to one not claiming under him; neither does the award produce that effect; the grant remains in full force; the property conveyed is held by his grantee, and the state asserts no claim to it."

The same rule of construction is also stated in the case of Beatty v. The Lessee of Knowles, 4 Pet. 168; decided in this Court in 1830. In delivering their opinion in that case, the Court say:—"That a corporation is strictly limited to the exercise of those powers which are specifically conferred on it, will not be denied. The exercise of the cor-

porate franchise being restrictive of individual rights,
cannot be extended beyond the letter and spirit of the act
of incorporation."

But the case most analogous to this, and in which the
question came more directly before the Court, is the case
of the Providence Bank v. Billings & Pittmann, 4 Pet. 514;
and which was decided in 1830. In that case, it appeared
that the legislature of Rhode Island had chartered the
bank, in the usual form of such acts of incorporation. The
charter contained no stipulation on the part of the state,
that it would not impose a tax on the bank, nor any reserva-
tion of the right to do so. It was silent on this point.
Afterwards, a law was passed, imposing a tax on all banks
in the state; and the right to impose this tax was resisted
by the Providence Bank, upon the ground, that if the
state could impose a tax, it might tax so heavily as to
render the franchise of no value, and destroy the institution; that the charter was a contract, and that a power
which may in effect destroy the charter is inconsistent with
it, and is impliedly renounced by granting it. But the
Court said that the taxing power was of vital importance,
and essential to the existence of government; and that the
relinquishment of such a power is never to be assumed.
And in delivering the opinion of the Court, the late Chief
Justice states the principle, in the following clear and emphatic language. Speaking of the taxing power, he says, "as
the whole community is interested in retaining it undiminished, that community has a right to insist that its
abandonment ought not to be presumed, in a case in which
the deliberate purpose of the state to abandon it does not
appear." The case now before the Court, is, in principle,
precisely the same. It is a charter from a state. The act
of incorporation is silent in relation to the contested
power. The argument in favour of the proprietors of the
Charles River Bridge, is the same, almost in words, with
that used by the Providence Bank; that is, that the power
claimed by the state, if it exists, may be so used as to
destroy the value of the franchise they have granted to the
corporation. The argument must receive the same answer;

and the fact that the power has been already exercised so as to destroy the value of the franchise, cannot in any degree affect the principle. The existence of the power does not, and cannot depend upon the circumstance of its having been exercised or not.

It may, perhaps, be said, that in the case of the Providence Bank, this Court were speaking of the taxing power; which is of vital importance to the very existence of every government. But the object and end of all government is to promote the happiness and prosperity of the community by which it is established; and it can never be assumed, that the government intended to diminish its power of accomplishing the end for which it was created. And in a country like ours, free, active, and enterprising, continually advancing in numbers and wealth; new channels of communication are daily found necessary, both for travel and trade; and are essential to the comfort, convenience, and prosperity of the people. A state ought never to be presumed to surrender this power, because, like the taxing power, the whole community have an interest in preserving it undiminished. And when a corporation alleges, that a state has surrendered for seventy years, its power of improvement and public accommodation, in a great and important line of travel, along which a vast number of its citizens must daily pass; the community have a right to insist, in the language of this Court above quoted, "that its abandonment ought not to be presumed, in a case, in which the deliberate purpose of the state to abandon it does not appear." The continued existence of a government would be of no great value, if by implications and presumptions, it was disarmed of the powers necessary to accomplish the ends of its creation; and the functions it was designed to perform, transferred to the hands of privileged corporations. The rule of construction announced by the Court, was not confined to the taxing power; nor is it so limited in the opinion delivered. On the contrary, it was distinctly placed on the ground that the interests of the community were concerned in preserving, undiminished, the power then in question; and whenever

any power of the state is said to be surrendered or diminished, whether it be the taxing power or any other
affecting the public interest, the same principle applies,
and the rule of construction must be the same. No one will
question that the interests of the great body of the people
of the state, would, in this instance, be affected by the surrender of this great line of travel to a single corporation,
with the right to exact toll, and exclude competition for
seventy years. While the rights of private property are
sacredly guarded, we must not forget that the community
also have rights, and that the happiness and well being of
every citizen depends on their faithful preservation.

Adopting the rule of construction above stated as the
settled one, we proceed to apply it to the charter of 1785,
to the proprietors of the Charles River Bridge. This act of
incorporation is in the usual form, and the privileges such
as are commonly given to corporations of that kind. It
confers on them the ordinary faculties of a corporation,
for the purpose of building the bridge; and establishes
certain rates of toll, which the company are authorized to
take. This is the whole grant. There is no exclusive privilege given to them over the waters of Charles river, above
or below their bridge. No right to erect another bridge
themselves, nor to prevent other persons from erecting one.
No engagement from the state, that another shall not be
erected; and no undertaking not to sanction competition,
nor to make improvements that may diminish the amount
of its income. Upon all these subjects the charter is
silent; and nothing is said in it about a line of travel, so
much insisted on in the argument, in which they are to
have exclusive privileges. No words are used, from which
an intention to grant any of these rights can be inferred. If
the plaintiff is entitled to them, it must be implied,
simply, from the nature of the grant; and cannot be inferred from the words by which the grant is made.

The relative position of the Warren Bridge has already
been described. It does not interrupt the passage over the
Charles River Bridge, nor make the way to it or from
it less convenient. None of the faculties or franchises

granted to that corporation, have been revoked by the legislature; and its right to take the tolls granted by the charter remains unaltered. In short, all the franchises and rights of property enumerated in the charter, and there mentioned to have been granted to it, remain unimpaired. But its income is destroyed by the Warren Bridge; which, being free, draws off the passengers and property which would have gone over it, and renders their franchise of no value. This is the gist of the complaint. For it is not pretended, that the erection of the Warren Bridge would have done them any injury, or in any degree affected their right of property; if it had not diminished the amount of their tolls. In order then to entitle themselves to relief, it is necessary to show, that the legislature contracted not to do the act of which they complain; and that they impaired, or in other words, violated that contract by the erection of the Warren Bridge.

The inquiry then is, does the charter contain such a contract on the part of the state? Is there any such stipulation to be found in that instrument? It must be admitted on all hands, that there is none—no words that even relate to another bridge, or to the diminution of their tolls, or to the line of travel. If a contract on that subject can be gathered from the charter, it must be by implication; and cannot be found in the words used. Can such an agreement be implied? The rule of construction before stated is an answer to the question. In charters of this description, no rights are taken from the public, or given to the corporation, beyond those which the words of the charter, by their natural and proper construction, purport to convey. There are no words which import such a contract as the plaintiffs in error contend for, and none can be implied; and the same answer must be given to them that was given by this Court to the Providence Bank. The whole community are interested in this inquiry, and they have a right to require that the power of promoting their comfort and convenience, and of advancing the public prosperity, by providing safe, convenient, and cheap ways for the transportation of produce, and the purposes of travel, shall not be construed to have been surrendered or diminished by the state; unless it shall appear by plain words, that it was intended to be done.

But the case before the Court is even still stronger against any such implied contract, as the plaintiffs in error contend for. The Charles River Bridge was completed in 1786. The time limited for the duration of the corporation by their original charter, expired in 1826. When, therefore, the law passed authorizing the erection of the Warren Bridge, the proprietors of Charles River Bridge held their corporate existence under the law of 1792, which extended their charter for thirty years; and the rights, privileges, and franchises of the company, must depend upon the construction of the last mentioned law, taken in connection with the act of 1785.

The act of 1792, which extends the charter of this bridge, incorporates another company to build a bridge over Charles river; furnishing another communication with Boston, and distant only between one and two miles from the old bridge.

The first six sections of this act incorporate the proprietors of the West Boston Bridge, and define the privileges, and describe the duties of that corporation. In the seventh section there is the following recital: "And whereas the erection of Charles River Bridge was a work of hazard and public utility, and another bridge in the place of West Boston Bridge may diminish the emoluments of Charles River Bridge; therefore, for the encouragement of enterprise," they proceed to extend the charter of the Charles River Bridge, and to continue it for the term of seventy years from the day the bridge was completed; subject to the conditions prescribed in the original act, and to be entitled to the same tolls. It appears, then, that by the same act that extended this charter, the legislature established another bridge, which they knew would lessen its profits; and this, too, before the expiration of the first charter, and only seven years after it was granted; thereby showing, that the state did not suppose that, by the terms it had used in the first law, it had deprived itself of the power of making such public improvements as might impair the profits of the Charles River Bridge; and from the language used in the clauses of the law by which the charter is extended, it would seem, that the legislature were especially careful to exclude any inference that the extension was made upon the ground of compromise with the Bridge Company, or as a compensation for rights impaired.

On the contrary, words are cautiously employed to exclude that conclusion; and the extension is declared to be granted as a reward for the hazard they had run, and "for the encouragement of enterprise." The extension was given because the company had undertaken and executed a work of doubtful success; and the improvements which the legislature then contemplated, might diminish the emoluments they had expected to receive from it. It results from this statement, that the legislature in the very law extending the charter, asserts its rights to authorize improvements over Charles river which would take off a portion of the travel from this bridge and diminish its profits; and the Bridge Company accept the renewal thus given, and thus carefully connected with this assertion of the right on the part of the state. Can they, when holding their corporate existence under this law, and deriving their franchises altogether from it; add to the privileges expressed in their charter an implied agreement, which is in direct conflict with a portion of the law from which they derive their corporate existence? Can the legislature be presumed to have taken upon themselves an implied obligation, contrary to its own acts and declarations contained in the same law? It would be difficult to find a case justifying such an implication, even between individuals; still less will it be found where sovereign rights are concerned, and where the interests of a whole community would be deeply affected by such an implication. It would, indeed, be a strong exertion of judicial power, acting upon its own views of what justice required, and the parties ought to have done; to raise, by a sort of judicial coercion, an implied contract, and infer it from the nature of the very instrument in which the legislature appear to have taken pains to use words which disavow and repudiate any intention, on the part of the state, to make such a contract.

Indeed, the practice and usage of almost every state in the Union, old enough to have commenced the work of internal improvement, is opposed to the doctrine contended for on the part of the plaintiffs in error. Turnpike roads have been made in succession, on the same line of travel; the later ones interfering materially with the profits of the first. These corporations have, in some instances, been utterly ruined by the introduction of newer and better modes of transportation, and travelling. In some cases, rail roads have rendered the turnpike roads on the same line of travel so entirely useless, that the franchise of the turnpike corporation is not worth preserving. Yet in none of these cases have the corporations supposed that their privileges were invaded, or any contract violated on the part of the state. Amid the multitude of cases which have occurred, and have been daily occurring for the last forty or fifty years, this is the first instance in which such an implied contract has been contended for, and this Court called upon to infer it from an ordinary act of incorporation, containing nothing more than the usual stipulations and provisions to be found in every such law. The absence of any such controversy, when there must have been so many occasions to give rise to it, proves that neither states, nor individuals, nor corporations, ever imagined that such a contract could be implied from such charters. It shows that the men who voted for these laws, never imagined that they were forming such a contract; and if we maintain that they have made it, we must create it by a legal fiction, in opposition to the truth of the fact, and the obvious intention of the party. We cannot deal thus with the rights reserved to the states; and by legal intendments and mere technical reasoning, take away from them any portion of that power over their own internal police and improvement, which is so necessary to their well being and prosperity.

And what would be the fruits of this doctrine of implied contracts on the part of the states, and of property in a line of travel by a corporation, if it should now be sanctioned by this Court? To what results would it lead us? If it is to be found in the charter to this bridge, the same process of reasoning must discover it, in the various acts which have been passed, within the last forty years, for turnpike companies. And what is to be the extent of the privileges of exclusion on the different sides of the road? The counsel who have so ably argued this case, have not attempted to define it by any certain boundaries. How far must the new improvement be distant from the old one? How near may you approach without invading its rights in the privileged line? If this Court should establish the principles now contended for, what is to become of the numerous rail roads established on the same line of travel with turnpike companies; and which have rendered the franchises of the turnpike corporations of no value? Let it once be understood that such charters carry with them these implied contracts, and give this unknown and undefined property in a line of travelling; and you will soon find the old turnpike corporations awakening from their sleep, and calling upon this Court to put down the improvements which have taken their place. The millions of property which have been invested in rail roads and canals, upon lines of travel which had been before occupied by turnpike corporations, will be put in jeopardy. We shall be thrown back to the improvements of the last century, and obliged to stand still, until the claims of the old turnpike corporations shall be satisfied; and they shall consent to permit these states to avail themselves of the lights of modern science, and to partake of the benefit of those improvements which are now adding to the wealth and prosperity, and the convenience and comfort, of every other part of the civilized world. Nor is this all. This Court will find itself compelled to fix, by some arbitrary rule, the width of this new kind of property in a line of travel; for if such a right of property exists, we have no lights to guide us in marking out its extent, unless, indeed, we resort to the old feudal grants, and to the exclusive rights of ferries, by prescription, between towns; and are prepared to decide that when a turnpike road from one town to another, had been made, no rail road or canal, between these two points, could afterwards be established. This Court are not prepared to sanction principles which must lead to such results. . . .

29

Divorce of Bank and State*

THOMAS HART BENTON

Anyone who reads the *Register of Debates* for the Jacksonian decade quickly discovers that Senator Thomas Hart Benton was the strong right arm of the Democratic party in the Senate. He was the stalwart supporter of Jackson's veto of the Bank bill and of the removal of deposits from the Bank of the United States. He was the battering ram of the opposition to the Senate resolution of censure against the President's removal policy, and his ceaseless efforts were finally crowned with victory when the Senate, in January of 1837, adopted his Expunging Resolution which wiped away the symbolic blot on the administration's record. "Solitary and alone," Benton declaimed, "and amidst the taunts and jeers of my opponents, I put this ball in motion."

The following selection from one of Benton's speeches as recorded in his *Thirty Years' View* is an interesting exhibit of the perplexities that beset the Jacksonian conception of social power by the end of President Jackson's administration. The speculative boom of 1835–36 and the panic of 1837 had revealed clearly that the social evils of the banking system came not only from the monopolistic power of the Bank of the United States, but also from the many small units of economic power represented by the state banks. Somehow, the diffusion of economic power through a system of competing smaller banks did not become an adequate mechanism for a fair distribution of wealth and comfort to the

* From Thomas Hart Benton, *Thirty Years' View; or, the History of the Working of the American Government for Thirty Years, from 1820 to 1850* (New York, 1854–56), II, 56–60, abridged.

honest producers. Indeed, Benton recognizes that the crisis came because "the weak [banks] govern the strong,"—that in the interdependent relation of credit which has grown up in the American economy, "banks have all become links of one chain" and the weak links, not the strong, determine the solvency of the whole system.

Because he was a hard-money man, Senator Benton eagerly embraced the remedy of the Van Buren administration—the divorce of bank and state by the refusal to deposit government funds in any private banks, state or otherwise, and to keep all government funds in an independent treasury system. Here again, we are faced with a very limited technique of governmental power. Even if the intoxicating influence of government deposits is to be removed from the banking system, will the mischiefs of banking system be controlled? Even if we suppose that free banking laws will be introduced as another form of the general laws of incorporation which militant Jacksonians are advocating, does the experience of 1835–36 justify a continued reliance on the free competition of many banks as a means of limiting the speculative gains of the men who make commerce "a game of hap-hazard" instead of a moral drama in which prudent and industrious habits are justly rewarded?

The bill is to divorce the government from the banks, or rather is to declare the divorce, for the separation has already taken place by the operation of law and by the delinquency of the banks. The bill is to declare the divorce; the amendment is to exclude their notes from revenue payments, not all at once, but gradually, and to be accomplished by the 1st day of January, 1841. Until then the notes of specie-paying banks may be received, diminishing one-fourth annually; and after that day, all payments to and from the federal government are to be made in hard money. Until that day, payments from the United States will be governed by existing laws. The amendment does not affect the Post Office department until January, 1841; until then, the fiscal operations of that Department remain under the present laws; after that day they fall under the principle of the bill, and all payments to and from that department will be made in hard money. The effect of the whole amendment will be to restore the currency of the constitution to the federal government—to re-establish the great acts of 1789 and of 1800—declaring that the revenues should be collected in gold and silver coin only; those early statutes which were enacted by the hard money men who made the constitution, who had seen and felt the evils of that paper money, and intended to guard against these evils in future by creating, not a paper, but a hard-money government.

I am for this restoration. I am for restoring to the federal treasury the currency of the constitution. I am for carrying back this government to the solidity projected by its founders. This is a great object in itself—a reform of the first magnitude—a reformation with healing on its wings, bringing safety to the government and blessings to the people. The currency is a thing which reaches every individual, and every institution. From the government to the washerwoman, all are reached by it, and all concerned in it; and, what seems paradoxical, all are concerned to the same degree; for all are concerned to the whole extent of their property and dealings; and all is all, whether it be much or little. The government with its many ten millions of revenue, suffers no more in proportion than the humble and meritorious laborer who works from sun to sun for the shillings which give food and raiment to his family. The federal government has deteriorated the currency, and carried mischief to the whole community, and lost its own revenues, and subjected itself to be trampled upon by corporations, by departing from the constitution, and converting this government from a hard-money to a paper money government. The object of the amendment and the bill is to reform these abuses, and it is a reform worthy to be called a reformation—worthy to engage the labor of patriots—worthy to unite the exertions of different parties—worthy to fix the attention of the age—

worthy to excite the hopes of the people, and to invoke upon its success the blessings of heaven.

Great are the evils,—political, pecuniary, and moral,— which have flowed from this departure from our constitution. Through the federal government alone—through it, not by it—two millions and a half of money have been lost in the last four months. Thirty-two millions of public money was the amount in the deposit banks when they stopped payment; of this sum twenty-five millions have been paid over to government creditors, or transferred to the States. But how paid, and how transferred? In what? In real money, or its equivalent? Not at all! But in the notes of suspended banks—in notes depreciated, on an average, ten per cent. Here then were two and a half millions lost. Who bore the loss? The public creditors and the States. Who gained it? for where there is a loss to one, there must be a gain to another. Who gained the two and a half millions, thus sunk upon the hands of the creditors and the States? The banks were the gainers; they gained it; the public creditors and the States lost it; and to the creditors it was a forced loss. It is in vain to say that they consented to take it. They had no alternative. It was that or nothing. The banks forced it upon the government; the government forced it upon the creditor. Consent was out of the question. Power ruled and that power was in the banks; and they gained the two and a half millions which the States and the public creditors lost.

I do not pretend to estimate the moneyed losses, direct and indirect, to the government alone, from the use of local bank notes in the last twenty-five years, including the war, and covering three general suspensions. Leaving the people out of view, as a field of losses beyond calculation, I confine myself to the federal government, and say, its losses have been enormous, prodigious, and incalculable. We have had three general stoppages of the local banks in the short space of twenty-two years. It is at the average rate of one in seven years; and who is to guaranty us from another, and from the consequent losses, if we continue to receive their bills in payment of public dues? Another stoppage must come, and that, reasoning from all analogies, in less than seven years after the resumption. Many must perish in the attempt to resume, and would do better to wind up at once, without attempting to go on, without adequate means, and against appalling obstacles. Another revulsion must come. Thus it was after the last resumption. The banks recommenced payments in 1817—in two years, the failures were more disastrous than ever. Thus it was in England after the long suspension of twenty-six years. Payments recommenced in 1823—in 1825 the most desolating crash of banks took place which had ever been known in the kingdom, although the Bank of England had imported, in less than four years, twenty millions sterling in gold,—about one hundred millions of dollars, to recommence upon. Its effects reached this country, crushed the cotton houses in New Orleans, depressed the money market, and injured all business.

The senators from New York and Virginia (Messrs. Tallmadge and Rives) push this point of confidence a little further; they address a question to me, and ask if I would lose confidence in all steamboats, and have them all discarded, if one or two blew up in the Mississippi? I answer the question in all frankness, and say, that I should not. But if, instead of one or two in the Mississippi, all the steamboats in the Union should blow up at once—in every creek, river and bay—while all the passengers were sleeping in confidence, and the pilots crying out all is well; if the whole should blow up from one end of the Union to the other just as fast as they could hear each other's explosions; then, indeed, I should lose confidence in them, and never again trust wife, or child, or my own foot, or any thing not intended for destruction, on board such sympathetic and contagious engines of death. I answer further, and tell the gentlemen, that if only one or two banks had stopped last May in New York, I should not have lost all confidence in the remaining nine hundred and ninety-nine; but when the whole thousand stopped at once; tumbled down together—fell in a lump—lie there—and when ONE

of their number, by a sign with the little finger, can make
the whole lie still, then, indeed, confidence is gone! And
this is the case with the banks. They have not only stopped
altogether, but in a season of profound peace, with eighty
millions of specie in the country, and just after the annual
examinations by commissioners and legislative committees,
and when all was reported well. With eighty millions in
the country, they stop even for change! It did not take a
national calamity—a war—to stop them! They fell in time
of peace and prosperity! We read of people in the West
Indies, and in South America, who rebuild their cities on
the same spot where earthquakes had overthrown them;
we are astonished at their fatuity; we wonder that they
will build again on the same perilous foundations. But
these people have a reason for their conduct; it is, that
their cities are only destroyed by earthquakes; it takes an
earthquake to destroy them; and when there is no earthquake, they are safe. But suppose their cities fell down
without any commotion in the earth, or the air—fell in a
season of perfect calm and serenity—and after that the
survivors should go to building again in the same place;
would not all the world say that they were demented,
and were doomed to destruction? So of the government of
the United States by these banks. If it continues to use
them, and to receive their notes for revenue, after what has
happened, and in the face of what now exists, it argues
fatuity, and a doom to destruction.

Resume when they will, or when they shall, and the
longer it is delayed the worse for themselves, the epoch of
resumption is to be a perilous crisis to many. This stopping
and resuming by banks, is the realization of the poetical
description of the descent into hell, and the return from
it. *Facilis descensus Averni—sed revocare gradum—hic
opus, hic labor est.* Easy is the descent into the regions below, but to return! this is work, this is labor indeed! Our
banks have made the descent; they have gone down with
ease; but to return—to ascend the rugged steps, and behold again the light above, how many will falter, and fall
back into the gloomy regions below.

Banks of circulation are banks of hazard and of failure. It is an incident of their nature. Those without circulation rarely fail. That of Venice has stood seven hundred years; those of Hamburgh, Amsterdam, and others, have stood for centuries. The Bank of England, the great mother of banks of circulation, besides an actual stoppage of a quarter of a century, has had her crisis and convulsion in average periods of seven or eight years, for the last half century—in 1783, '93, '97, 1814, '19, '25, '36—and has only been saved from repeated failure by the powerful support of the British government, and profuse supplies of exchequer bills. Her numerous progeny of private and joint stock banks of circulation have had the same convulsions; and not being supported by the government, have sunk by hundreds at a time. All the banks of the United States are banks of circulation; they are all subject to the inherent dangers of that class of banks, and are, besides, subject to new dangers peculiar to themselves. From the quantity of their stock held by foreigners, the quantity of other stocks in their hands, and the current foreign balance against the United States, our paper system has become an appendage to that of England. As such, it suffers from sympathy when the English system suffers. In addition to this, a new doctrine is now broached—that our first duty is to foreigners! and, upon this principle, when the banks of the two countries are in peril, ours are to be sacrificed to save those of England!

The power of a few banks over the whole, presents a new feature of danger in our system. It consolidates the banks of the whole Union into one mass, and subjects them to one fate, and that fate to be decided by a few, without even the knowledge of the rest. An unknown divan of bankers sends forth an edict which sweeps over the empire, crosses the lines of States with the facility of a Turkish firman, prostrating all State institutions, breaking up all engagements, and levelling all law before it. This is consolidation of a kind which the genius of Patrick Henry had not even conceived. But while this firman is thus potent and irresistible for prostration, it is impotent and powerless for resurrection. It goes out in vain, bidding the prostrate banks to rise. A *veto* power intervenes. One voice is sufficient to keep all down; and thus we have seen one word from Philadelphia annihilate the New York proposition for resumption, and condemn the many solvent banks to the continuation of a condition as mortifying to their feelings as it is injurious to their future interests.

Again, from the mode of doing business among our banks—using each other's paper to bank upon, instead of holding each other to weekly settlements, and liquidation of balances in specie, and from the fatal practice of issuing notes at one place, payable at another—our banks have all become links of one chain, the strength of the whole being dependent on the strength of each. A few govern all. Whether it is to fail, or to resume, the few govern; and not only the few, but the weak. A few weak banks fail; a panic ensues, and the rest shut up; many strong ones are ready to resume; the weak are not ready, and the strong must wait. Thus the principles of safety, and the rules of government, are reversed. The weak govern the strong; the bad govern the good; and the insolvent govern the solvent. This is our system, if system it can be called, which has no feature of consistency, no principle of safety, and which is nothing but the floating appendage of a foreign and overpowering system.

The federal government and its creditors have suffered great pecuniary losses from the use of these banks and their paper; they must continue to sustain such losses if they continue to use such depositories and to receive such paper. The pecuniary losses have been, now are, and must be hereafter great; but, great as they have been, now are, and may be hereafter, all that loss is nothing compared to the political dangers which flow from the same source. These dangers affect the life of the government. They go to its existence. They involve anarchy, confusion, violence, dissolution! They go to deprive the government of support—of the means of living; they strip it in an instant of every shilling of revenue, and leave it penniless, helpless, lifeless. The late stoppage might have broken up the gov-

ernment, had it not been for the fidelity and affection of
the people to their institutions and the eighty millions
of specie which General Jackson had accumulated in the
country. That stoppage presented a peculiar feature of
peril which has not been brought to the notice of the
public; it was the stoppage of the sums standing in the
names of disbursing officers, and wanted for daily payments in all the branches of the public service. These
sums amounted to about five millions of dollars. They
had been drawn from the Treasury, they were no longer
standing to the credit of the United States; they had gone
into the hands of innumerable officers and agents, in all
parts of the Union, and were temporarily, and for mere
safe-keeping from day to day, lodged with these deposit
banks, to be incessantly paid out to those who were doing work and labor, performing contracts, or rendering
service, civil or military, to the country. These five millions were stopped with the rest! In an instant, as if by
enchantment, every disbursing officer, in every part of the
Union, was stripped of the money which he was going to
pay out! All officers of the government, high and low,
the whole army and navy, all the laborers and contractors, post offices and all, were suddenly, instantaneously,
left without pay; and consequently without subsistence. It
was tantamount to a disbandment of the entire government. It was like a decree for the dissolution of the body
politic. It was celebrated as a victory—as a conquest—as a
triumph, over the government. The least that was expected
was an immediate civil revolution—the overthrow of the
democratic party, the change of administration, the re-
ascension of the federal party to power, and the re-estab-
lishment of the condemned Bank of the United States.
These consequences were counted upon; and that they did
not happen was solely owing to the eighty millions of
hard money which kept up a standard of value in the
country, and prevented the dishonored bank notes from
sinking too low to be used by the community. But it is not
merely stoppage of the banks that we have to fear: collisions with the States may ensue. State legislatures may

sanction the stoppage, withhold the poor right of suing, and thus interpose their authority between the federal government and its revenues. This has already happened, not in hostility to the government, but in protection of themselves; and the consequence was the same as if the intention had been hostile. It was interposition between the federal government and its depositories; it was deprivation of revenue; it was an act the recurrence of which should be carefully guarded against in future.

This is what we have seen; this is a danger which we have just escaped; and if these banks shall be continued as depositories of public money, or, which is just the same thing, if the government shall continue to receive their "paper promises to pay," the same danger may be seen again, and under far more critical circumstances. A similar stoppage of the banks may take place again—will inevitably take place again—and it may be when there is little specie in the country, or when war prevails. All history is full of examples of armies and navies revolting for want of pay; all history is full of examples of military and naval operations miscarried for want of money; all history is full of instances of governments overturned from deficits of revenue and derangements of finances. And are we to expose ourselves recklessly, and with our eyes open, to such dangers? And are we to stake the life and death of this government upon the hazards and contingencies of banking—and of such banking as exists in these United States? Are we to subject the existence of this government to the stoppages of the banks, whether those stoppages result from misfortune, improvidence, or bad faith? Are we to subject this great and glorious political fabric, the work of so many wise and patriotic heads, to be demolished in an instant, and by an unseen hand? Are we to suffer the machinery and the working of our boasted constitution to be arrested by a spring-catch, applied in the dark? Are men, with pens sticking behind their ears, to be allowed to put an end to this republic? No, sir! never. If we are to perish prematurely, let us at least have a death worthy of a great nation; let us at least have a field covered with the bodies of heroes and of patriots, and consecrated forever to the memory of a subverted empire. Rome had her Pharsalia—Greece her Chæronea—and many barbarian kingdoms have given immortality to the spot on which they expired; and shall this great republic be subjected to extinction on the contingencies of trade and banking? . . .

30

"He has collected and embodied the wishes of the people . . ."*

WILLIAM M. HOLLAND

Despite the failure of the Jackson administration to prevent the speculative excesses which led to the panic of 1837, Andrew Jackson's two terms in office provide an amazing record of resourceful and effective uses of presidential power. Many of his economic policies, affecting internal improvements, the sale of public lands, as well as banking and credit, were carried out against the opposition of hostile majorities in the Congress and of a majority of the newspapers in the country. How are we to account for such successful leadership against opposing political and social forces stronger and more numerous than any his predecessors had faced?

William Holland, author of a semi-authorized campaign biography of Martin Van Buren, tried to answer these questions in 1835. In his view, Jackson's great strength results from the ardent support of the great mass of the people. The men of "wealth, fashion, and inherited distinction" assume that the people have been misled by demagogues and artful partisans who control the Democratic party organization through their intrigues. Holland, however, denies that the popular support for Jackson is the result of manipulation and chicanery. He argues instead that there is an intuitive bond between the President and the common man—that the plain farmer or the mechanic "feels that the breast of the President beats in unison with his own."

* From William M. Holland, *The Life and Political Opinions of Martin Van Buren* (Hartford, Connecticut, 1835), pp. 357–60, abridged.

. . . If the great mass of the community are led by sophistry and the artful representations of ingenious men, how happens it that their opinions are formed to their present standard? It may be safely stated that two thirds of the public presses in this country, are opposed to the principles of the present administration. The periodical reviews and literary journals lean against the democratic cause without a single exception. Public seminaries of instruction, the learned professions and a vast preponderance of the literary and oratorical talent of the country, are under the same bias. English literature so extensively circulated among us is pervaded by the same principles. Wealth, fashion and inherited distinction are, to a great extent, arrayed against the democratic cause. How then does it happen that the people are guided by opposite sentiments? If they may be imposed upon by plausible demagogues, or cajoled by flattery, or alarmed by exaggeration, or blindly led by example, why has the unceasing application of all these means, by the horror-stricken enemies of popular misrule, hitherto failed to produce its natural effect?

The true answer to this question is, that the great mass of the American people are not so meanly endowed and so unhappily constituted. There is an honest love of truth, a blunt native judgment, a piercing sagacity, in the great mass of the people, which cannot be widely led astray from the principles of truth, patriotism and virtue. The demagogue can never meet the approbation of these sentiments. Intrigue and hollow-hearted patriotism wither before them. They are attracted, instinctively, by the capable and honest public servant; they recoil from the political gambler.

One would think that the experience of the past would have taught designing politicians, that the combined influence of unbounded wealth and a partizan press can never turn public sentiment, for any considerable period, from the channel of truth.

The democratic usage, of selecting those men for office who will faithfully express the will of the people, leads to that coincidence of sentiment, between republicans and their public agents, which is characterized by their opponents as servility. It is illustrated in the example of General Jackson. The leading measures of his administration have been ardently approved by the democracy. This results it is said, from blind attachment to a leader, without the capacity to form a just judgment of his public measures. The democratic party, it is alledged, are so organized and drilled by the artful partizans of the President, as to follow him, whither soever he may lead.

But the true cause of the surprizing harmony which exists between the President and the people, is either not understood by the anti-democratic party or is misrepresented. The truth is, that the President has been sustained in his measures, because they have all been based upon a careful observation, and thorough knowledge, of the popular will. The President has had the sagacity to observe the sentiments of the great body of the people and the integrity and firmness to carry them into effect. He has collected and embodied the wishes of the people; he has felt himself, constantly, to be their agent and minister; and if he has seemed to lead public opinion, it has been because he is endued with a penetration which has enabled him to foresee its current, and by throwing himself at its head, to bring its full force to sustain him. Guided by the fundamental principle, that the will of the majority should, in all cases, control, he has never attempted to defeat that will. He has earnestly endeavored to ascertain the wishes of his constituents, and having ascertained them, he has labored, with astonishing firmness, vigor and capacity, to carry them into effect. This is the source of that attachment which binds the heart of every true republican to the great political father of the democracy. Many a plain farmer or mechanic, reflecting amid his solitary labors, on the "Great American System," the Bank, and other deeply contrived measures of general policy, and gradually forming his own mind into a clear view of their bearing upon the interests of the country, has been astonished to find a veto message or proclamation, from the chief magistrate of the nation, suddenly lighting up his mind, unlocking as it were his own secret thoughts, coinciding with his own internal convictions, but displaying them with such clearness and strength as to leave him no longer in doubt. He sees that the President has reasoned as he is reasoning, but with greater rapidity and vigor; he feels that the breast of the President beats in unison with his own; that he is truly one of the people, identical in his wishes and feelings with the plain farmer at the plough. It is impossible for him not to repose confidence in such a man and fasten affection upon him. It is evident that the same sympathetic cord, which binds the hearts of true republicans to each other throughout the Union, unites them all to their firm and faithful friend at the head of the government. . . .

31

"Great men always wear the imprints of the times . . ."*

FRANCIS J. GRUND

William Holland's effort to account for the successful leadership of President Jackson exhibits not only the preference of the Jacksonian generation for the man of common sense and intuitive wisdom, but also the growing disposition of American intellectuals to accept a transcendentalist view of the possibilities of knowledge and understanding that had already been developed by the romantic poets and philosophers of Europe. A more precise analysis of the style and method of Jackson's leadership can be seen in the following record of an interesting conversation taken from Francis Grund's *Aristocracy in America*. Grund was another European observer who was moved to write a commentary on American society. Unlike most of the Europeans who visited America in the 1830s, Grund settled down in America and became an American citizen. He carried on an active career in journalism and in the writing of elementary textbooks for American schools. In addition, he developed a keen interest in politics, actually stumping and writing on behalf of the Jacksonian Democratic party. Consequently, his observations about America have an anecdotal character which reflects his experience of working and living with Americans.

The selection that follows is an account of a conversation Grund had with two Democratic Senators about the reasons for Jackson's success as a political leader. They, too, recognize the importance of the intuitive

*From Francis J. Grund, *Aristocracy in America* (London, 1839), II, 239–46, abridged.

bond that exists between Jackson and the people, but they try to assess the various ingredients that make Jackson the symbol of the age—his military record, his low level of literacy, his iron will, his skillful use of patronage and party organization. There is much in this selection that anticipates the considerations that must be included in any modern analysis of Jackson's leadership.

. . . "General Jackson," said one of the senators, "understands the people of the United States twenty times better than his antagonists; and, if his successor have but half the same tact, the Whigs may give up the hope of governing the country for the next half century."

"You ought not to say '*tact*,'" interrupted the other senator, "for that alone will not do it; he must have the same manners as our present President. General Jackson has a peculiar way of addressing himself to the feelings of every man with whom he comes in contact. His simple, unostentatious manners carry into every heart the conviction of his honesty; while the firmness of his character inspires his friends with the hope of success. His motto always was, '*Never sacrifice a friend to an enemy;*' or, '*Make yourself strong with your friends, and you need not fear your foes.*' These things, however, must be *born* with a man; they must be spontaneous, and felt as such by the people, or they lose the best part of their effect. All the tact in the world will not answer the same purpose; for, in exactly the same proportion as we perceive a man is prudent, we become cautious ourselves,—and then farewell to popularity!

"When the people give their suffrages to a man, they never do so on a rigid examination of his political principles; for this task the labouring classes of any country neither have the time nor the disposition, and it is wholly needless to attempt to persuade them to a different course by a long and tedious argument. The large masses act in politics pretty much as they do in religion. Every doctrine is with them, more or less, a matter of *faith*; received, principally, on account of their trust in the apostle. If the latter fail to captivate their hearts, no reasoning in the world is capable of filling the vacancy: and the more natural and corrupt the people are, the less are they to be moved by abstract reasoning, whether the form of government be republican, monarchical, or despotic."

"Precisely so," ejaculated the member. "General Jackson is popular, just because he is General Jackson; so much so, that if a man were to say a word against him in the Western States, he would be '*knocked into eternal smash.*'"

"And this sort of popularity," continued the senator, "our Northern people consider as the mere consequence of the battle of New Orleans. The battle, and General Jackson's military character, had undoubtedly a great deal to do with it, but they were not of themselves sufficient to elevate him to the Presidency. In a country in which so large a portion of the people consider the acquiring of a fortune the only rational object of pursuit,—in which so great and so exclusive an importance is attached to money, that, with a few solitary exceptions, it is the only means of arriving at personal distinction,—a character like Jackson's, so perfectly disinterested, and so entirely devoted to what he at least deemed the good of his country, could not but excite astonishment and admiration among the natural, and therefore more susceptible, people of the Western States. The appearance of General Jackson was a phenomenon, and would at the present time have been one in every country. He called himself 'the people's friend,' and gave proofs of his sincerity and firmness in adhering to his friends, and of his power to protect them. The people believed in General Jackson as much as the Turks in their prophet, and would have followed him wherever he chose to lead them. With this species of popularity it is in vain to contend; and it betrays little knowledge of the world, and the springs of human action, to believe those who possess it men of ordinary capacity.

"What the French call '*le génie du caractère,*' which is the true talisman of popular favour, is perhaps the highest talent with which mortals can be endowed. It is a pure gift of Heaven, and has accomplished the noblest deeds in history. When Napoleon reproached Voltaire with not having sufficiently appreciated the character of Mahomed, whom the French poet introduced in the drama of the same name as a mere impostor, he felt that none but a great mind could have conceived and executed what to ordinary men would have appeared absurd or chimerical; and that he who had the power to instil a lasting enthusiasm for a new cause into millions, and on that enthusiasm to establish an empire which has spread over half the world, must have been more than a mere charlatan, for he must have been possessed of a thorough knowledge of human character. This is a thing a man cannot acquire by study, if he do not possess it by intuition; and hence it can neither be defined nor understood by men not similarly gifted, who, applying their own scale to what is truly incommensurable, are always astonished at the success of those whom they were all their lives accustomed to look upon as second or third rate men.

"Have we not heard it objected to Napoleon, that he could not write an elegant epistle? Do the French not pity Shakspeare for having been so little of a scholar, and so inelegant in his expressions? And yet wherein consisted the particular genius of these men, so entirely opposite to one another, if it was not, principally, in the perfect knowledge which truly intuitively they possessed of human character?

"In the same manner it has been said of General Jackson that he is incapable of writing a good English sentence, as if this were the standard by which to measure the capacity of a political chief, especially in America, where, out of a hundred senators and representatives, scarcely one has received what in Europe would be called a literary education. If classical learning were to constitute the scale by which to measure the talents of our statesmen, how far would they not rank behind the paltriest Prussian schoolmaster! General Jackson understood the people of the United States better than, perhaps, any President before him, and developed as much energy in his administration as any American statesman. I do not here speak as a partisan, nor do I wish to inquire whether all his measures were beneficial to the people; but they were, at least, all in unison with his political doctrines, and carried through with an iron consequence, notwithstanding the enormous opposition that wealth, and, in a great degree, also talent, put in the way of their execution. And yet they call Jackson a second-rate man, because he is not a regular *speechifyer*, or has never published a long article in the newspapers!

"To judge of a man like General Jackson, one must not analyze him after the manner of a chemist; one must not separate his talents—his oratory—his style of composition—his generalship, &c.; but take the *tout ensemble* of the man, and I venture to say there is not such another in the United States. It is useless to draw envious comparisons between him and Washington, Wellington, Napoleon, Jefferson, and so forth. Great men always wear the imprints of the times and circumstances which call their talents into action; but history is sure to preserve the name of any man who has had the strength and genius to stamp his own character on the people over whose destinies he presided. General Jackson has many political enemies, and his political doctrines are perhaps only maintained—I will not say maintainable—by his own great personality. His successor in office may not be able to continue to make head against the opposition;—another party may get into power, and introduce different doctrines into the administration of the country;—but the impulse which General Jackson has given to the democracy of America will always continue to be felt, and impel the government in a more or less popular direction."

"You are a great friend of General Jackson," said I, "from the animated defence you make of his character."

"I certainly am, sir," said he; "and I do not know a single man of our party that is not warmly attached to him. Not that I approve of all his political principles;

but I like the man, and would rather see *him* President than any other."

"You have spoken my very heart," cried the other senator. "I like *Old Hickory*, because he is just the man for the people, and as immovable as a rock. One always knows where to find him."

"He is just the man our party wanted," rejoined the first senator, "in order to take the lead."

"And I like Old Ironhead," said the member, "because he is a man after my own sort. When he once says he is your friend, he *is* your friend; but once your enemy, then *look out for breakers.*"

"And, what is more," interrupted the senator, "his hatred is of that pure Saxon kind which is always coupled with moral horror; and, for that reason, irreconcileable."

"And, what is better than all," cried the member, chuckling, "he has a good memory; he never forgets a man who has rendered him a service, nor does he ever cease to remember an injury. The former is sure of being rewarded, the latter will with difficulty escape punishment. Mr. Adams, during his Presidency, was pusillanimous enough to endeavour to reconcile his enemies by all sorts of *douceurs*; he appointed them to office, invited them to dinner, and distinguished them even before his friends. This conduct naturally alienated the latter; while the former, perceiving his drift, did not think themselves bound to be grateful for his attentions. General Jackson introduced the doctrine of reward and punishment, and has 'got along' with it much better than his warmest friends anticipated. He appointed his friends to office, and dismissed his antagonists the moment they had taken an active part in politics. That principle, sir, is the proper one to go upon. The hope of reward, and the fear of punishment, govern men in politics and religion." . . .

32

David Crockett Enters Politics*

COLONEL DAVID CROCKETT

One of the great and enduring folk heroes created by
the Jacksonian generation was Davy Crockett, the brag-
gart of the West Tennessee canebrakes who once boasted
that he could "whip his weight in wild-cats . . . and
hug a bear too close for comfort, and eat any man opposed to Jackson." Davy Crockett was already a legendary figure in his own lifetime. Somehow, this resourceful backwoodsman appealed to a deeply felt American
admiration for the man of action, common sense, and
self-assurance. Beginning in 1833, a series of autobio-
graphical sketches of the life of David Crockett began to
appear in print and were eagerly read throughout the
United States. Although it is doubtful whether Crockett
himself had a hand in writing any but the first of these,
they became the basis of the flourishing myth of Davy
Crockett. Other myth-makers added further to the developing legend. James Kirke Paulding wrote two plays
about Crockett, a "Crockett March" was composed in
his honor, and between 1835 and the Civil War, fifty
Crockett Almanacs were issued, in New York, Boston,
Philadelphia, Baltimore, and Nashville. The flare of
glory in which his life was ended at the Alamo simply
gave further emotive power to the Crockett myth.

There was a political dimension to the Crockett myth
that was more visible to the Jacksonian than to later
generations. Crockett had a political career which included several terms in Congress during the Jackson
administrations. He began as a follower of Jackson but
soon found himself at odds with the President over his

* From *Life of David Crockett* (Philadelphia, 1885), pp. 109–
17, unabridged.

Indian policy, his land policy, and the removal of the deposits from the Bank of the United States. Crockett was then taken up by the Whigs who recognized that he was a valuable asset in the new style of democratic politics. Crockett's characteristic motto—"go ahead"—was exploited as an expression of the essential spirit of the newly created Whig party.

The selection from Crockett's "Autobiography" that follows is rich in many of the popular symbols of the Jacksonian generation. Common sense and natural wisdom are exalted above a knowledge of Latin, "law-learning," and fine speechmaking. Even more interesting is the ready acceptance of demagoguery and deception as a necessary means for political success. At a later point in the "Autobiography," Crockett says of his political methods, "I was as cunning as a little red fox, and wouldn't risk my tail in a 'committal trap.'"

Something significant seems to be taking place in American mythologizing. Earlier, the backwoodsman and frontier farmer had been celebrated for natural virtue free from the vice and artifice of sophisticated city dwellers. Can we not say that the David Crockett myth fuses new symbols with the old? Are Americans in the Jacksonian era ready to assume that natural wisdom and common sense go hand-in-hand with manipulative skill and cunning in politics?

. . . The place on which I lived was sickly, and I was determined to leave it. I therefore set out the next fall to look at the country which had been purchased of the Chickasaw tribe of Indians. I went on to a place called Shoal Creek, about eighty miles from where I lived, and here again I got sick. I took the ague and fever, which I supposed was brought on by my camping out. I remained here for some time, as I was unable to go farther; and in that time I became so well pleased with the country about there, that I resolved to settle in it. It was just only a little distance in the purchase, and no order had been established there; but I thought I could get along without order as well as anybody else. And so I moved and settled myself down on the head of Shoal Creek. We remained here some two or three years, without any law at all; and so many bad characters began to flock in upon us, that we found it necessary to set up a sort of temporary government of our own. I don't mean that we made any president, and called him the "government," but we met and made what we called a corporation; and I reckon we called *it* wrong, for it wasn't a bank, and hadn't any deposites; and now they call the bank a corporation. But be this as it may, we lived in the backwoods, and didn't profess to know much, and no doubt used many wrong words. But we met, and appointed magistrates and constables to keep order. We didn't fix any laws for them, though; for we supposed they would know law enough, whoever they might be; and so we left it to themselves to fix the laws.

I was appointed one of the magistrates; and when a man owed a debt, and wouldn't pay it, I and my constable ordered our warrant, and then he would take the man, and bring him before me for trial. I would give judgment against him, and then an order for an execution would easily scare the debt out of him. If any one was charged with marking his neighbor's hogs, or with stealing anything,—which happened pretty often in those days,—I would have him taken, and if there were tolerable grounds for the charge, I would have him well whipp'd and cleared. We kept this up till our Legislature added us to the white settlements in Giles county, and appointed magistrates by law, to organize matters in the parts where I lived. They appointed nearly every man a magistrate who had belonged to our corporation. I was then, of course, made a squire, according to law; though now the honor rested more heavily on me than before. For, at first, whenever I told my constable, says I—"Catch that fellow and bring him up for trial,"—away he went, and the fellow must come, dead or alive; for we considered this a good warrant, though it was only in verbal writing. But after I was appointed by the assembly, they told me my warrants must be in real writing, and signed; and that I must keep a book, and write my proceedings in it. This was a hard business on me, for I could just barely write my own name; but to do this, and write the warrants too, was at least a huckleberry over my persimmon. I had a pretty well informed constable, however, and he aided me very much in this business. Indeed, I had so much confidence in him, that I told him, when we should happen to be out anywhere, and see that a warrant was necessary, and would have a good effect, he needn't take the trouble to come all the way to me to get one, but he could just fill out one; and then on the trial I could correct the whole business if he had committed any error. In this way I got on pretty well, till by care and attention I improved my handwriting in such a manner as to be able to prepare my warrants, and keep my record book without much difficulty. My judgments were never appealed from, and if they had been, they would have stuck like wax, as I gave my decisions on the principles of common justice and honesty between man and man, and relied on natural born sense, and not on law learning to guide me; for I had never read a page in a law book in all my life. . . .

About the time we were getting under good headway in our new government, a Captain Matthews came to me and told me he was a candidate for the office of colonel of a regiment, and that I must run for first major in the same regiment. I objected to this, telling him that I thought I had done my share of fighting, and that I wanted nothing to do with military appointments.

He still insisted, until at last I agreed, and of course had every reason to calculate on his support in my election. He was an early settler in that country, and made rather more corn than the rest of us; and knowing it would afford him a good opportunity to electioneer a little, he made a great corn husking, and a great frolic, and gave a general treat, asking everybody over the whole country. Myself and my family were, of course, invited. When I got there, I found a very large collection of people, and some friend of mine soon informed me that the captain's son was going to offer against me for the office of major, which he had seemed so anxious for me to get. I cared nothing about the office, but it put my dander up high enough to see, that after he had pressed me so hard to offer, he was countenancing, if not encouraging, a secret plan to beat me.

I took the old gentleman out, and asked him about it. He told me it was true his son was going to run as a candidate, and that he hated worse to run against me than any man in the county. I told him his son need give himself no uneasiness about that; that I shouldn't run against him for major, but against his daddy for colonel. He took me by the hand, and we went into the company. He then made a speech and informed the people that I was his opponent. I mounted up for a speech too. I told the people the cause of my opposing him, remarking that as I had the whole family to run against any way, I was determined to levy on the head of the mess. When the time for election came, his son was opposed by another man for major; and he and his daddy were both badly beaten. I just now began to take a rise, as in a little time I was asked to offer for the Legislature in the counties of Lawrence and Heckman.

I offered my name in the month of February, and started about the first of March with a drove of horses to the lower part of the State of North Carolina. This was in the year 1821, and I was gone upwards of three months. I returned, and set out electioneering, which was a bran-fire new business to me. It now became necessary that I should tell the people something about the government, and an eternal sight of other things that I knowed nothing more about than I did about Latin, and law, and such things as that. I have said before that in those days none of us called General Jackson the government, nor did he seem in as fair a way to become so as I do now; but I knowed so little about it, that if any one had told me he was "the government," I should have believed it, for I had never read even a newspaper in my life, or anything else, on the subject.

But over all my difficulties, it seems to me I was born for luck, though it would be hard for any one to guess what sort. I will, however, explain that hereafter.

I went first into Heckman county, to see what I could do among the people as a candidate. Here they told me that they wanted to move their town nearer to the centre of the county, and I must come out in favor of it. There's no devil if I knowed what this meant, or how the town was to be moved; and so I kept dark, going on the identical same plan that I now find is called "*non-committal*." About this time there was a great squirrel hunt on Duck river, which was among my people. They were to hunt two days; then to meet and count the scalps, and have a big barbecue, and what might be called a tip-top country frolic. The dinner, and a general treat, was all to be paid for by the party having taken the fewest scalps. I joined one side, taking the place of one of the hunters, and got a gun ready for the hunt. I killed a great many squirrels, and when we counted scalps, my party was victorious.

The company had every thing to eat and drink that could be furnished in so new a country, and much fun and good humor prevailed. But before the regular frolic commenced, I mean the dancing, I was called on to make a speech as a candidate; which was a business I was as ignorant of as an outlandish negro.

A public document I had never seen, nor did I know there were such things; and how to begin I couldn't tell. I made many apologies, and tried to get off, for I know'd I had a man to run against who could speak prime, and I know'd, too, that I wasn't able to shuffle and cut with him. He was there, and knowing my ignorance as well as I did myself, he also urged me to make a speech. The truth is, he thought my being a candidate was a mere matter of sport; and didn't think for a moment, that he was in any danger from an ignorant backwoods bear hunter. But I found I couldn't get off, and so I determined just to go ahead, and leave it to chance what I should say. I got up and told the people I reckoned they know'd what I had come for, but if not, I could tell them. I had come for their votes, and if they didn't watch mighty close I'd get them too. But the worst of all was, that I could not tell them anything about government. I tried to speak about something, and I cared very little what, until I choked up as bad as if my mouth had been jamm'd and cramm'd chock full of dry mush. There the people stood, listening all the while, with their eyes, mouths, and ears all open, to catch every word I would speak.

At last I told them I was like a fellow I had heard of not long before. He was beating on the head of an empty barrel near the road-side, when a traveler, who was passing along, asked him what he was doing that for? The fellow replied that there was some cider in that barrel a few days before, and he was trying to see if there was any then, but if there was he couldn't get at it. I told them that there had been a little bit of a speech in me a while ago, but I believed I couldn't get it out. They all roared out in a mighty laugh, and I told some other anecdotes, equally amusing to them, and believing I had them in a first-rate way, I quit and got down, thanking the people for their attention. But I took care to remark that I was as dry as a powder-horn, and that I thought it was time for us all to wet our whistles a little: and so I put off to the liquor stand, and was followed by the greater part of the crowd.

I felt certain this was necessary, for I knowed my competitor could talk government matters to them as easy as he pleased. He had, however, mighty few left to hear him, as I continued with the crowd, now and then taking a horn, and telling good-humored stories, till he was done speaking. I found I was good for the votes at the hunt, and when we broke up I went on to the town of Vernon, which was the same they wanted me to move. Here they pressed me again on the subject, and I found I could get either party by agreeing with them. But I told them I didn't know whether it would be right or not, and so couldn't promise either way.

Their court commenced on the next Monday, as the barbecue was on a Saturday, and the candidates for Governor and for Congress, as well as my competitor and myself, all attended.

The thought of having to make a speech made my knees feel mighty weak, and set my heart to fluttering almost as bad as my first love scrape with the Quaker's niece. But as good luck would have it, these big candidates spoke nearly all day, and when they quit, the people were worn out with fatigue, which afforded me a good apology for not discussing the government. But I listened mighty close to them, and was learning pretty fast about political matters. When they were all done, I got up and told some laughable story, and quit. I found I was safe in those parts, and so I went home, and did not go back again till after the election was over. But to cut this matter short, I was elected, doubling my competitor, and nine votes over. . . .

33

"We have taught them how to conquer us!"*

THE DEMOCRATIC REVIEW

The Jacksonians sensed very early the importance of newspapers in a democratic society. The inner circle of advisers in President Jackson's first administration made arrangements for the establishing of a new party newspaper, the Washington *Globe*. The *Globe* became the recognized spokesman for Jacksonian policies and its editorials were copied or paraphrased in a wide network of local Democratic newspapers. In 1837, the *United States Magazine and Democratic Review* was launched and also became a vigorous formulator of Democratic opinion and taste in politics, literature, and the arts.

The selection below is unusually revealing. It is taken from a remarkable editorial entitled "The War of the Five Campaigns" written in the midst of the campaign for the Presidency in 1840. The Whig tactics of the "Log Cabin and Hard Cider" campaign are fully exposed. Yet, in a backhanded way, the *Democratic Review* seems to admit that these manipulations of popular symbols were first used successfully by the Democrats and that the Whigs have finally learned the secret of democratic politics. Recent studies of voting behavior in the 1830s demonstrate clearly that there was a great upsurge of voter participation in American politics in the 1830s climaxed by the tremendous outpouring of voters in 1840. Whatever else is revealed by this editorial, we can see how quickly the Jacksonian generation perceived that the skills of manipulating public opinion and of organizing political associations were the necessitous

* From the *United States Magazine and Democratic Review*, VII (1840), 485–87, abridged.

means for the control and use of power in the age of the common man.

. . . Such, then, have been the first four campaigns of the holy war in which we are engaged—the struggle of the Democratic party for financial reform, in the action of the General Government, against enormous accumulations of money-power, controlling two-thirds of the press, and in offensive and defensive alliance with a great political party, ambitious, vigilant, violent and indefatigable. We are now in the midst of the fifth—the fifth, and we trust and believe, the last. Each one of these, it will readily be perceived, has been a separate movement from the preceding —all differing in their distinct characteristics, though alike in the mutual bitterness of party spirit which they have unfortunately engendered; and alike too in their result. The Democratic party, in possession of the administration, has throughout been on the defensive, and throughout victorious in that attitude. The Opposition have been the party of attack; and in the successive forms in which they have varied their assaults, with the varying progress of events, their leaders have certainly exhibited much ingenuity in keeping alive the delusions and excitement of their followers, as well as a perseverance and courage worthy perhaps of a better cause and a better fate. But in their present campaign they have brought a deep disgrace not only on themselves, but on our common country, and the institutions of democracy.

This must be called the "Log Cabin and Hard Cider" campaign—and must unquestionably stand without a parallel in our past political history. It presents, as before remarked, a totally new phase in our party politics—a new experiment upon our institutions. We were justified in inferring, a year ago, from the past history and present aspect of the party contest, that no other alternative but dissolution remained to the Whigs—that no farther chance of success, no farther ground to be occupied, was left to them; for though the prediction has not been realized, yet is it very certain that the expedient to which they have had recourse was one to which there has been no former precedent to direct our attention. They have not yet gone to pieces. They have not yet given up the vain struggle in despair. On the contrary they are making a more zealous and active effort than ever before—and apparently with an infatuation of hope and confidence unknown in any of their former assaults upon the democratic ascendency. One struggle more—one last rally, to concentrate the courage and energy of despair for a sudden and bold dash, which may yet retrieve with a sweeping success all their past losses and atone for all their past defeats—this is the idea of their present movement. The Presidential election of this year affords the opportunity—one or two coincident circumstances seem to favor it—it can never in all probability return, and certainly not for four years—and the most powerful motives of interest, of ambition and of partisan passion stimulate to the effort of taking advantage of it. They remember that it was thus that Bonaparte conquered at Marengo—but they forget that he tried in vain the same tactics at Waterloo.

They have struck upon a new idea. Like the Messenians of old from the Spartans, or the Russians of Pultowa from Charles, they have at last learned from defeat the very art of victory! We have taught them how to conquer us! It was the dazzle of a military title that was the secret of General Jackson's inexplicable popularity—why, then, might not the name of General Harrison 'tickle the ears of the groundlings' with the same charm that made that of the old hero of New Orleans such a tower of strength? The hickory-tree, too, played a conspicuous part in the old Jackson days, as a popular rallying cry of the friends of the stout and stalwart old man, of whose characteristic traits its uprightness, firmness, and excellent serviceable qualities seemed to constitute it a natural symbol and representative—why, then, might not the watchword of a "Log Cabin and Hard Cider," however unmeaning and ridiculously inappropriate, answer a similar purpose of rousing the hurrah of a popular enthusiasm?

Thus has Federalism reasoned—and thus has it actually reasoned itself into the delusion that after all its successive disappointments, this new campaign is to succeed in overthrowing the Administration that has triumphed over all its former attacks, and is to turn back that mighty movement of democratic reform which it is the mission of this Administration to carry forward!

In the prosecution of this idea, we see them straining every nerve to affect a popular character—at the same time that they in reality betray, more clearly even than when it was not disavowed, that contempt for the intelligence of the People which constitutes the foundation of their entire political theory. The plan of operations was organized at the Harrisburg Convention, and has been zealously carried out ever since, throughout every section of the country. It consists in avoiding all public expositions of their principles, of the views and intentions which they would bring with them into power if successful—in carrying on an active opposition on every available point, of a mere partisan character—in keeping up a series of elaborate demonstrations, on the grandest scale that the number and means of a large and wealthy party will permit, of a popular enthusiasm, which it is imagined will tend to create that which it feigns to be—and in playing off before the ignorant mass upon whom all this is designed to operate a great variety of silly mummeries calculated for the presumed level of their capacity, in which log cabins and cider barrels play the chief parts. This is the strategy of the fifth campaign in which we are now engaged.

In furtherance of this ludicrously impudent imposture, we see too the attempt to appropriate the name to which they also ascribe much of our popular strength. They are now, forsooth, the "*Democratic* Whigs"—and it must be confessed that so far as regards external demeanor they carry it out bravely enough—out-Heroding Herod—though it must be confessed that like the sudden metamorphoses we sometimes witness in the course of the plots and intrigues of the stage, they do enact the unfamiliar part with an elaborate superfluity of swagger which cannot but betray the grossness of the deception to every eye but that of the most determined blindness.

Widely, widely do they miscalculate, when they expect to succeed in such a contest by such means; and we shall confess ourselves grievously disappointed if they do not receive at the coming election a lesson, a punishment, commensurate with the grossness of the national insult of which, by such appeals to the popular ignorance and folly, they are guilty. If the institutions of democracy are now for a while brought into contempt in the eyes of the rest of the world, by the spectacle which our country now presents—with one of its great parties canvasing on a Presidential campaign on such a plan of operations—the disgrace must be redeemed, the wrong atoned for, by the severity of the rebuke with which it must be repelled by the just indignation of an insulted People. We have not been wrong when we have relied upon the sober intelligence, the instinctive sagacity, of the democratic mass of our citizens to judge rightly between the true and false, when fairly exhibited in contrast before them, as has been amply done in the present contest, as well by the practical developement of events as by theoretical argument. We have no fear that our staunch Democracy who have so firmly withstood all the open attacks and ambushed snares of Federalism during the past ten years of struggle between the two antagonist parties and principles, are to succumb now to the feeblest of their attacks, and the shallowest as well as most impudent of their stratagems. Their main reliance, to favor the success of their present movement, is upon the fact of the general reduction of the prices of labor and of agricultural produce, caused by the present contraction of the currency consequent upon the recent double collapse of the credit system. True, this circumstance—the only new element entering into the question since our great electoral victories of 1838 and 1839—may constitute the present struggle a somewhat severe test of the intelligence and firmness of the people; but it is a test which we are well assured they will pass through with honor and triumph. . . .

34

Of the Relation between Public Associations and the Newspapers*

ALEXIS DE TOCQUEVILLE

We cannot fully understand the new conformation of power in the Jacksonian generation unless we look at the devices of influencing public opinion and of organizing social action. It is true that many of the establishments that had seemed to represent order in an earlier generation—the established colonial churches, the landholding and merchant aristocracies, the bench, and the bar—were stripped of much of their power by the time of the Jacksonian decade. Can we, therefore, assume that Americans were becoming anti-institutional in their thought and action? To be sure, they were opposed to all of the earlier institutions which smacked of privilege and aristocratic pretensions, but should we not say that the Jacksonian generation created new structures of power? Did not the political party become the new church, did not the party press become the pulpit from which public morality was defined, and did not the stump speaker replace the aristocratic gentleman as the formulator of social goals?

Among Tocqueville's more perceptive observations are those which deal with the importance of associations in American life. He describes the "immense assemblage of associations" in America and concluded that ". . . the most democratic country on the face of the earth is that in which men have, in our time, carried to the highest perfection the art of pursuing in common

* From Alexis de Tocqueville, *Democracy in America*, Francis Bowen, ed. (Cambridge, Massachusetts, 1863), II, 129–39, unabridged.

the object of their common desires. . . ." In the selections below, Tocqueville is particularly concerned to explain the intimate connection between public associations and the newspapers.

[OF THE USE WHICH THE AMERICANS MAKE OF PUBLIC ASSOCIATIONS IN CIVIL LIFE]

I do not propose to speak of those political associations by the aid of which men endeavor to defend themselves against the despotic action of a majority, or against the aggressions of regal power. That subject I have already treated. If each citizen did not learn, in proportion as he individually becomes more feeble, and consequently more incapable of preserving his freedom single-handed, to combine with his fellow-citizens for the purpose of defending it, it is clear that tyranny would unavoidably increase together with equality.

Those associations only which are formed in civil life, without reference to political objects, are here adverted to. The political associations which exist in the United States are only a single feature in the midst of the immense assemblage of associations in that country. Americans of all ages, all conditions, and all dispositions, constantly form associations. They have not only commercial and manufacturing companies, in which all take part, but associations of a thousand other kinds,—religious, moral, serious, futile, general or restricted, enormous or diminutive. The Americans make associations to give entertainments, to found seminaries, to build inns, to construct churches, to diffuse books, to send missionaries to the antipodes; they found in this manner hospitals, prisons, and schools. If it be proposed to inculcate some truth, or to foster some feeling, by the encouragement of a great example, they form a society. Wherever, at the head of some new undertaking, you see the government in France, or a man of rank in England, in the United States you will be sure to find an association.

I met with several kinds of associations in America of which I confess I had no previous notion; and I have often admired the extreme skill with which the inhabitants of the United States succeed in proposing a common object to the exertions of a great many men, and in inducing them voluntarily to pursue it.

I have since travelled over England, whence the Americans have taken some of their laws and many of their customs; and it seemed to me that the principle of association was by no means so constantly or adroitly used in that country. The English often perform great things singly, whereas the Americans form associations for the smallest undertakings. It is evident that the former people consider association as a powerful means of action, but the latter seem to regard it as the only means they have of acting.

Thus, the most democratic country on the face of the earth is that in which men have, in our time, carried to the highest perfection the art of pursuing in common the object of their common desires, and have applied this new science to the greatest number of purposes. Is this the result of accident? or is there in reality any necessary connection between the principle of association and that of equality?

Aristocratic communities always contain, amongst a multitude of persons who by themselves are powerless, a small number of powerful and wealthy citizens, each of whom can achieve great undertakings single-handed. In aristocratic societies, men do not need to combine in order to act, because they are strongly held together. Every wealthy and powerful citizen constitutes the head of a permanent and compulsory association, composed of all those who are dependent upon him, or whom he makes subservient to the execution of his designs.

Amongst democratic nations, on the contrary, all the citizens are independent and feeble; they can do hardly anything by themselves, and none of them can oblige his fellow-men to lend him their assistance. They all, therefore, become powerless, if they do not learn voluntarily to help each other. If men living in democratic countries had no right and no inclination to associate for political purposes, their independence would be in great jeopardy; but they might long preserve their wealth and their cultivation: whereas, if they never acquired the habit of forming associations in ordinary life, civilization itself would be endangered. A people amongst whom individuals should lose the power of achieving great things single-handed, without acquiring the means of producing them by united exertions, would soon relapse into barbarism.

Unhappily, the same social condition which renders associations so necessary to democratic nations, renders their formation more difficult amongst those nations than amongst all other. When several members of an aristocracy agree to combine, they easily succeed in doing so: as each of them brings great strength to the partnership, the number of its members may be very limited; and when the members of an association are limited in number, they may easily become mutually acquainted, understand each other, and establish fixed regulations. The same opportunities do not occur amongst democratic nations, where the associated members must always be very numerous for their association to have any power.

I am aware that many of my countrymen are not in the least embarrassed by this difficulty. They contend, that, the more enfeebled and incompetent the citizens become, the more able and active the government ought to be rendered, in order that society at large may execute what individuals can no longer accomplish. They believe this answers the whole difficulty, but I think they are mistaken.

A government might perform the part of some of the largest American companies; and several States, members of the Union, have already attempted it; but what political power could ever carry on the vast multitude of lesser undertakings which the American citizens perform every day, with the assistance of the principle of association? It is easy to foresee that the time is drawing near when man will be less and less able to produce, of himself alone, the commonest necessaries of life. The task of the governing power will therefore perpetually increase, and its very efforts will extend it every day. The more it stands in the place of associations, the more will individuals, losing the notion of combining together, require its assistance: these are causes and effects which unceasingly create each other. Will the administration of the country ultimately assume the management of all the manufactures which no single citizen is able to carry on? And if a time at length arrives when, in consequence of the extreme subdivision of landed property, the soil is split into an infinite number of parcels, so that it can only be cultivated by companies of husbandmen, will it be necessary that the head of the government should leave the helm of state to follow the plough? The morals and the intelligence of a democratic people would be as much endangered as its business and manufactures, if the government ever wholly usurped the place of private companies.

Feelings and opinions are recruited, the heart is enlarged, and the human mind is developed, only by the reciprocal influence of men upon each other. I have shown that these influences are almost null in democratic countries; they must therefore be artificially created, and this can only be accomplished by associations.

When the members of an aristocratic community adopt a new opinion, or conceive a new sentiment, they give it a station, as it were, beside themselves, upon the lofty platform where they stand; and opinions or sentiments so conspicuous to the eyes of the multitude are easily introduced into the minds or hearts of all around. In democratic countries, the governing power alone is naturally in a condition to act in this manner; but it is easy to see that its action is always inadequate, and often dangerous. A government can no more be competent to keep alive and to renew the circulation of opinions and feelings amongst a great people, than to manage all the speculations of productive industry. No sooner does a government attempt to go beyond its political sphere, and to enter upon this new track, than it exercises, even unintentionally, an insupportable tyranny; for a government can only dictate strict rules, the opinions which it favors are rigidly enforced, and it is never easy to discriminate between its advice and its commands. Worse still will be the case, if the government really believes itself interested in preventing all circulation of ideas; it will then stand motionless and oppressed by the heaviness of voluntary torpor. Governments, therefore, should not be the only active powers: associations ought, in democratic nations, to stand in lieu of those powerful private individuals whom the equality of conditions has swept away.

As soon as several of the inhabitants of the United States have taken up an opinion or a feeling which they wish to promote in the world, they look out for mutual assistance; and as soon as they have found each other out, they combine. From that moment they are no longer isolated men, but a power seen from afar, whose actions serve for an example, and whose language is listened to. The first time I heard in the United States that a hundred thousand men had bound themselves publicly to abstain from spirituous liquors, it appeared to me more like a joke than a serious engagement; and I did not at once perceive why these temperate citizens could not content themselves with drinking water by their own firesides. I at last understood that these hundred thousand Americans, alarmed by the progress of drunkenness around them, had made up their minds to patronize temperance. They acted just in the same way as a man of high rank who should dress very plainly, in order to inspire the humbler orders with a contempt of luxury. It is probable that, if these hundred thousand men had lived in France, each of them would singly have memorialized the government to watch the public houses all over the kingdom.

Nothing, in my opinion, is more deserving of our attention than the intellectual and moral associations of America. The political and industrial associations of that country strike us forcibly; but the others elude our observation, or, if we discover them, we understand them imperfectly, because we have hardly ever seen anything of the kind. It must, however, be acknowledged, that they are as necessary to the American people as the former, and perhaps more so. In democratic countries, the science of association is the mother of science; the progress of all the rest depends upon the progress it has made.

Amongst the laws which rule human societies, there is one which seems to be more precise and clear than all others. If men are to remain civilized, or to become so, the art of associating together must grow and improve in the same ratio in which the equality of conditions is increased.

[Of the Relation between Public Associations and the Newspapers]

When men are no longer united amongst themselves by firm and lasting ties, it is impossible to obtain the co-operation of any great number of them, unless you can persuade every man whose help you require that his private interest obliges him voluntarily to unite his exertions to the exertions of all the others. This can be habitually and conveniently effected only by means of a newspaper: nothing but a newspaper can drop the same thought into a thousand minds at the same moment. A newspaper is an adviser who does not require to be sought, but who comes of his own accord, and talks to you briefly every day of the common weal, without distracting you from your private affairs.

Newspapers therefore become more necessary in proportion as men become more equal, and individualism more to be feared. To suppose that they only serve to protect freedom would be to diminish their importance: they maintain civilization. I shall not deny that, in democratic countries, newspapers frequently lead the citizens to launch together into very ill-digested schemes; but if there were no newspapers, there would be no common activity. The evil which they produce is therefore much less than that which they cure.

The effect of a newspaper is not only to suggest the same purpose to a great number of persons, but to furnish means for executing in common the designs which they

may have singly conceived. The principal citizens who inhabit an aristocratic country discern each other from afar;
and if they wish to unite their forces, they move towards
each other, drawing a multitude of men after them. It frequently happens, on the contrary, in democratic countries,
that a great number of men who wish or who want to combine cannot accomplish it, because, as they are very insig-
nificant and lost amidst the crowd, they cannot see, and
know not where to find, one another. A newspaper then
takes up the notion or the feeling which had occurred
simultaneously, but singly, to each of them. All are then
immediately guided towards this beacon; and these wan-
dering minds, which had long sought each other in darkness, at length meet and unite. The newspaper brought
them together, and the newspaper is still necessary to keep
them united.

In order that an association amongst a democratic people should have any power, it must be a numerous body.
The persons of whom it is composed are therefore scattered
over a wide extent, and each of them is detained in the
place of his domicile by the narrowness of his income, or
by the small unremitting exertions by which he earns it.
Means must then be found to converse every day without
seeing each other, and to take steps in common without
having met. Thus, hardly any democratic association can
do without newspapers.

There is, consequently, a necessary connection between
public associations and newspapers: newspapers make associations, and associations make newspapers; and if it has
been correctly advanced, that associations will increase in
number as the conditions of men become more equal, it
is not less certain that the number of newspapers increases
in proportion to that of associations. Thus it is, in America,
that we find at the same time the greatest number of
associations and of newspapers.

This connection between the number of newspapers and
that of associations leads us to the discovery of a further
connection between the state of the periodical press and
the form of the administration in a country, and shows

that the number of newspapers must diminish or increase amongst a democratic people, in proportion as its administration is more or less centralized. For, amongst democratic nations, the exercise of local powers cannot be intrusted to the principal members of the community, as in aristocracies. Those powers must either be abolished, or placed in the hands of very large numbers of men, who then in fact constitute an association permanently established by law, for the purpose of administering the affairs of a certain extent of territory; and they require a journal, to bring to them every day, in the midst of their own minor concerns, some intelligence of the state of their public weal. The more numerous local powers are, the greater is the number of men in whom they are vested by law; and as this want is hourly felt, the more profusely do newspapers abound.

The extraordinary subdivision of administrative power has much more to do with the enormous number of American newspapers, than the great political freedom of the country and the absolute liberty of the press. If all the inhabitants of the Union had the suffrage,—but a suffrage which should extend only to the choice of their legislators in Congress,—they would require but few newspapers, because they would have to act together only on very important, but very rare, occasions. But within the great national association, lesser associations have been established by law in every county, every city, and indeed in every village, for the purposes of local administration. The laws of the country thus compel every American to co-operate every day of his life with some of his fellow-citizens for a common purpose, and each one of them requires a newspaper to inform him what all the others are doing.

I am of opinion that a democratic people, without any national representative assemblies, but with a great number of small local powers, would have in the end more newspapers than another people governed by a centralized administration and an elective legislature. What best explains to me the enormous circulation of the daily press in the United States is, that, amongst the Americans, I find the utmost national freedom combined with local freedom of every kind.

There is a prevailing opinion in France and England, that the circulation of newspapers would be indefinitely increased by removing the taxes which have been laid upon the press. This is a very exaggerated estimate of the effects of such a reform. Newspapers increase in numbers, not according to their cheapness, but according to the more or less frequent want which a great number of men may feel for intercommunication and combination.

In like manner, I should attribute the increasing influence of the daily press to causes more general than those by which it is commonly explained. A newspaper can only subsist on the condition of publishing sentiments or principles common to a large number of men. A newspaper, therefore, always represents an association which is composed of its habitual readers. This association may be more or less defined, more or less restricted, more or less numerous; but the fact that the newspaper keeps alive, is a proof that at least the germ of such an association exists in the minds of its readers.

This leads me to a last reflection, with which I shall conclude this chapter. The more equal the conditions of men become, and the less strong men individually are, the more easily do they give way to the current of the multitude, and the more difficult is it for them to adhere by themselves to an opinion which the multitude discard. A newspaper represents an association; it may be said to address each of its readers in the name of all the others, and to exert its influence over them in proportion to their individual weakness. The power of the newspaper press must therefore increase as the social conditions of men become more equal.

35

Jacksonian Political Caricature

(See Plates 13–16 following page 214.)

The Jacksonian era was a great period of political caricature in American political history. The intensified political
controversy during the Jacksonian generation provided
abundant opportunities for the use of caricature. Further-
more, the development of lithography in those years made
for a great increase in cartooning. Lithography was simple
and inexpensive and cartoonists responded to this technical advance by raising their art to a higher level. The illustrations described below are examples of some of the more
interesting political cartoons of the Jacksonian period.

PLATE 13. *The Downfall of Mother Bank*. By E. W.
Clay (?).

The bitter controversy over Jackson's veto of the bill to
recharter the Bank of the United States and his removal
of deposits stimulated a great deal of activity by the
political cartoonists, mostly hostile to President Jackson.
The cartoon entitled "The Downfall of Mother Bank"
and "drawn by Zek Downing" was one of the few favorable to the President. This drawing is sometimes
attributed to Edward W. Clay, one of the great carica-
turists of the Jacksonian era. In the cartoon, Jackson
holds aloft his order for the removal of the public deposits while lightning bolts from his upraised hand cause
the pillars of the Bank to crash down upon Whig editors
and politicians and upon Nicholas Biddle, the powerful
president of the Bank of the United States.

PLATE 14. *King Andrew the First*. Artist unknown.

"King Andrew the First," issued as a broadside, probably
in 1834, is a classic image in the mythology of the Amer-

ican Whigs. In this lithograph, Jackson is depicted in regal robes, trampling on the "Constitution of the United States of America," "Virtue, Liberty, and Independence," "Internal Improvements," "U. S. Bank." Below the lithograph are twenty lines of print attacking Jackson and raising the question "Shall he reign over us, or shall the People rule?" This caricature contains a marvelous collection of many of the key symbols in the political ideology of the Whigs.

PLATE 15. *The Times*, by E. W. Clay.

This Whig cartoon was produced by Edward W. Clay for the political campaign of 1840 and must have had great appeal to those who had unhappy memories of the Panic of 1837 and the economic distress which followed. The elaborate print depicts various aspects of economic and social misery. There is a run on the "Mechanics Bank"; idle shipping is tied up at the wharf; unemployed and barefoot workmen are standing in front of a billboard which advertises a lottery scheme; and stocks of peaches and flour stand unsold. Only the pawnbroker and the liquor store seem to be doing a thriving trade, while across the river the prison is receiving a new cartload of inmates.

PLATE 16. *The New Era Whig Trap* Sprung. By Napoleon Sarony (?).

This lithograph, signed "Boneyshanks" and sometimes attributed to Napoleon Sarony, another of the more notable cartoonists of the Jacksonian era, was published in Washington, D.C., during the campaign of 1840. In this drawing, Van Buren is imprisoned in a log cabin, with logs bearing the names of states and with an American eagle perched on top. Jackson is trying to overturn the cabin with a lever labeled "Hickory" resting against a base labeled "New-Orleans." Inside the cabin, Van Buren is expressing his lack of hope that Jackson will be able to free him even with such powerful symbols because much of the cabin is "all chinked up with *Clay*."

PART IV

The Reconstruction of Ideologies

36

The Office of the People in Art, Government, and Religion*

GEORGE BANCROFT

Educated at Harvard and Göttingen, George Bancroft became one of the major carriers into American thought of ideas taken from German idealistic philosophy as developed by Kant, Fichte, Heeren, and Herder. In 1834, he issued the first volume of his twelve-volume *History of the United States from the Discovery of the American Continent,* and when the final two volumes were completed in 1882, he had achieved a reputation as the greatest and most widely read historian in America.

Entering politics actively in 1834, Bancroft scandalized the Brahmins of Boston and Harvard by casting his lot with the Jacksonian Democratic party. Thereafter, his considerable intellectual talents were given to the defense of Jacksonian policies in public lectures and in letters to leading newspapers. At the same time, the first volume of his monumental history already revealed his conviction that a "favoring Providence, calling our institutions into being, has conducted the country to its present happiness and glory." If every page of this and succeeding volumes do not actually "vote for Jackson," there are many passages that exalt the common man as the creative source of freedom and happiness in America. Bancroft was well rewarded by the Jacksonians for his efforts; he became Collector of Customs in Boston and, by virtue of the control of Custom House patronage, became a powerful leader in the Democratic party of

* From George Bancroft, *Literary and Historical Miscellanies* (New York, 1840), pp. 408–35, abridged.

Massachusetts. In the Polk administration, he served as Secretary of the Navy and, in later years, he held diplomatic posts as minister to England and to Prussia.

The following oration, delivered at Williams College in 1835, is one of the more remarkable documents of the Jacksonian decade. At first glance, it seems incredible that a scholar trained at Harvard and Göttingen could say that "the decision of the whole is to be preferred to the judgment of the enlightened few" or that "the universal decision is the nearest criterion of truth," and that "the common mind . . . is the sieve which separates error from certainty." There is something here that appears to resemble the anti-intellectualism in the populistic utterances of Davy Crockett and others of the Jacksonian generation who disparaged book learning. Yet Bancroft cannot be disposed of so easily. In this oration, he is clearly trying to give a philosophical basis to the cult of the common man; he is drawing upon the creative world of German idealism in order to shape a transcendental democratic philosophy. In his distinction between the intelligence that is based upon the experience of the senses and the intelligence that is based on an "internal sense" which is informed by intuitive evidence, Bancroft anticipates the transcendentalist philosophy of Ralph Waldo Emerson; by his fervent faith in farmers, mechanics, the masses, and "lowly humanity" he anticipates the poetic utterances of Walt Whitman's *Leaves of Grass.*

I

The material world does not change in its masses or in its powers. The stars shine with no more lustre than when they first sang together in the glory of their birth. The flowers that gemmed the fields and the forests, before America was discovered, now bloom around us in their season. The sun that shone on Homer shines on us in unchanging lustre. The bow that beamed on the patriarch still glitters in the clouds. Nature is the same. For her no new forces are generated; no new capacities are discovered.

The earth turns on its axis, and perfects its revolutions, and renews its seasons, without increase or advancement.

But a like passive destiny does not attach to the inhabitants of the earth. For them the expectations of social improvement are no delusion; the hopes of philanthropy are more than a dream. The five senses do not constitute the whole inventory of our sources of knowledge. They are the organs by which thought connects itself with the external universe; but the power of thought is not merged in the exercise of its instruments. We have functions which connect us with heaven, as well as organs which set us in relation with earth. We have not merely the senses opening to us the external world, but an internal sense, which places us in connexion with the world of intelligence and the decrees of God.

There is a *spirit in man:* not in the privileged few; not in those of us only who by the favor of Providence have been nursed in public schools: IT IS IN MAN: it is the attribute of the race. The spirit, which is the guide to truth, is the gracious gift to each member of the human family.

Reason exists within every breast. I mean not that faculty which deduces inferences from the experience of the senses, but that higher faculty, which from the infinite treasures of its own consciousness, originates truth, and assents to it by the force of intuitive evidence; that faculty which raises us beyond the control of time and space, and gives us faith in things eternal and invisible. There is not the difference between one mind and another, which the pride of philosophers might conceive. To them no faculty is conceded, which does not belong to the meanest of their countrymen. In them there can not spring up a truth, which does not equally have its germ in every mind. They have not the power of creation; they can but reveal what God has implanted in every breast.

The intellectual functions, by which relations are perceived, are the common endowments of the race. The differences are apparent, not real. The eye in one person may be dull, in another quick, in one distorted, and in another tranquil and clear; yet the relation of the eye to light is in all men the same. Just so judgment may be liable in individual minds to the bias of passion, and yet its relation to truth is immutable, and is universal.

In questions of practical duty, conscience is God's umpire, whose light illumines every heart. There is nothing in books, which had not first, and has not still its life within us. Religion itself is a dead letter, wherever its truths are not renewed in the soul. Individual conscience may be corrupted by interest, or debauched by pride, yet the rule of morality is distinctly marked; its harmonies are to the mind like music to the ear; and the moral judgment, when carefully analyzed and referred to its principles, is always founded in right. The eastern superstition, which bids its victims prostrate themselves before the advancing car of their idols, springs from a noble root, and is but a melancholy perversion of that self-devotion, which enables the Christian to bear the cross, and subject his personal passions to the will of God. Immorality of itself never won to its support the inward voice; conscience, if questioned, never forgets to curse the guilty with the memory of sin, to cheer the upright with the meek tranquillity of approval. And this admirable power, which is the instinct of Deity, is the attribute of every man; it knocks at the palace gate, it dwells in the meanest hovel. Duty, like death, enters every abode, and delivers its message. Conscience, like reason and judgment, is universal.

That the moral affections are planted every where, needs only to be asserted to be received. The savage mother loves her offspring with all the fondness that a mother can know. Beneath the odorous shade of the boundless forests of Chili, the native youth repeats the story of love as sincerely as it was ever chanted in the valley of Vaucluse. The affections of family are not the growth of civilization. The charities of life are scattered every where; enamelling the vales of human being, as the flowers paint the meadows. They are not the fruit of study, nor the privilege of refinement, but a natural instinct.

Our age has seen a revolution in works of imagination. The poet has sought his theme in common life. Never is the genius of Scott more pathetic, than when, as in the Antiquary, he delineates the sorrows of a poor fisherman, or as in the Heart of Mid Lothian, he takes his heroine from a cottage. And even Wordsworth, the purest and most original poet of the day, in spite of the inveterate character of his political predilections, has thrown the light of genius on the walks of commonest life; he finds a lesson in every grave of the village churchyard; he discloses the boundless treasures of feeling in the peasant, the laborer and the artisan; the strolling peddler becomes, through his genius, a teacher of the sublimest morality; and the solitary wagoner, the lonely shepherd, even the feeble mother of an idiot boy, furnishes lessons in the reverence for Humanity.

If from things relating to truth, justice, and affection, we turn to those relating to the beautiful, we may here still further assert, that the sentiment for the beautiful resides in every breast. The lovely forms of the external world delight us from their adaptation to our powers.

> Yea, what were mighty Nature's self?
> Her features could they win us,
> Unhelped by the poetic voice
> That hourly speaks within us?

The Indian mother, on the borders of Hudson's Bay, decorates her manufactures with ingenious devices and lovely colors, prompted by the same instinct which guided the pencil and mixed the colors of Raphael. The inhabitant of Nootka Sound tattoos his body with the method of harmonious Arabesques. Every form, to which the hands of the artist have ever given birth, sprung first into being as a conception of his mind, from a natural faculty, which belongs not to the artist exclusively, but to man. Beauty, like truth and justice, lives within us; like virtue and like moral law, it is a companion of the soul. The power which leads to the production of beautiful forms, or to the perception of them in the works which God has made, is an attribute of Humanity. . . .

II

If it be true, that the gifts of mind and heart are universally diffused, if the sentiment of truth, justice, love, and beauty exists in every one, then it follows, as a necessary consequence, that the common judgment in taste, politics, and religion, is the highest authority on earth, and the nearest possible approach to an infallible decision. From the consideration of individual powers I turn to the action of the human mind in masses.

If reason is a universal faculty, the universal decision is the nearest criterion of truth. The common mind winnows opinions; it is the sieve which separates error from certainty. The exercise by many of the same faculty on the same subject would naturally lead to the same conclusions. But if not, the very differences of opinion that arise prove the supreme judgment of the general mind. Truth is one. It never contradicts itself. One truth cannot contradict another truth. Hence truth is a bond of union. But error not only contradicts truth, but may contradict itself; so that there may be many errors, and each at variance with the rest. Truth is therefore of necessity an element of harmony; error as necessarily an element of discord. Thus there can be no continuing universal judgment but a right one. Men cannot agree in an absurdity; neither can they agree in a falsehood.

If wrong opinions have often been cherished by the masses, the cause always lies in the complexity of the ideas presented. Error finds its way into the soul of a nation, only through the channel of truth. It is to a truth that men listen; and if they accept error also, it is only because the error is for the time so closely interwoven with the truth, that the one cannot readily be separated from the other.

Unmixed error can have no existence in the public mind. Wherever you see men clustering together to form a party, you may be sure that however much error may be there, truth is there also. Apply this principle boldly; for it contains a lesson of candor, and a voice of encouragement.

There never was a school of philosophy, nor a clan in the realm of opinion, but carried along with it some important truth. And therefore every sect that has ever flourished has benefited Humanity; for the errors of a sect pass away and are forgotten; its truths are received into the common inheritance. To know the seminal thought of every prophet and leader of a sect, is to gather all the wisdom of mankind.

> By heaven! there should not be a seer, who left
> The world one doctrine, but I'd task his lore,
> And commune with his spirit. All the truth
> Of all the tongues of earth, I'd have them all,
> Had I the powerful spell to raise their ghosts.

The sentiment of beauty, as it exists in the human mind, is the criterion in works of art, inspires the conceptions of genius, and exercises a final judgment on its productions. For who are the best judges in matters of taste? Do you think the cultivated individual? Undoubtedly not; but the collective mind. The public is wiser than the wisest critic. In Athens, the arts were carried to perfection, when "the fierce democracie" was in the ascendant; the temple of Minerva and the works of Phidias were planned and perfected to please the common people. When Greece yielded to tyrants, her genius for excellence in art expired; or rather, the purity of taste disappeared; because the artist then endeavored to gratify a patron, and therefore, humored his caprice; while before he had endeavored to delight the race. . . .

III

In like manner the best government rests on the people and not on the few, on persons and not on property, on the free development of public opinion and not on authority; because the munificent Author of our being has conferred the gifts of mind upon every member of the human race without distinction of outward circumstances. Whatever of other possessions may be engrossed, mind asserts its own independence. Lands, estates, the produce of mines, the prolific abundance of the seas, may be usurped by a privileged class. Avarice, assuming the form of ambitious power, may grasp realm after realm, subdue continents, compass the earth in its schemes of aggrandizement, and sigh after other worlds; but mind eludes the power of appropriation; it exists only in its own individuality; it is a property which cannot be confiscated and cannot be torn away; it laughs at chains; it bursts from imprisonment; it defies monopoly. A government of equal rights must, therefore, rest upon mind; not wealth, not brute force, the sum of the moral intelligence of the community should rule the State. Prescription can no more assume to be a valid plea for political injustice; society studies to eradicate established abuses, and to bring social institutions and laws into harmony with moral right; not dismayed by the natural and necessary imperfections of all human effort, and not giving way to despair, because every hope does not at once ripen into fruit.

The public happiness is the true object of legislation, and can be secured only by the masses of mankind themselves awakening to the knowledge and the care of their own interests. Our free institutions have reversed the false and ignoble distinctions between men; and refusing to gratify the pride of caste, have acknowledged the common mind to be the true material for a commonwealth. Every thing has hitherto been done for the happy few. It is not possible to endow an aristocracy with greater benefits than they have already enjoyed; there is no room to hope that individuals will be more highly gifted or more fully developed than the greatest sages of past times. The world can advance only through the culture of the moral and intellectual powers of the people. To accomplish this end by means of the people themselves, is the highest purpose of government. If it be the duty of the individual to strive after a perfection like the perfection of God, how much more ought a nation to be the image of Deity. The common mind is the true Parian marble, fit to be wrought into likeness to a God. The duty of America is to secure the culture and the happiness of the masses by their reliance on themselves.

The absence of the prejudices of the old world leaves us here the opportunity of consulting independent truth; and man is left to apply the instinct of freedom to every social relation and public interest. We have approached so near to nature, that we can hear her gentlest whispers; we have made Humanity our lawgiver and our oracle; and, therefore, the nation receives, vivifies and applies principles, which in Europe the wisest accept with distrust. Freedom of mind and of conscience, freedom of the seas, freedom of industry, equality of franchises, each great truth is firmly grasped, comprehended and enforced; for the multitude is neither rash nor fickle. In truth, it is less fickle than those who profess to be its guides. Its natural dialectics surpass the logic of the schools. Political action has never been so consistent and so unwavering, as when it results from a feeling or a principle, diffused through society. The people is firm and tranquil in its movements, and necessarily acts with moderation, because it becomes but slowly impregnated with new ideas; and effects no changes, except in harmony with the knowledge which it has acquired. Besides, where it is permanently possessed of power, there exists neither the occasion nor the desire for frequent change. It is not the parent of tumult; sedition is bred in the lap of luxury, and its chosen emissaries are the beggared spendthrift and the impoverished libertine. The government by the people is in very truth the strongest government in the world. Discarding the implements of terror, it dares to rule by moral force, and has its citadel in the heart.

Such is the political system which rests on reason, reflection, and the free expression of deliberate choice. There may be those who scoff at the suggestion, that the decision of the whole is to be preferred to the judgment of the enlightened few. They say in their hearts that the masses are ignorant; that farmers know nothing of legislation; that mechanics should not quit their workshops to join in forming public opinion. But true political science does indeed venerate the masses. It maintains, not as has been perversely asserted, that "the people can make right," but that the people can DISCERN right. Individuals are but shadows, too often engrossed by the pursuit of shadows; the race is immortal: individuals are of limited sagacity; the common mind is infinite in its experience: individuals are languid and blind; the many are ever wakeful: individuals are corrupt; the race has been redeemed: individuals are timeserving; the masses are fearless: individuals may be false, the masses are ingenuous and sincere: individuals claim the divine sanction of truth for the deceitful conceptions of their own fancies; the Spirit of God breathes through the combined intelligence of the people. Truth is not to be ascertained by the impulses of an individual; it emerges from the contradictions of personal opinions; it raises itself in majestic serenity above the strifes of parties and the conflict of sects; it acknowledges neither the solitary mind, nor the separate faction as its oracle; but owns as its only faithful interpreter the dictates of pure reason itself, proclaimed by the general voice of mankind. The decrees of the universal conscience are the nearest approach to the presence of God in the soul of man.

Thus the opinion which we respect is, indeed, not the opinion of one or of a few, but the sagacity of the many. It is hard for the pride of cultivated philosophy to put its ear to the ground, and listen reverently to the voice of lowly humanity; yet the people collectively are wiser than the most gifted individual, for all his wisdom constitutes but a part of theirs. When the great sculptor of Greece was endeavoring to fashion the perfect model of beauty, he did not passively imitate the form of the loveliest woman of his age; but he gleaned the several lineaments of his faultless work from the many. And so it is, that a perfect judgment is the result of comparison, when error eliminates error, and truth is established by concurring witnesses. The organ of truth is the invisible decision of the unbiased world; she pleads before no tribunal but public opinion; she owns no safe interpreter but the common mind; she knows no court of appeals but the soul of humanity. It is when the multitude give counsel, that right purposes find safety; theirs is the fixedness that cannot be shaken; theirs is the understanding which exceeds in wisdom; theirs is the heart, of which the largeness is as the sand on the sea-shore. . . .

37

"The Democratic Principle"*

THE DEMOCRATIC REVIEW

The introductory editorial in the first number of the *United States Magazine and Democratic Review*, presumably written by the editor, John L. O'Sullivan, asserts a determination to advocate "that high and holy DEMOCRATIC PRINCIPLE which was designed to be the fundamental element of the new social and political system created by the 'American experiment'. . . ." Considering the character and intended role of the *Democratic Review*, this editorial can be taken as an authoritative codification of the democratic ideas held by the followers of Jackson after a decade of political conflict.

In view of the political and social changes during the Jacksonian decade, the most striking aspect of the editorial is the archaism of the conceptions of government and of the social norms articulated by its writer. It is evident that the Jeffersonian heritage is an indispensable part of the total composition of the mythology of the Jacksonian party and a highly cherished element in its sense of the past. Hence much of the editorial seems to be little more than a reiteration of Jeffersonian principles. To be sure, there are some subtle differences which reflect the social experience of the Jacksonian generation. For example, the Jeffersonian formulation concerning the supremacy of the will of the majority with due respect for the rights of minorities is there, but "public opinion" and the "popular will" are set more strongly in opposition to knowledge and talent than in any of Jefferson's writings. Yet the Jeffersonian belief

* From the *United States Magazine and Democratic Review*,
I (January 1838), 2–15, abridged.

that "the best government is that which governs least" and the Jeffersonian faith in a social order that operates according to "spontaneous action and self-regulation" are repeated without the slightest indication of how these conceptions might still apply to the changing conditions of the economic and social order. Indeed, much of the anti-democratic influence of the times is assumed to proceed from the cities "where wealth accumulates, where luxury gradually unfolds its corrupting tendencies, where aristocratic habits and social classifications form and strengthen themselves, where the congregation of men stimulates and exaggerates all ideas. . . ."

Somehow, the Jacksonians were intellectually and emotionally predisposed to see life with a Jeffersonian vision of government and society. There is nothing in the editorial of the *Democratic Review* which suggests any attempt to reshape the Jeffersonian ideas in relation to the new forms of enterprise or to take account of the current proposals to give business corporations a more democratic basis. Hence we are faced with a difficult problem of historical explanation. Is this a genuine incapacity on the part of Jacksonians to develop a democratic ideology relevant to the new economic realities of American society? Is the Jacksonian ideology an example of what Karl Mannheim has called "false consciousness"? Or, remembering the emergence of the new techniques of mass politics, should we say, perhaps, that the Jefferson symbol was being used largely as a manipulative symbol?

. . . So many false ideas have insensibly attached themselves to the term "democracy," as connected with our party politics, that we deem it necessary here, at the outset, to make a full and free profession of the cardinal principles of political faith on which we take our stand; principles to which we are devoted with an unwavering force of conviction and earnestness of enthusiasm which, ever since they were first presented to our minds, have constantly grown and strengthened by contemplation of them, and of the incalculable capabilities of social improvement of which they contain the germs.

We believe, then, in the principle of *democratic republicanism*, in its strongest and purest sense. We have an abiding confidence in the virtue, intelligence, and full capacity for self-government, of the great mass of our people —our industrious, honest, manly, intelligent millions of freemen.

We are opposed to all self-styled "wholesome restraints" on the free action of the popular opinion and will, other than those which have for their sole object the prevention of precipitate legislation. This latter object is to be attained by the expedient of the division of power, and by causing all legislation to pass through the ordeal of successive forms; to be sifted through the discussions of co-ordinate legislative branches, with mutual suspensive veto powers. Yet all should be dependant with equal directness and promptness on the influence of public opinion; the popular will should be equally the animating and moving spirit of them all, and ought never to find in any of its own creatures a self-imposed power, capable (when misused either by corrupt ambition or honest error) of resisting itself, and defeating its own determined object. We cannot, therefore, look with an eye of favor on any such forms of representation as, by length of tenure of delegated power, tend to weaken that universal and unrelaxing responsibility to the vigilance of public opinion, which is the true conservative principle of our institutions.

The great question here occurs, which is of vast importance to this country, (was it not once near dissolving the Union, and plunging it into the abyss of civil war?)—of the relative rights of majorities and minorities. Though we go for the republican principle of the supremacy of the will of the majority, we acknowledge, in general, a strong sympathy with minorities, and consider that their rights have a high moral claim on the respect and justice of majorities; a claim not always fairly recognised in practice by the latter, in the full sway of power, when flushed with triumph, and impelled by strong interests. This has ever been the point of the democratic cause most open to assault, and most difficult to defend. This difficulty does not arise from any intrinsic weakness. The democratic theory is perfect and harmonious in all its parts; and if this point is not so self-evidently clear as the rest is generally, in all candid discussion, conceded to be, it is because of certain false principles of government, which have, in all practical experiments of the theory, been interwoven with the democratic portions of the system, being borrowed from the example of anti-democratic systems of government. We shall always be willing to meet this question frankly and fairly. The great argument against pure democracy, drawn from this source, is this:

Though the main object with reference to which all social institutions ought to be modelled is undeniably, as stated by the democrat, "the greatest good of the greatest number," yet it by no means follows that the greatest number always rightly understands its own greatest good. Highly pernicious error has often possessed the minds of nearly a whole nation; while the philosopher in his closet, and an enlightened few about him, powerless against the overwhelming current of popular prejudice and excitement, have alone possessed the truth, which the next generation may perhaps recognise and practice, though its author, now sainted, has probably, in his own time, been its martyr. The original adoption of the truth would have saved perhaps oceans of blood, and mountains of misery and crime. How much stronger, then, the case against the absolute supremacy of the opinion and will of the majority, when its numerical preponderance is, as often happens, comparatively small. And if the larger proportion of the more wealthy and cultivated classes of the society are found on the side of the minority, the disinterested observer may well be excused if he hesitate long before he awards the judgment, in a difficult and complicated question, in favor of the mere numerical argument. Majorities are often as liable to error of opinion, and not always free from a similar proneness to selfish abuse of power, as minorities; and a vast amount of injustice may often be perpetrated, and consequent general social injury be done, before the evil reaches that extreme at which it rights itself by revolution, moral or physical.

We have here, we believe, correctly stated the anti-democratic side of the argument on this point. It is not to be denied that it possesses something more than plausibility. It has certainly been the instrument of more injury to the cause of the democratic principle than all the bayonets and cannon that have ever been arrayed in support of it against that principle. The inference from it is, that the popular opinion and will must not be trusted with the supreme and absolute direction of the general interests; that it must be subjected to the "conservative checks" of minority interests, and to the regulation of the "more enlightened wisdom" of the "better classes," and those to whom the possession of a property "test of merit" gives what they term "a stake in the community." And here we find ourselves in the face of the great stronghold of the anti-democratic, or *aristocratic*, principle.

It is not our purpose, in this place, to carry out the discussion of this question. The general scope and tendency of the present work are designed to be directed towards the refutation of this sophistical reasoning and inference. It will be sufficient here to allude to the leading ideas by which they are met by the advocate of the pure democratic cause.

In the first place, the greatest number are *more likely*, at least, as a general rule, to understand and follow their own greatest good, than is the minority.

In the second, a minority is much more likely to abuse power for the promotion of its own selfish interests, at the expense of the majority of numbers—the substantial and producing mass of the nation—than the latter is to oppress unjustly the former. The social evil is also, in that case, proportionately greater. This is abundantly proved by the history of all aristocratic interests that have existed, in various degrees and modifications, in the world. A majority cannot subsist upon a minority; while the natural, and in fact uniform, tendency of a minority entrusted with governmental authority is, to surround itself with wealth, splendor, and power, at the expense of the producing mass, creating and perpetuating those artificial social distinctions which violate the natural equality of rights of the human race, and at the same time offend and degrade the true dignity of human nature.

In the third place, there does not naturally exist any such original superiority of a minority class above the great mass of a community, in intelligence and competence for the duties of government—even putting out of view its constant tendency to abuse from selfish motives, and the safer honesty of the mass. The general diffusion of education; the facility of access to every species of knowledge important to the great interests of the community; the freedom of the press, whose very licentiousness cannot materially impair its permanent value, in this country at least, make the pretensions of those self-styled "better classes" to the sole possession of the requisite intelligence for the management of public affairs, too absurd to be entitled to any other treatment than an honest, manly contempt. As far as superior knowledge and talent confer on their possessor a natural charter of privilege to control his associates, and exert an influence on the direction of the general affairs of the community, the free and natural action of that privilege is best secured by a perfectly free democratic system, which will abolish all artificial distinctions, and, preventing the accumulation of any social obstacles to advancement, will permit the free developement of every germ of talent, wherever it may chance to exist, whether on the proud mountain summit, in the humble valley, or by the wayside of common life.

But the question is not yet satisfactorily answered, how the relation between majorities and minorities, in the frequent case of a collision of sentiments and particular interests, is to be so adjusted as to secure a mutual respect of rights, to preserve harmony and good will, and save society from the *malum extremum discordia*, from being as a house divided against itself—and thus to afford free scope to that competition, discussion, and mutual moral influence, which cannot but result, in the end, in the ascendency of the truth, and in "the greatest good of the greatest number." On the one side, it has only been shown that the absolute government of the majority does not always afford a perfect guarantee against the misuse of its numerical power over the weakness of the minority. On the other, it has been shown that this chance of misuse is, as a general rule, far less than in the opposite relation of the ascendency of a minority; and that the evils attendant upon it are infinitely less, in every point of view, in the one case than the other. But this is not yet a complete or satisfactory solution of the problem. Have we but a choice of evils? Is there, then, such a radical deficiency in the moral elements implanted by its Creator in human society, that no other alternative can be devised by which both evils shall be avoided, and a result attained more analogous to the beautiful and glorious harmony of the rest of his creation?

It were scarcely consistent with a true and living faith in the existence and attributes of that Creator, so to believe; and such is not the democratic belief. The reason of the plausibility with which appeal may be made to the experience of so many republics, to sustain this argument against democratic institutions, is, that the true theory of national self-government has been hitherto but imperfectly understood; bad principles have been mixed up with the good; and the republican government has been administered on ideas and in a spirit borrowed from the strong governments of the other forms; and to the corruptions and manifold evils which have never failed, in the course of time, to evolve themselves out of these seeds of destruction, is ascribable the eventual failure of those experiments, and the consequent doubt and discredit which have attached themselves to the democratic principles on which they were, in the outset, mainly based.

It is under the word *government*, that the subtle danger lurks. Understood as a central consolidated power, managing and directing the various general interests of the society, all government is evil, and the parent of evil. A strong and active democratic *government*, in the common sense of the term, is an evil, differing only in degree and mode of operation, and not in nature, from a strong despotism. This difference is certainly vast, yet, inasmuch as these strong governmental powers must be wielded by human agents, even as the powers of the despotism, it is, after all, only a difference in degree; and the tendency to demoralization and tyranny is the same, though the developement of the evil results is much more gradual and slow in the one case than in the other. Hence the demagogue—hence the faction—hence the mob—hence the violence, licentiousness, and instability—hence the ambitious struggles of parties and their leaders for power—hence the abuses of that power by majorities and their leaders—hence the indirect oppressions of the general by partial interests—hence (fearful symptom) the demoralization of the great men of the nation, and of the nation itself, proceeding (unless checked in time by the more healthy and patriotic portion of the mind of the nation rallying itself to reform the principles and sources of the evil) gradually to that point of maturity at which relief from the tumult of moral and physical confusion is to be found only under the shelter of an energetic armed despotism.

The best government is that which governs least. No human depositories can, with safety, be trusted with the power of legislation upon the general interests of society so as to operate directly or indirectly on the industry and property of the community. Such power must be perpetually liable to the most pernicious abuse, from the natural imperfection, both in wisdom of judgment and purity of purpose, of all human legislation, exposed constantly to the pressure of partial interests; interests which, at the same time that they are essentially selfish and tyrannical, are ever vigilant, persevering, and subtle in all the arts of deception and corruption. In fact, the whole history of human society and government may be safely appealed to, in evidence that the abuse of such power a thousand fold more than overbalances its beneficial use. Legislation has been the fruitful parent of nine-tenths of all the evil, moral and physical, by which mankind has been afflicted since the creation of the world, and by which human nature has been self-degraded, fettered, and oppressed. Government should have as little as possible to do with the general business and interests of the people. If it once undertake these functions as its rightful province of action, it is impossible to say to it "thus far shalt thou go, and no farther." It will be impossible to confine it to the public interests of the *commonwealth*. It will be perpetually tampering with private interests, and sending forth seeds of corruption which will result in the demoralization of the society. Its domestic action should be confined to the administration of justice, for the protection of the natural equal rights of the citizen, and the preservation of social order. In all other respects, the VOLUNTARY PRINCIPLE, the principle of FREEDOM, suggested to us by the analogy of the divine government of the Creator, and already recognised by us with perfect success in the great social interest of Religion, affords the true "golden rule" which is alone abundantly competent to work out the best possible general result of order and happiness from that chaos of characters, ideas, motives, and interests—human society. Afford but the single nucleus of a system of administration of justice between man and man, and, under the sure operation of this principle, the floating atoms will distribute and combine themselves, as we see in the beautiful natural process of crystallization, into a far more perfect and harmonious result than if government, with its "fostering hand," undertake to disturb, under the plea of directing, the process. The natural laws which will establish themselves and find their own level are the best laws. The same hand was the Author of the moral, as of the physical world; and we feel clear and strong in the assurance that we cannot err in trusting, in the former, to the same fundamental principles of spontaneous action and self-regulation which produce the beautiful order of the latter.

This is then, we consider, the true theory of government, the one simple result towards which the political science of the world is gradually tending, after all the long

and varied experience by which it will have dearly earned
the great secret—the elixir of political life. This is the fundamental principle of the philosophy of democracy, to
furnish a system of administration of justice, and then
leave all the business and interests of society to themselves, to free competition and association—in a word to
the VOLUNTARY PRINCIPLE—

> Let man be fettered by no duty, save
> His brother's right—like his, inviolable.

It is borrowed from the example of the perfect self-
government of the physical universe, being written in letters of light on every page of the great bible of Nature. It
contains the idea of full and fearless faith in the providence of the Creator. It is essentially involved in Christianity, of which it has been well said that its pervading
spirit of democratic equality among men is its highest fact,
and one of its most radiant internal evidences of the divin-
ity of its origin. It is the essence and the one general result
of the science of political economy. And this principle
alone, we will add, affords a satisfactory and perfect solution of the great problem, otherwise unsolved, of the relative rights of majorities and minorities.

This principle, therefore, constitutes our "point of departure." It has never yet received any other than a very
partial and imperfect application to practice among men,
all human society having been hitherto perpetually chained
down to the ground by myriads of lilliputian fetters of
artificial government and prescription. Nor are we yet prepared for its full adoption in this country. Far, very far
indeed, from it; yet is our gradual tendency toward it clear
and sure. How many generations may yet be required before our theory and practice of government shall be sifted
and analysed down to the lowest point of simplicity consistent with the preservation of some degree of national
organization, no one can presume to prophecy. But that we
are on the path toward that great result, to which mankind
is to be guided down the long vista of future years by the
democratic principle,—walking hand in hand with the sister

spirit of Christianity,—we feel a faith as implicit as that with which we believe in any other great moral truth.

This is all generalization, and therefore, though necessary, probably dull. We have endeavored to state the theory of the Jeffersonian democracy, to which we profess allegiance, in its abstract essence, however unpopular it appears to be, in these latter days, to "theorize." These are the original ideas of American democracy; and we would not give much for that "practical knowledge" which is ignorant of, and affects to disregard, the essential and abstract principles which really constitute the animating soul of what were else lifeless and naught. The application of these ideas to practice, in our political affairs, is obvious and simple. Penetrated with a perfect faith in their eternal truth, we can never hesitate as to the direction to which, in every practical case arising, they must point with the certainty of the magnetized needle; and we have no desire to shrink from the responsibility, at the outset, of a frank avowal of them in the broadest general language.

But having done so, we will not be further misunderstood, and we hope not misrepresented, as to immediate practical views. We deem it scarcely necessary to say that we are opposed to all precipitate radical changes in social institutions. Adopting "Nature as the best guide," we cannot disregard the lesson which she teaches, when she accomplishes her most mighty results of the good and beautiful by the silent and slow operation of great principles, without the convulsions of too rapid action. *Festina lente* is an invaluable precept, if it be not abused. On the other hand, that specious sophistry ought to be no less watchfully guarded against, by which old evils always struggle to perpetuate themselves by appealing to our veneration for "the wisdom of our fathers," to our inert love of present tranquillity, and our natural apprehension of possible danger from the untried and unknown—

> Better to bear the present ills we know,
> Than fly to others that we know not of.

We are not afraid of that much dreaded phrase, "untried experiment," which looms so fearfully before the eyes of some of our most worthy and valued friends. The whole history of the progress hitherto made by humanity, in every respect of social amelioration, records but a series of "*experiments.*" The American revolution was the greatest of "experiments," and one of which it is not easy at this day to appreciate the gigantic boldness. Every step in the onward march of improvement by the human race is an "experiment;" and the present is most emphatically an age of "experiments." The eye of man looks naturally *forward*; and as he is carried onward by the progress of time and truth, he is far more likely to stumble and stray if he turn his face backward, and keep his looks fixed on the thoughts and things of the past. We feel safe under the banner of the democratic principle, which is borne onward by an unseen hand of Providence, to lead our race toward the high destinies of which every human soul contains the God-implanted germ; and of the advent of which—certain, however distant—a dim prophetic presentiment has existed, in one form or another, among all nations in all ages. We are willing to make every reform in our institutions that may be commanded by the test of the democratic principle—to *democratize* them—but only so rapidly as shall appear, to the most cautious wisdom, consistent with a due regard to the existing developement of public opinion and to the permanence of the progress made. Every instance in which the action of *government* can be simplified, and one of the hundred giant arms curtailed, with which it now stretches around its fatal protecting grasp over almost all the various interests of society, to substitute the truly healthful action of the free voluntary principle—every instance in which the operation of the public opinion and will, fairly signified, can be brought to bear more directly upon the action of delegated powers—we would regard as so much gained for the true interest of the society and of mankind at large. In this path we cannot go wrong; it is only necessary to be cautious not to go too fast.

Such is, then, our democracy. It of course places us in

the school of the strictest construction of the constitution; and in that appears to be involved a full committal of opinion on all the great political questions which now agitate the public mind, and to which we deem it unnecessary here to advert in detail. One necessary inference from the views expressed above is, that we consider the preservation of the present ascendency of the democratic party as of great, if not vital, importance to the future destinies of this holy cause. Most of its leading members we know to possess all the qualifications that should entitle men to the confidence and attachment of their country; and the arduous functions of the executive department of the government are administered with an efficiency, and a strictness and purity of principle, which, considering their nature, extent, and complexity, are indeed remarkable. And even without a particular knowledge of the men, the principle alone would still of necessity attach us to that party. The acquisition of the vast influence of the executive department by the present Opposition principles, we could not look upon but as a staggering blow to the cause of democracy, and all the high interests committed with it; from which it would take a long and indefinite period of years to recover—even if the loss of time in national progress would not, in that event, have to be reckoned by generations! We shall therefore, while devoting ourselves to preserve and improve the purity of our democratic institutions, labor to sustain the present democratic administration, by fair appeal to argument, with all the earnestness due to the gravity of the principles and interests involved.

We are admonished by the prescribed limits of this introductory article, to curtail various topics of interest to which we had intended to allude in it. The important subject of national literature cannot, however, be passed without a slight notice.

What is the cause, is sometimes asked among the disciples of the democratic school of political philosophy, of that extensive anti-democratic corruption of sentiment in some portions of our people, especially in the young mind of the nation, which is certainly so just a subject of surprise and alarm? It has lately been a topic of newspaper remark, that nineteen-twentieths of the youth of one of the colleges of Virginia were opposed to the democratic principles. The very exaggeration is good evidence of the lamentable truth; and it is well known that a very large proportion of the young men who annually leave our colleges, carry with them a decided anti-popular bias, to swell the ranks of that large majority of the *"better classes"* already ranged on that side, and to exercise the influence of their cultivated talents in a cause at variance with the genius of our country, the spirit of the age, the best interests and true dignity of humanity, and the highest truths of the science of political morals.

And yet the democratic cause is one which not only ought to engage the whole mind of the American nation, without any serious division of its energies,—to carry forward the noble mission entrusted to her, of going before the nations of the world as the representative of the democratic principle and as the constant living exemplar of its results; but which ought peculiarly to commend itself to the generosity of youth, its ardent aspirations after the good and beautiful, its liberal and unselfish freedom from narrow prejudices of interest.

For Democracy is the cause of Humanity. It has faith in human nature. It believes in its essential equality and fundamental goodness. It respects, with a solemn reverence to which the proudest artificial institutions and distinctions of society have no claim, the human soul. It is the cause of philanthropy. Its object is to emancipate the mind of the mass of men from the degrading and disheartening fetters of social distinctions and advantages; to bid it walk abroad through the free creation "in its own majesty;" to war against all fraud, oppression, and violence; by striking at their root, to reform all the infinitely varied human misery which has grown out of the old and false ideas by which the world has been so long misgoverned; to dismiss the hireling soldier; to spike the cannon, and bury the bayonet; to burn the gibbet, and open the debtor's dungeon; to substitute harmony and mutual respect for the jealousies and discord now subsisting between different classes of society, as the consequence of their artificial classification. It is the cause of Christianity, to which a slight allusion has been already made, to be more fully developed hereafter. And that portion of the peculiar friends and ministers of religion who now, we regret to say, cast the weight of their social influence against the cause of democracy, under the false prejudice of an affinity between it and infidelity, (no longer, in this century, the case, and which, in the last, was but a consequence of the overgrown abuses of religion found, by the reforming spirit that then awakened in Europe, in league with despotism,) understand but little either its true spirit, or that of their own faith. It is, moreover, a cheerful creed, a creed of high hope and universal love, noble and ennobling; while all others, which imply a distrust of mankind, and of the natural moral principles infused into it by its Creator, for its own self-developement and self-regulation, are as gloomy and selfish, in the tone of moral sentiment which pervades them, as they are degrading in their practical tendency, and absurd in theory, when examined by the light of original principles.

Then whence this remarkable phenomenon, of the young mind of our country so deeply tainted with antidemocratic sentiment—a state of things lamentable in itself, and portentous of incalculable future evil?

Various partial causes may be enumerated in explanation of it; among which we may refer to the following: In the first place, the possession of the executive power (as it exists in our system) is, in one point of view, a great disadvantage to the principles of that ascendant party. The Administration occupies a position of defence; the Opposition, of attack. The former is by far the more arduous task. The lines of fortification to be maintained against the never relaxing onsets from every direction, are so extensive and exposed, that a perpetual vigilance and devotion to duty barely suffice to keep the enemy at bay. The attacking cause, ardent, restless, ingenious, is far more attractive to the imagination of youth than that of the defence. It is, moreover, difficult, if not impossible, to preserve a perfect purity from abuse and corruption throughout all the countless ramifications of the action of such an executive system as ours, however stern may be the integrity, and high the patriotism, of the presiding spirit which, from its head, animates the whole. Local abuses in the management of party affairs are the necessary consequence of the long possession of the ascendancy. The vast official patronage of the executive department is a weight and clog under which it is not easy to bear up. This must lay any administration open to perpetual assault at great disadvantage; and especially if the great party campaign present at any time such a phase as may render it necessary to put forth, to the full limits of constitutional right, the energies of the executive department, to resist the accumulated pressure of attack, bearing along in its train evils, to avert which almost any means would seem justifiable. This we have seen, in a remarkable manner, the case during the two terms of the late administration. Our natural jealousy of power affords a string to which, when played upon by the bold and skilful hands that are never found wanting, the very spirit of democratic freedom never fails to respond; and many are confused by sophistry and clamor, and carried away by the power of eloquence—divine, even though misused—to array themselves against their own best and most honest friends, under leaders, in truth, the worst enemies of the American principles for which they believe themselves contending.

In the second place, we may refer to a cause which we look upon with deep pain, as one of the worst fruits of the evil principles to which allusion has already been made above as existing in our system—the demoralization of many of the great men of the nation. How many of these master-spirits of their day, to whom their country had long been accustomed to look with generous affection as her hope and pride, have we not seen seduced from the path of their early promise by the intrigues of party and the allurements of ambition, in the pursuit of that too dazzling prize, and too corrupting both in the prospect and the possession—the presidential office! To how many a one could we point, within the history of the last quarter of a century, to whom we might well apply Milton's famous description of Lucifer, the Son of the Morning:

> He above the rest,
> In shape and gesture proudly eminent,
> Stood like a tower; his form had not yet lost
> All her original brightness, nor appeared
> Less than archangel ruined, and the excess
> Of glory obscured; as when the sun new risen
> Looks through the horizontal misty air,
> Shorn of his beams, or from behind the moon,
> In dim eclipse, disastrous twilight sheds
> On half the nations, and with fear of change
> Perplexes monarchs. Darkened so, yet shone
> Above them all the archangel; but his face
> Deep scars of thunder had entrench'd, and care
> Sat on his faded cheek, but under brows
> Of dauntless courage and considerate pride,
> Waiting revenge, &c.

The influence of such men, (especially on the minds of the young,) commanding by their intellectual power, misleading by their eloquence, and fascinating by the natural sympathy which attaches itself to greatness still proud in its "fallen estate," produces certainly a powerful effect in our party contests.

We might also refer to the fact, that the anti-democratic cause possesses at least two-thirds of the press of the country, and that portion of it which is best supported by talent and the resources of capital, under the commercial patronage of our cities. To the strong influence that cities,—where wealth accumulates, where luxury gradually unfolds its corrupting tendencies, where aristocratic habits and social classifications form and strengthen themselves, where the congregation of men stimulates and exaggerates all ideas,—to the influence that cities exert upon the country, no inconsiderable effect is to be ascribed. From the influence of the mercantile classes, too, (extensively anti-democratic) on the young men of the professions, especially that of the law, creating an insensible bias, from the dependence of the latter mainly on the patronage of the former, these young men becoming again each the centre of a small sphere of social influence; from that of the religious ministry, silently and insensibly exerted, from the false prejudice slightly touched upon above; from these and some other minor influences, on which we cannot here pause, a vast and active power on public opinion is perpetually in operation. And it is only astonishing that the democratic party should be able to bear up against them all so successfully as we in fact witness. This is to be ascribed (under that Providence whose unseen hand we recognise in all human affairs) only to the sterling honesty and good sense of the great industrious mass of our people, its instinctive perception of, and yearning after, the democratic truth, and the unwavering generosity of its support of those public servants whom it has once tried well and long, and with whom it has once acknowledged the genuine sympathy of common sentiments and a common cause. Yet still the democratic principle can do little more than hold its own. The moral energies of the national mind are, to a great extent, paralyzed by division; and instead of bearing forward the ark of democratic truth, entrusted to us as a chosen people, towards the glorious destiny of its future, we must fain be content, if we can but stem with it the perpetual tide of attack which would bear it backward towards the ideas and habits of past dark ages.

But a more potent influence than any yet noticed, is that of our national literature. Or rather we have no national literature. We depend almost wholly on Europe, and particularly England, to think and write for us, or at least to furnish materials and models after which we shall mould our own humble attempts. We have a considerable number of writers; but not in that consists a national literature. The vital principle of an American national literature must be democracy. Our mind is enslaved to the past and present literature of England. Rich and glorious as is that vast collection of intellectual treasure, it would have been far better for us had we been separated from it by the ocean of a difference of language, as we are from the country itself by our sublime Atlantic. Our mind would then have been compelled to think for itself and to express itself, and its animating spirit would have been our democracy. As it now is, we are cowed by the mind of England. We follow feebly and afar in the splendid track of a literature moulded on the whole (notwithstanding a number of noble exceptions) by the ideas and feelings of an utterly anti-democratic social system. We give back but a dim reflection—a faint echo of the expression of the English mind. No one will misunderstand us as disparaging the literature of our mother language—far from it. We appreciate it with a profound veneration and gratitude, and would use it, without abusing it by utterly submitting our own minds to it; but we look upon it, as we do upon the political system of the country, as a something magnificent, venerable, splendid, and powerful, and containing a considerable infusion of the true principle; yet the one no more suitable to be adopted as our own, or as a model for slavish imitation, than the other. In the spirit of her literature we can never hope to rival England. She is immeasurably in advance of us, and is rich with ever active energies, and resources of literary habits and capital (so to speak) which mock our humble attempts at imitation. But we should not follow in her wake; a radiant path invites us forward in another direction. We have a principle —an informing soul—of our own, our democracy, though we allow it to languish uncultivated; this must be the animating spirit of our literature, if, indeed, we would have a national American literature. There is an immense field open to us, if we would but enter it boldly and cultivate it as our own. All history has to be re-written; political science and the whole scope of all moral truth have to be considered and illustrated in the light of the democratic principle. All old subjects of thought and all new questions arising, connected more or less directly with human existence, have to be taken up again and re-examined in this point of view. We *ought* to exert a powerful moral influence on Europe, and yet we are entirely unfelt; and as it is only by its literature that one nation can utter itself and make itself known to the rest of the world, we are really entirely unknown. In the present general fermentation of popular ideas in Europe, turning the public thoughts naturally to the great democracy across the Atlantic, the voice of America might be made to produce a powerful and beneficial effect on the developement of truth; but as it is, American writings are never translated, because they almost always prove to be a diluted and tardy second edition of English thought.

The anti-democratic character of our literature, then, is a main cause of the evil of which we complain; and this is both a mutual cause and effect, constantly acting and re-acting. Our "better educated classes" drink in an anti-democratic habit of feeling and thinking from the copious, and it must be confessed delicious, fountain of the literature of England; they give the same spirit to our own, in which we have little or nothing that is truly democratic and American. Hence this tone of sentiment of our literary institutions and of our learned professions, poisoning at the spring the young mind of our people.

If the "United States Magazine and Democratic Review" shall be able, by the influence of example and *the most liberal* encouragement, to contribute in any degree towards the remedy of this evil, (as of the other evils in our institutions which may need reform,) by vindicating the true glory and greatness of the democratic principle, by infusing it into our literature, and by rallying the mind of the nation from the state of torpor and even of demoralization in which so large a proportion of it is sunk, one of the main objects of its establishment will have been achieved.

38

The Laboring Classes*

ORESTES A. BROWNSON

Orestes A. Brownson is a remarkable example of the restless searching after new truths and new loyalties which beset so many reformers in the uncertainties of the Jacksonian age. He had been successively a Presbyterian, a Universalist, and an agnostic before reaching a temporary accommodation with Unitarianism in the later years of the 1830s. Earlier in the decade, he had worked briefly with Frances Wright in the New York Workingmen's Party but, by 1836, he was established in Chelsea, on the outskirts of Boston, where he founded his Society for Christian Union and Progress, an organization devoted to promoting the elevation of the laboring class by moral exhortations.

In the political controversies of the Van Buren administration, Brownson gave more and more support to the policies of the Democratic party. George Bancroft gave him encouragement and financial aid in starting the *Boston Quarterly Review,* and the new review quickly became an organ for Democratic intellectuals in Boston. In his editorials, Brownson increasingly favored the principles of the radical, Locofoco, wing of the Democratic party.

The selection that follows appeared in the *Boston Quarterly Review* in July 1840 and represents one of the most radical utterances by a Democratic intellectual in the Jacksonian generation. Brownson sets forth a startling vision of class warfare, drawing a sharp dividing line between the propertyless workers and the middle class. When we remember that Jacksonian leaders, again

* From the *Boston Quarterly Review,* III (July 1840), 366–95, abridged.

and again, had defended the honest capitalist as well as the honest farmer and the honest mechanic, we are entitled to ask whether Brownson's conception of a class struggle between labor and capital ever had any chance of being incorporated in the Jacksonian ideology. Indeed, we can also ask whether Brownson's proposed remedy for the oppression of the laboring classes—the abolition of all laws of inheritance—really constitutes a war of labor against capital. Is it not really a proposal to create a system of social competition for self-made men in which there are no initial social advantages whatsoever?

. . . No one can observe the signs of the times with much care, without perceiving that a crisis as to the relation of wealth and labor is approaching. It is useless to shut our eyes to the fact, and like the ostrich fancy ourselves secure because we have so concealed our heads that we see not the danger. We or our children will have to meet this crisis. The old war between the King and the Barons is well nigh ended, and so is that between the Barons and the Merchants and Manufacturers,—landed capital and commercial capital. The business man has become the peer of my Lord. And now commences the new struggle between the operative and his employer, between wealth and labor. Every day does this struggle extend further and wax stronger and fiercer; what or when the end will be God only knows.

In this coming contest there is a deeper question at issue than is commonly imagined; a question which is but remotely touched in your controversies about United States Banks and Sub Treasuries, chartered Banking and free Banking, free trade and corporations, although these controversies may be paving the way for it to come up. We have discovered no presentiment of it in any king's or queen's speech, nor in any president's message. It is embraced in no popular political creed of the day, whether christened Whig or Tory, *Juste-milieu* or Democratic. No popular senator, or deputy, or peer seems to have any glimpse of it; but it is working in the hearts of the million, is struggling to shape itself, and one day it will be uttered, and in thunder tones. Well will it be for him, who, on that day, shall be found ready to answer it.

What we would ask is, throughout the Christian world, the actual condition of the laboring classes, viewed simply and exclusively in their capacity of laborers? They constitute at least a moiety of the human race. We exclude the nobility, we exclude also the middle class, and include only actual laborers, who are laborers and not proprietors, owners of none of the funds of production, neither houses, shops, nor lands, nor implements of labor, being therefore solely dependent on their hands. We have no means of ascertaining their precise proportion to the whole number of the race; but we think we may estimate them at one half. In any contest they will be as two to one, because the large class of proprietors who are not employers, but laborers on their own lands or in their own shops will make common cause with them.

Now we will not so belie our acquaintance with political economy, as to allege that these alone perform all that is necessary to the production of wealth. We are not ignorant of the fact, that the merchant, who is literally the common carrier and exchange dealer, performs a useful service, and is therefore entitled to a portion of the proceeds of labor. But make all necessary deductions on his account, and then ask what portion of the remainder is retained, either in kind or in its equivalent, in the hands of the original producer, the workingman? All over the world this fact stares us in the face, the workingman is poor and depressed, while a large portion of the non-workingmen, in the sense we now use the term, are wealthy. It may be laid down as a general rule, with but few exceptions, that men are rewarded in an inverse ratio to the amount of actual service they perform. Under every government on earth the largest salaries are annexed to those offices, which demand of their incumbents the least amount of actual labor either mental or manual. And this is in perfect harmony with the whole system of repartition of the fruits of industry, which obtains in every department of society. Now here is the system which prevails, and here is its result. The whole class of simple laborers are poor, and in general unable to procure anything beyond the bare necessaries of life.

In regard to labor two systems obtain; one that of slave labor, the other that of free labor. Of the two, the first is, in our judgment, except so far as the feelings are concerned, decidedly the least oppressive. If the slave has never been a free man, we think, as a general rule, his sufferings are less than those of the free laborer at wages. As to actual freedom one has just about as much as the other. The laborer at wages has all the disadvantages of freedom and none of its blessings, while the slave, if denied the blessings, is freed from the disadvantages. We are no advocates of slavery, we are as heartily opposed to it as any modern abolitionist can be; but we say frankly that, if there must always be a laboring population distinct from proprietors and employers, we regard the slave system as decidedly preferable to the system at wages. It is no pleasant thing to go days without food, to lie idle for weeks, seeking work and finding none, to rise in the morning with a wife and children you love, and know not where to procure them a breakfast, and to see constantly before you no brighter prospect than the almshouse. Yet these are no unfrequent incidents in the lives of our laboring population. Even in seasons of general prosperity, when there was only the ordinary cry of "hard times," we have seen hundreds of people in a not very populous village, in a wealthy portion of our common country, suffering for the want of the necessaries of life, willing to work, and yet finding no work to do. Many and many is the application of a poor man for work, merely for his food, we have seen rejected. These things are little thought of, for the applicants are poor; they fill no conspicuous place in society, and they have no biographers. But their wrongs are chronicled in heaven. It is said there is no want in this country. There may be less than in some other countries. But death by actual starvation in this country is, we apprehend,

no uncommon occurrence. The sufferings of a quiet, un-
assuming but useful class of females in our cities, in general sempstresses, too proud to beg or to apply to the almshouse, are not easily told. They are industrious; they do all
that they can find to do; but yet the little there is for
them to do, and the miserable pittance they receive for
it, is hardly sufficient to keep soul and body together. And
yet there is a man who employs them to make shirts,
trousers, &c., and grows rich on their labors. He is one of
our respectable citizens, perhaps is praised in the newspapers for his liberal donations to some charitable institution. He passes among us as a pattern of morality, and is
honored as a worthy Christian. And why should he not be,
since our *Christian* community is made up of such as he,
and since our clergy would not dare question his piety,
lest they should incur the reproach of infidelity, and lose
their standing, and their salaries? Nay, since our clergy
are raised up, educated, fashioned, and sustained by such
as he? Not a few of our churches rest on Mammon for
their foundation. The basement is a trader's shop.

We pass through our manufacturing villages, most of
them appear neat and flourishing. The operatives are well
dressed, and we are told, well paid. They are said to be
healthy, contented, and happy. This is the fair side of the
picture; the side exhibited to distinguished visitors. There
is a dark side, moral as well as physical. Of the common
operatives, few, if any, by their wages, acquire a competence. A few of what Carlyle terms not inaptly the
body-servants are well paid, and now and then an agent or
an overseer rides in his coach. But the great mass wear
out their health, spirits, and morals, without becoming
one whit better off than when they commenced labor. The
bills of mortality in these factory villages are not striking,
we admit, for the poor girls when they can toil no longer
go home to die. The average life, working life we mean,
of the girls that come to Lowell, for instance, from Maine,
New Hampshire, and Vermont, we have been assured, is
only about three years. What becomes of them then? Few
of them ever marry; fewer still ever return to their native

places with reputations unimpaired. "She has worked in a Factory," is almost enough to damn to infamy the most worthy and virtuous girl. We know no sadder sight on earth than one of our factory villages presents, when the bell at break of day, or at the hour of breakfast, or dinner, calls out its hundreds or thousands of operatives. We stand and look at these hard working men and women hurrying in all directions, and ask ourselves, where go the proceeds of their labors? The man who employs them, and for whom they are toiling as so many slaves, is one of our city nabobs, revelling in luxury; or he is a member of our legislature, enacting laws to put money in his own pocket; or he is a member of Congress, contending for a high Tariff to tax the poor for the benefit of the rich; or in these times he is shedding crocodile tears over the deplorable condition of the poor laborer, while he docks his wages twenty-five per cent.; building miniature log cabins, shouting Harrison and "hard cider." And this man too would fain pass for a Christian and a republican. He shouts for liberty, stickles for equality, and is horrified at a Southern planter who keeps slaves.

One thing is certain; that of the amount actually produced by the operative, he retains a less proportion than it costs the master to feed, clothe, and lodge his slave. Wages is a cunning device of the devil, for the benefit of tender consciences, who would retain all the advantages of the slave system, without the expense, trouble, and odium of being slave-holders.

Messrs. Thome and Kimball, in their account of emancipation in the West Indies, establish the fact that the employer may have the same amount of labor done, twenty-five per cent. cheaper than the master. What does this fact prove, if not that wages is a more successful method of taxing labor than slavery? We really believe our Northern system of labor is more oppressive, and even more mischievous to morals, than the Southern. We, however, war against both. We have no toleration for either system. We would see the slave a man, but a free man, not a mere operative at wages. This he would not be were he now emancipated. Could the abolitionists effect all they propose, they would do the slave no service. Should emancipation work as well as they say, still it would do the slave no good. He would be a slave still, although with the title and cares of a freeman. If then we had no constitutional objections to abolitionism, we could not, for the reason here implied, be abolitionists.

The slave system, however, in name and form, is gradually disappearing from Christendom. It will not subsist much longer. But its place is taken by the system of labor at wages, and this system, we hold, is no improvement upon the one it supplants. Nevertheless the system of wages will triumph. It is the system which in name sounds honester than slavery, and in substance is more profitable to the master. It yields the wages of iniquity, without its opprobrium. It will therefore supplant slavery, and be sustained—for a time.

Now, what is the prospect of those who fall under the operation of this system? We ask, is there a reasonable chance that any considerable portion of the present generation of laborers, shall ever become owners of a sufficient portion of the funds of production, to be able to sustain themselves by laboring on their own capital, that is, as independent laborers? We need not ask this question, for everybody knows there is not. Well, is the condition of a laborer at wages the best that the great mass of the working people ought to be able to aspire to? Is it a condition,—nay can it be made a condition,—with which a man should be satisfied; in which he should be contented to live and die?

In our own country this condition has existed under its most favorable aspects, and has been made as good as it can be. It has reached all the excellence of which it is susceptible. It is now not improving but growing worse. The actual condition of the workingman to-day, viewed in all its bearings, is not so good as it was fifty years ago. If we have not been altogether misinformed, fifty years ago, health and industrious habits, constituted no mean stock in trade, and with them almost any man might aspire to competence and independence. But it is so no longer. The wilderness has receded, and already the new lands are beyond the reach of the mere laborer, and the employer has him at his mercy. If the present relation subsist, we see nothing better for him in reserve than what he now possesses, but something altogether worse.

We are not ignorant of the fact that men born poor become wealthy, and that men born to wealth become poor; but this fact does not necessarily diminish the numbers of the poor, nor augment the numbers of the rich. The relative numbers of the two classes remain, or may remain, the same. But be this as it may; one fact is certain, no man born poor has ever, by his wages, as a simple operative, risen to the class of the wealthy. Rich he may have become, but it has not been by his own manual labor. He has in some way contrived to tax for his benefit the labor of others. He may have accumulated a few dollars which he has placed at usury, or invested in trade; or he may, as a master workman, obtain a premium on his journeymen; or he may have from a clerk passed to a partner, or from a workman to an overseer. The simple market wages for ordinary labor, has never been adequate to raise him from poverty to wealth. This fact is decisive of the whole controversy, and proves that the system of wages must be supplanted by some other system, or else one half of the human race must forever be the virtual slaves of the other.

Now the great work for this age and the coming, is to raise up the laborer, and to realize in our own social arrangements and in the actual condition of all men, that equality between man and man, which God has established between the rights of one and those of another. In other words, our business is to emancipate the proletaries, as the past has emancipated the slaves. This is our work. There must be no class of our fellow men doomed to toil through life as mere workmen at wages. If wages are tolerated it must be, in the case of the individual operative, only under such conditions that by the time he is of a proper age to settle in life, he shall have accumulated

enough to be an independent laborer on his own capital,
—on his own farm or in his own shop. Here is our work.
How is to to be done?

Reformers in general answer this question, or what they
deem its equivalent, in a manner which we cannot but
regard as very unsatisfactory. They would have all men
wise, good, and happy; but in order to make them so, they
tell us that we want not external changes, but internal;
and therefore instead of declaiming against society and
seeking to disturb existing social arrangements, we should
confine ourselves to the individual reason and conscience;
seek merely to lead the individual to repentance, and to
reformation of life; make the individual a practical, a truly
religious man, and all evils will either disappear, or be
sanctified to the spiritual growth of the soul.

This is doubtless a capital theory, and has the advantage that kings, hierarchies, nobilities,—in a word, all who
fatten on the toil and blood of their fellows, will feel no
difficulty in supporting it. Nicholas of Russia, the Grand
Turk, his Holiness the Pope, will hold us their especial
friends for advocating a theory, which secures to them the
odor of sanctity even while they are sustaining by their
anathemas or their armed legions, a system of things of
which the great mass are and must be the victims. If you
will only allow me to keep thousands toiling for my pleasure or my profit, I will even aid you in your pious efforts
to convert their souls. I am not cruel; I do not wish either
to cause, or to see suffering; I am therefore disposed to
encourage your labors for the souls of the workingman,
providing you will secure to me the products of his bodily
toil. So far as the salvation of his soul will not interfere
with my income, I hold it worthy of being sought; and if
a few thousand dollars will aid you, Mr. Priest, in recon-
ciling him to God, and making fair weather for him hereafter, they are at your service. I shall not want him to
work for me in the world to come, and I can indemnify
myself for what your salary costs me, by paying him less
wages. A capital theory this, which one may advocate without incurring the reproach of a disorganizer, a jacobin, a

leveller, and without losing the friendship of the rankest aristocrat in the land.

This theory, however, is exposed to one slight objection, that of being condemned by something like six thousand years' experience. For six thousand years its beauty has been extolled, its praises sung, and its blessings sought, under every advantage which learning, fashion, wealth, and power can secure; and yet under its practical operations, we are assured, that mankind, though totally depraved at first, have been growing worse and worse ever since. . . .

Now the evils of which we have complained are of a social nature. That is, they have their root in the constitution of society as it is, and they have attained to their present growth by means of social influences, the action of government, of laws, and of systems and institutions upheld by society, and of which individuals are the slaves. This being the case, it is evident that they are to be removed only by the action of society, that is, by government, for the action of society is government.

But what shall government do? Its first doing must be an *un*doing. There has been thus far quite too much government, as well as government of the wrong kind. The first act of government we want, is a still further limitation of itself. It must begin by circumscribing within narrower limits its powers. And then it must proceed to repeal all laws which bear against the laboring classes, and then to enact such laws as are necessary to enable them to maintain their equality. We have no faith in those systems of elevating the working classes, which propose to elevate them without calling in the aid of the government. We must have government, and legislation expressly directed to this end.

But again what legislation do we want so far as this country is concerned? We want first the legislation which shall free the government, whether State or Federal, from the control of the Banks. The Banks represent the interest of the employer, and therefore of necessity interests adverse to those of the employed; that is, they represent the interests of the business community in opposition to the laboring community. So long as the government remains under the control of the Banks, so long it must be in the hands of the natural enemies of the laboring classes, and may be made, nay, will be made, an instrument of depressing them yet lower. It is obvious then that, if our object be the elevation of the laboring classes, we must destroy the power of the Banks over the government, and place the government in the hands of the laboring classes themselves, or in the hands of those, if such there be, who have an identity of interest with them. But this cannot be done so long as the Banks exist. Such is the subtle influence of credit, and such the power of capital, that a banking system like ours, if sustained, necessarily and inevitably becomes the real and efficient government of the country. We have been struggling for ten years in this country against the power of the banks, struggling to free merely the Federal government from their grasp, but with humiliating success. At this moment, the contest is almost doubtful,—not indeed in our mind, but in the minds of a no small portion of our countrymen. The partizans of the Banks count on certain victory. The Banks discount freely to build "log cabins," to purchase "hard cider," and to defray the expense of manufacturing enthusiasm for a cause which is at war with the interests of the people. That they will succeed, we do not for one moment believe; but that they could maintain the struggle so long, and be as strong as they now are, at the end of ten years' constant hostility, proves but all too well the power of the Banks, and their fatal influence on the political action of the community. The present character, standing, and resources of the Bank party, prove to a demonstration that the Banks must be destroyed, or the laborer not elevated. Uncompromising hostility to the whole banking system should therefore be the motto of every working man, and of every friend of Humanity. The system must be destroyed. On this point there must be no misgiving, no subterfuge, no palliation. The system is at war with the rights and interest of labor, and it must go.

Every friend of the system must be marked as an enemy to his race, to his country, and especially to the laborer. No matter who he is, in what party he is found, or what name he bears, he is, in our judgment, no true democrat, as he can be no true Christian.

Following the distruction of the Banks, must come that of all monopolies, of all PRIVILEGE. There are many of these. We cannot specify them all; we therefore select only one, the greatest of them all, the privilege which some have of being born rich while others are born poor. It will be seen at once that we allude to the hereditary descent of property, an anomaly in our American system, which must be removed, or the system itself will be destroyed. We cannot now go into a discussion of this subject, but we promise to resume it at our earliest opportunity. We only say now, that as we have abolished hereditary monarchy and hereditary nobility, we must complete the work by abolishing hereditary property. A man shall have all he honestly acquires, so long as he himself belongs to the world in which he acquires it. But his power over his property must cease with his life, and his property must then become the property of the state, to be disposed of by some equitable law for the use of the generation which takes his place. Here is the principle without any of its details, and this is the grand legislative measure to which we look forward. We see no means of elevating the laboring classes which can be effectual without this. And is this a measure to be easily carried? Not at all. It will cost infinitely more than it cost to abolish either hereditary monarchy or hereditary nobility. It is a great measure, and a startling. The rich, the business community, will never voluntarily consent to it, and we think we know too much of human nature to believe that it will ever be effected peaceably. It will be effected only by the strong arm of physical force. It will come, if it ever come at all, only at the conclusion of war, the like of which the world as yet has never witnessed, and from which, however inevitable it may seem to the eye of philosophy, the heart of Humanity recoils with horror.

We are not ready for this measure yet. There is much previous work to be done, and we should be the last to bring it before the legislature. The time, however, has come for its free and full discussion. It must be canvassed in the public mind, and society prepared for acting on it. No doubt they who broach it, and especially they who support it, will experience a due share of contumely and abuse. They will be regarded by the part of the community they oppose, or may be thought to oppose, as "graceless varlets," against whom every man of substance should set his face. But this is not, after all, a thing to disturb a wise man, nor to deter a true man from telling his whole thought. He who is worthy of the name of man, speaks what he honestly believes the interests of his race demand, and seldom disquiets himself about what may be the consequences to himself. Men have, for what they believed the cause of God or man, endured the dungeon, the scaffold, the stake, the cross, and they can do it again, if need be. This subject must be freely, boldly, and fully discussed, whatever may be the fate of those who discuss it.

39

"The whigs of 1840 stand . . . where the whigs of the Revolution were . . ."*

HENRY CLAY

Henry Clay is one of the more fascinating figures in American politics of the first half of the nineteenth century. He began his career as a Jeffersonian-Republican and became one of the leading war hawks of the country at the time of the War of 1812. After the war, Clay became the pre-eminent leader of the National Republicans in developing the policies of economic nationalism. He extended Alexander Hamilton's original case for tariff protection by expanding the "home market" argument in order to persuade American farmers that industrialism would create an assured and profitable domestic market for anything that they could raise. By his advocacy of the "American system" of tariffs and internal improvements, Clay became one of the chief prophets of the transportation revolution which developed apace during his long political career.

Henry Clay was a man of great popular gifts. He was a splendid orator who possessed a remarkable ability to stir a crowd with visions of a glorious future of material growth and comfort. Yet the fascination of his personality and the fire of his rhetoric could not prevail against Andrew Jackson. Clay was Jackson's opponent in 1832 and went down in a crushing defeat which weakened and demoralized the National Republicans. Nevertheless, Clay continued to fight Jacksonian policies in the Senate and became one of the chief architects of the new coalition of National Republicans, Anti-

* From *The Works of Henry Clay*, Calvin Colton, ed. (New York, 1904), VIII, 197–213, abridged.

masons, and disgruntled Democrats which formed the
Whig party in 1834.

Although Whiggery attracted men who were charmed
by the vision of national possibilities promised by the
"American system," Clay himself did not adequately
symbolize the aspirations of many of the newer and
younger men in the party. Hence Clay was passed over
by the Whig Convention in 1840, and the nomination
for the presidency was given to a military hero, William Henry Harrison, at the insistence of men like
Thurlow Weed who had learned the techniques of mass
politics in New York. Clay, nevertheless, took an active
part in the campaign of 1840 and, with men like Daniel
Webster and Horace Greeley, contributed the solid
statements of Whig principles that accompanied the
demagoguery of the "Log Cabin and Hard Cider" campaign.

The selection below is from a speech that Clay made
near his birthplace in Hanover County, Virginia, during the campaign of 1840. We can certainly take this
address as one of the best summations of Whig principles and policies. Indeed, we can assume that the principles presented in this speech represent the basic Whig
consensus as it had been formed in the political battles
of the 1830s. Central to this consensus was the charge
of "executive usurpation" against the Jacksonians, and
an elaborated Whig theory of the presidency which
urges the narrowest limitations for executive power that
can be found anywhere in public discourse in the nineteenth century. Thus, the historian finds the Whigs
caught in an ideological trap of their own making. The
Whig economic program required vigorous and positive
action by the government—but did not the Whig theory
of limited executive power weaken the possibilities of
positive action by the government? In view of the growing intensity of sectional and group politics, could they
hope to get anything more from the legislative branch
than legislative stalemate? Were not the Whigs caught
in an ideological distortion created by their common
hatred of "King Andrew" Jackson?

See page 360 for description of Plates 17–24.

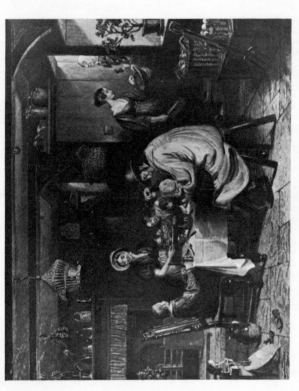

[17] *Fruits of Industry.* Painted by F. Prentis and engraved by A. L. Dick. Courtesy of Forbes Library, Northampton, Massachusetts.

[18] *Fruits of Idleness*. Painted by F. Prentis and engraved by A. L. Dick. Courtesy of Forbes Library, Northampton, Massachusetts.

[19] *Pat Lyon at the Forge*. Painting by John Neagle. Courtesy of the Boston Athenaeum. On loan to the Museum of Fine Arts, Boston.

[20] *Power Loom Weaving* Engraver unknown.

[21] *The Exchange and Girard's Bank, Philadelphia.* Engraved by W. H. Bartlett.

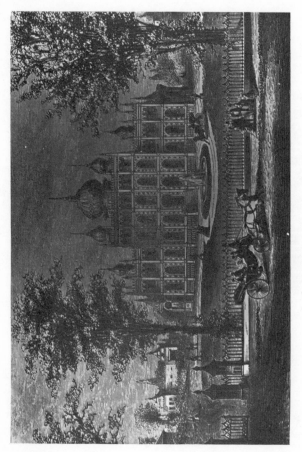

[22] *Iranistan*. Engraver unknown.

[23] *The United States Senate*, A.D. 1850. Engraver unknown. Courtesy of the Mead Art Collection, Amherst College.

[24] *Stump Speaking.* Hand-colored lithograph by Gautier after a painting by George Caleb Bingham. Courtesy of the Mead Art Collection, Amherst College.

What are the positions of the two great parties of the present day? Modern democracy has reduced the federal theory of a strong and energetic executive to practical operation. It has turned from the people, the natural ally of genuine democracy, to the executive, and, instead of vigilance, jealousy, and distrust, has given to that department all its confidence, and made to it a virtual surrender of all the powers of government. The recognized maxim of royal infallibility is transplanted from the British monarchy into modern American democracy, and the president can do no wrong! This new school adopts, modifies, changes, renounces, renews opinions at the pleasure of the executive. Is the bank of the United States a useful and valuable institution? Yes, unanimously pronounces the democratic Legislature of Pennsylvania. The president vetoes it as a pernicious and dangerous establishment. The democratic majority in the same Legislature pronounce it to be pernicious and dangerous. The democratic majority of the House of Representatives of the United States, declare the deposits of the public money in the bank of the United States to be safe. The president says they are unsafe, and removes them. The democracy say they are unsafe, and approve the removal. The president says that a scheme of a sub-treasury is revolutionary and disorganizing. The democracy say it is revolutionary and disorganizing. The president says it is wise and salutary. The democracy say it is wise and salutary.

The whigs of 1840 stand where the republicans of 1798 stood, and where the whigs of the Revolution were, battling for liberty, for the people, for free institutions, against power, against corruption, against executive encroachments, against monarchy.

We are reproached with struggling for offices and their emoluments. If we acted on the avowed and acknowledged principle of our opponents, "that the spoils belong to the victors," we should indeed be unworthy of the support of the people. No! fellow-citizens; higher, nobler, more patriotic motives actuate the whig party. Their object is the restoration of the Constitution, the preservation of liberty, and rescue of the country. If they were governed by the sordid and selfish motives acted upon by their opponents, and unjustly imputed to them, to acquire office and emolument, they have only to change their names, and enter the presidential palace. The gate is always wide open, and the path is no narrow one which leads through it. The last comer, too, often fares best.

On a re-survey of the few past years we behold enough to sicken and sadden the hearts of true patriots. Executive encroachment has quickly followed upon executive encroachment; persons honored by public confidence, and from whom nothing but grateful and parental measures should have flowed, have inflicted stunning blow after blow, in such rapid succession, that, before the people could recover from the reeling effects of one, another has fallen heavily upon them. Had either of various instances of executive misrule stood out separate and alone, so that its enormity might have been seen and dwelt upon with composure, the condemnation of the executive would have long since been pronounced; but it has hitherto found safety and impunity in the bewildering effects of the multitude of its misdeeds. The nation has been in the condition of a man who, having gone to bed after his barn has been consumed by fire, is aroused in the morning to witness his dwelling-house wrapped in flames. So bold and presumptuous had the executive become, that, penetrating in its influence the hall of a co-ordinate branch of the government, by means of a submissive or instructed majority of the Senate, it has caused a record of the country to be effaced and expunged, the inviolability of which was guarantied by a solemn injunction of the Constitution! And that memorable and scandalous scene was enacted only because the offensive record contained an expression of disapprobation of an executive proceeding.

If this state of things were to remain—if the progress of executive usurpation were to continue unchecked, hopeless despair would seize the public mind, or the people would be goaded to acts of open and violent resistance. But, thank God, the power of the president, fearful and rapid as its strides have been, is not yet too great for the power of the elective franchise; and a bright and glorious prospect, in the election of William Henry Harrison, has opened upon the country. The necessity of a change of rulers has deeply penetrated the hearts of the people; and we everywhere behold cheering manifestations of that happy event. The fact of his election alone, without reference to the measures of his administration, will powerfully contribute to the security and happiness of the people. It will bring assurance of the cessation of that long series of disastrous experiments which have so greatly afflicted the people. Confidence will immediately revive, credit be restored, active business will return, prices of products will rise; and the people will feel and know that, instead of their servants being occupied in devising measures for their ruin and destruction, they will be assiduously employed in promoting their welfare and prosperity.

But grave and serious measures will, unquestionably, early and anxiously command the earnest attention of the new administration. I have no authority to announce, and do not pretend to announce, the purposes of the new president. I have no knowledge of them, other than that which is accessible to every citizen. In what I shall say as to the course of a new administration, therefore, I mean to express my own sentiments, to speak for myself, without compromising any other person. Upon such an interesting occasion as this is, in the midst of the companions of my youth, or their descendants, I have felt that it is due to them and to myself, explicitly to declare my sentiments, without reserve, and to show that I have been, and, as I sincerely believe, the friends with whom I have acted have been, animated by the disinterested desire to advance the best interests of the country, and to preserve its free institutions.

The first, and, in my opinion, the most important object, which should engage the serious attention of a new administration, is that of circumscribing the executive

power, and throwing around it such limitations and safeguards as will render it no longer dangerous to the public
liberties.

Whatever is the work of man necessarily partakes of his
imperfection and it was not to be expected, that, with all
the acknowledged wisdom and virtues of the framers of
our Constitution, they could have sent forth a plan of
government, so free from all defect, and so full of guar-
anties, that it should not, in the conflict of embittered
parties and of excited passions, be perverted and misin-
terpreted. Misconceptions or erroneous constructions of
the powers granted in the Constitution, would probably
have occurred, after the lapse of many years, in seasons
of entire calm, and with a regular and temperate administration of the government; but, during the last twelve
years, the machine, driven by a reckless charioteer, with
frightful impetuosity, has been greatly jarred and jolted,
and it needs careful examination and a thorough repair.

With the view, therefore, to the fundamental character
of the government itself, and especially of the executive
branch, it seems to me that, either by amendments of the
Constitution, when they are necessary, or by remedial legislation, when the object falls within the scope of the powers
of Congress, there should be,

First, a provision to render a person ineligible to the
office of President of the United States, after a service of
one term.

Much observation and deliberate reflection have satisfied me that too much of the time, the thoughts, and
the exertions of the incumbent, are occupied, during his
first term, in securing his re-election. The public business,
consequently, suffers; and measures are proposed or executed with less regard to the general prosperity than to
their influence upon the approaching election. If the limitation to one term existed, the president would be exclusively devoted to the discharge of his public duties; and
he would endeavor to signalize his administration by the
beneficence and wisdom of its measures.

Secondly, the veto power should be more precisely defined, and be subjected to further limitations and qualifications. Although a large, perhaps the largest, proportion of all the acts of Congress, passed at the short session of Congress since the commencement of the government, were passed within the three last days of the session, and when, of course, the president for the time being had not the ten days for consideration, allowed by the Constitution, President Jackson, availing himself of that allowance, has failed to return important bills. When not returned by the president, within the ten days, it is questionable whether they are laws or not. It is very certain that the next Congress can not act upon them by deciding whether or not they shall become laws, the president's objections notwithstanding. All this ought to be provided for.

At present, a bill, returned by the president, can only become a law by the concurrence of two thirds of the members of each House. I think if Congress passes a bill after discussion and consideration, and, after weighing the objections of the president, still believes it ought to pass, it should become a law provided a majority of *all* the members of each House concur in its passage. If the weight of his argument, and the weight of his influence conjointly, can not prevail on a majority, against their previous convictions, in my opinion, the bill ought not to be arrested. Such is the provision of the Constitutions of several of the States, and that of Kentucky among them.

Thirdly, the power of dismission from office, should be restricted, and the exercise of it be rendered responsible.

The constitutional concurrence of the Senate is necessary to the confirmation of all important appointments; but, without consulting the Senate, without any other motive than resentment or caprice, the president may dismiss, at his sole pleasure, an officer created by the joint action of himself and the Senate. The practical effect is, to nullify the agency of the Senate. There may be, occasionally, cases in which the public interest requires an immediate dismission without waiting for the assembling of the Senate; but, in all such cases, the president should be bound to communicate fully the grounds and motives of the dismission. The power would be thus rendered responsible. Without it, the exercise of the power is utterly repugnant to free institutions, the basis of which is perfect responsibility, and dangerous to the public liberty, as has been already shown.

Fourthly, the control over the treasury of the United States should be confided and confined exclusively to Congress; and all authority of the president over it, by means of dismissing the Secretary of the Treasury, or other persons having the immediate charge of it, be rigorously precluded.

You have heard much, fellow-citizens, of the divorce of banks and government. After crippling them and impairing their utility, the executive and its partisans have systematically denounced them. The executive and the country were warned again and again of the fatal course that has been pursued; but the executive nevertheless persevered, commencing by praising, and ending by decrying, the State banks. Under cover of the smoke which has been raised, the real object all along has been, and yet is, to obtain the possession of the money power of the Union. That accomplished and sanctioned by the people—the union of the sword and the purse in the hands of the president effectually secured—and farewell to American liberty. The sub-treasury is the scheme for effecting that union; and, I am told, that of all the days in the year, that which gave birth to our national existence and freedom, is the selected day to be disgraced by ushering into existence a measure imminently perilous to the liberty, which, on that anniversary, we commemorate in joyous festivals. Thus, in the spirit of destruction which animates our rulers, would they convert a day of gladness and of glory, into a day of sadness and mourning. Fellow-citizens, there is one divorce urgently demanded by the safety and the highest interests of the country—a divorce of the president from the treasury of the United States.

And, fifthly, the appointment of members of Congress to any office, or any but a few specific offices, during their continuance in office, and for one year thereafter, should be prohibited.

This is a hackneyed theme, but it is not less deserving of serious consideration. The Constitution now interdicts the appointment of a member of Congress to any office created, or the emoluments of which have been increased while he was in office. In the purer days of the republic, that restriction might have been sufficient, but in these more degenerate times, it is necessary, by an amendment of the Constitution, to give the principle greater extent.

These are the subjects, in relation to the permanent character of the government itself, which, it seems to me, are worthy of the serious attention of the people, and of a new administration. There are others of an administrative nature, which require prompt and careful consideration.

First, the currency of the country, its stability and uniform value, and as intimately and indissolubly connected with it, the insurance of the faithful performance of the fiscal services, necessary to the government, should be maintained and secured by exercising all the powers requisite to these objects with which Congress is constitutionally invested. These are the great ends to be aimed at; the means are of subordinate importance. Whether these ends, indispensable to the well-being of both the people and the government, are to be attained by sound and safe State banks, carefully selected, and properly distributed, or by a new bank of the United States, with such limitations, conditions, and restrictions, as have been indicated by experience, should be left to the arbitrament of enlightened public opinion.

Candor and truth require me to say, that, in my judgment, while banks continue to exist in the country, the services of a bank of the United States can not be safely dispensed with. I think that the power to establish such a bank is a settled question; settled by Washington and by Madison, by the people, by forty years' acquiescence, by the judiciary, and by both of the great parties which so long held sway in this country. I know and I respect the contrary opinion, which is entertained in this State. But, in my deliberate view of the matter, the power to establish such a bank being settled, and being a necessary and proper power, the only question is, as to the expediency of its exercise. And on questions of mere expediency, public opinion ought to have a controlling influence. Without banks, I believe we can not have a sufficient currency; without a bank of the United States, I fear we can not have a sound currency. But it is the end, that of a sound and sufficient currency, and a faithful execution of the fiscal duties of government, that should engage the dispassionate and candid consideration of the whole community. There is nothing in the name of the bank of the United States which has any magical charm, or to which any one need be wedded. It is to secure certain great objects, without which society can not prosper; and if, contrary to my apprehension, these objects can be accomplished by dispensing with the agency of a bank of the United States, and employing that of State banks, all ought to rejoice, and heartily acquiesce, and none would more than I should.

Second, that the public lands, in conformity with the trusts created expressly, or by just implication, on their acquisition, be administered in a spirit of liberality toward the new States and Territories, and a spirit of justice toward all the States.

The land bill which was rejected by President Jackson, and acts of occasional legislation, will accomplish both these objects. I regret that the time does not admit of my exposing here the nefarious plans and purposes of the administration as to this vast national resource. That, like every other great interest of the country, is administered with the sole view of the effect upon the interests of the party in power. A bill has passed the Senate, and is now pending before the House, according to which, forty millions of dollars are stricken from the real value of a certain portion of the public lands by a short process; and a citizen of Virginia, residing on the south-west side of the Ohio, is not allowed to purchase lands as cheap, by half a dollar per acre, as a citizen living on the north-west side of that river. I have no hesitation in expressing my conviction, that the whole public domain is gone if Mr. Van Buren be re-elected.

Third, that the policy of protecting and encouraging the production of American industry, entering into competition with the rival productions of foreign industry, be adhered to and maintained on the basis of the principles and in the spirit of the compromise of March, 1833.

Protection and national independence are, in my opinion, identical and synonymous. The principle of abandonment of the one can not be surrendered without a forfeiture of the other. Who, with just pride and national sensibility, can think of subjecting the products of our industry to all the taxation and restraints of foreign powers, without effort, on our part, to counteract their prohibitions and burdens, by suitable countervailing legislation? The question can not be, ought not to be, one of principle, but of measure and degree. I adopt that of the compromise act, not because that act is irrepealable, but because it met with the sanction of the nation. Stability, with moderate and certain protection, is far more important than instability, the necessary consequence of high protection. But the protection of the compromise act will be adequate, in most, if not as to all interests. The twenty per centum which it stipulates, cash duties, home valuations, and the list of free articles inserted in the act for the particular advantage of the manufacturer, will insure, I trust, sufficient protection. All together, they will amount probably to no less than thirty per centum, a greater extent of protection than was secured prior to the act of 1828, which no one stands up to defend. Now the valuation of foreign goods is made not by the American authority, except in suspected cases, but by foreigners and abroad. They assess the value, and we the duty; but, as the duty depends, in most cases, upon the value, it is manifest that those who assess the value fix the duty. The home valuation will give our government what it rightfully possesses, both the power to ascertain the true value of the thing which it taxes, as well as the amount of that tax.

Fourth, that a strict and wise economy in the disbursement of the public money be steadily enforced; and that, to that end, all useless establishments, all unnecessary offices and places, foreign and domestic, and all extravagance, either in the collection or expenditure of the public revenue, be abolished and repressed.

I have not time to dwell on details in the application of this principle. I will say that a pruning-knife, long, broad, and sharp, should be applied to every department of the government. There is abundant scope for honest and skillful surgery. The annual expenditure may, in reasonable time, be brought down from its present amount of about forty millions to nearly one third of that sum.

Fifth, the several States have made such great and gratifying progress in their respective systems of internal improvement, and have been so aided by the distribution under the deposit act, that, in future, the erection of new roads and canals should be left to them, with such further aid only from the general government, as they would derive from the payment of the last installment under that act, from an absolute relinquishment of the right of Congress to call upon them to refund the previous installments, and from their equal and just quotas, to be received by a future distribution of the net proceeds from the sales of the public lands.

And, sixth, that the right to slave property, being guarantied by the Constitution, and recognized as one of the compromises incorporated in that instrument by our ancestors, should be left where the Constitution has placed it, undisturbed and unagitated by Congress.

These, fellow-citizens, are views both of the structure of the government and of its administration, which appear to me worthy of commanding the grave attention of the public and its new servants. Although, I repeat, I have neither authority nor purpose to commit any body else, I believe most, if not all, of them are entertained by the political friends with whom I have acted. Whether the salutary reforms which they include will be effected or considered, depends upon the issue of that great struggle which is now going on throughout all this country. This contest has had no parallel since the period of the Revolution. In both instances, there is a similarity of object. That was to achieve, this is to preserve the liberties of the country. Let us catch the spirit which animated, and imitate the virtues which adorned our noble ancestors. Their devotion, their constancy, their untiring activity, their perseverance, their indomitable resolution, their sacrifices, their valor! If they fought for liberty or death, in the memorable language of one of the most illustrious of them, let us never forget that the prize now at hazard, is liberty or slavery. We should be encouraged by the fact, that the contest, to the success of which they solemnly pledged their fortunes, their lives, and their sacred honors, was far more unequal than that in which we are engaged. But, on the other hand, let us cautiously guard against too much confidence. History and experience prove that more has been lost by self-confidence and contempt of enemies than won by skill and courage. Our opponents are powerful in numbers, and in organization, active, insidious, possessed of ample means, and wholly unscrupulous in the use of them. They count upon success by the use of two words, democracy and federalism; democracy, which, in violation of all truth, they appropriate to themselves, and federalism, which, in violation of all justice, they apply to us. And allow me to conjure you not to suffer yourselves to be diverted, deceived, or discouraged by the false rumors which will be industriously circulated, between the present time and the period of the election, by our opponents. They will put them forth in every variety, and without number, in the most imposing forms, certified and sworn to by conspicuous names. They will brag, they will boast, they will threaten. Regardless of all their arts, let us keep steadily and faithfully and fearlessly at work. . . .

40

"This is a country of self-made men . . ."*

CALVIN COLTON

Calvin Colton is one of the more interesting intellectuals associated with American Whiggery in the Jacksonian era. A graduate of Yale, Colton enjoyed for a time a successful career in the ministry, in the course of which he wrote several works on the history of religion and missionary enterprise. In the 1830s, his interests ranged more widely, and he began to write political essays and travel sketches, among them *The Americans*, written in 1833, as a defense of American life against the aspersions of English critics. Leaving the ministry, Colton began an equally successful career as an editor and pamphleteer for the Whig party. In 1842–43, he was editor of the *True Whig* in Washington; and in 1844, he became Clay's official biographer and, still later, the editor of the collected speeches and writings of Henry Clay. In 1852, Colton was named to the chair of Political Economy at Trinity College, Hartford, where he served until his death.

In 1843–44, Colton wrote a series of political tracts under the name of "Junius." The ten Junius Tracts represent the most complete codification of all of the Whig positions, old and new. One does not have to read very far in these tracts to discover that Colton is strongly affected by the "revolution of 1840" in which the Whigs had won a great popular victory at the polls. Hence the Junius Tracts represent an interesting reconstruction of Whig principles, fusing the older ideas of Clay's American system with the equalitarian values that

* From Calvin Colton, *Labor and Capital*, The Junius Tracts, No. VII, 1844, abridged.

had gone through such a significant escalation in American life during the Jacksonian decade.

The following selection is taken from Junius Tract No. VII, entitled "Labor and Capital." This single tract contains the most fundamental statement of the new Whig philosophy. Colton emphasizes the essential harmony of interests in America between labor and capital. In addition, this tract clearly places the image of the self-made man at the center of the Whig mythology. "Ours is a country," he declares, "where men start from an humble origin, and from small beginnings rise gradually in the world, as the reward of merit and industry. . . ."

If we take Colton as a representative example, then the Whigs seem to be more successful than the Jacksonian Democrats in the construction of an ideology which is relevant to the changing social order. They exalt the entrepreneurial urge of the men on the make in America without the abashed tone that appears in so many of the utterances of Jacksonians. To the new Whigs, the self-made man is unequivocally a capitalist and all of the institutions of capitalism—corporations, banks, insurance companies, railroads—are thought of as being "well adapted to a democratic state of society." In Colton's tract, all attempts to defend the monopolistic privileges of a Bank of the United States or other large corporations have been eliminated from the Whig ideology. "Few and large corporations," he writes, "monopolizing powers in their own specific spheres, are objects of popular jealousy and justly so. But the multiplication of them, with moderate capital and powers . . . spreads them out over the surface of society. . . . It is a wider and more democratic distribution of power." Can we not say then, that Colton's statement of Whig principles is built upon an interesting marriage between democracy and capitalism—the two most powerful forces at work in American society in the Jacksonian era?

[§ 1. What Is Labor?]

It is any man's or woman's efforts to live and prosper,
whether of body or of mind, or of both; whether in agriculture, or commerce, or manufactures, or mechanics, or
in either of the numerous branches of these great and comprehensive pursuits; whether in the useful or fine arts, in
digging ditches or digging out the sciences; whether in a
professional career, or in making books; in teaching, or in
study; in legislation, or in government; in making pins, or
casting cannon; in the use of hands or of feet, of fingers
or of toes, of muscles or of brains; in search of knowledge,
or in its application; in inventions, or their uses; in making canals, or building ships; erecting railroads, or con-
structing locomotives; in burning lime or brick, in quarry-
ing or in masonry; in wielding a sledge-hammer, or making
watches; in grinding knives, or selling brick-dust; in fishing
for oysters, or harpooning whales; in any one of the thousand occupations, of the city or the country, on the land or
on the sea; and so on, and so on, to the end of that infinite
diversity of human pursuits, by which men and women
toil for a livelihood, and to get on in the world. In a free
country each one chooses his own vocation, and it is not
easy to say, whether mind work or muscular effort is
hardest.

[§ 2. What Is Capital?]

Money is usually called capital. But it is not exclusively
so, unless it is intended to comprehend everything that will
fetch money; or everything that is *worth* money. In this
sense labor is capital. Labor, certainly, is the foundation
and cause of wealth. All the world would be poor, and
come to nothing without it. Whatever any man has, which
others want, and which, being wanted, will fetch money,
whether it be a capacity for labor, or any species of prop-

erty, it is capital. For any man, therefore, to know how rich he is, or how much capital he has, he has only to inquire *what he can do and what he has* that will fetch money.

[§ 3. THE CAPITAL OF LABOR]

He who is able to work, and who can find employment with fair pay, is rich to begin with, and may become rich in the usual sense of the term. A power to labor, where labor is in demand, is the best, most independent, and most productive of all capital. Money at interest, or in stocks, usually produces, in this country, an income averaging perhaps six per cent. Some get more, some less, and some none at all. They are liable to go backward, and lose principal itself. But labor, with economy, can hardly ever be worth less than fifty per cent. That is, a laborer can live satisfactorily, and lay up, as vested capital, half of his wages. In some kinds of employment, he can lay up three-fourths, it may be more than that. Economy and skill in the management of his earnings, may also be made productive of wealth, in addition to the profits of his labor. Some laborers, by a careful use of past earnings, soon get to realize a hundred per cent. on their capital, including labor; and then they are growing rich, wealthy. Industrious labor of any kind, in a country like ours, with economy, and being applied where labor is in demand for wages, is a sure foundation of wealth. Man does not have to labor to acquire the power. It is a capital with which he is endowed by creation, an independent faculty, and more productive than any other.

[§ 4. SKILL IN LABOR, AND IN THE MANAGEMENT OF ITS AVAILS, IS CAPITAL]

Man has not only bones, sinews, muscles, and other powers of bodily labor, but he has mind to direct it, to improve in it, to make it more available, to put all its proceeds to a profitable use, and to improve even its uses. Labor turns bodily power to account, and skill mutiplies the profits of labor, so that when a man gets a-going in the world, he goes fast. Riches flow in, and wealth accumulates. A man's power of labor is limited; but his skill is unlimited. Skill is often a thousand times more productive than what is commonly called labor. But, it is to be remembered, that skill itself is the fruit of the labor of mind, or is the employment of mind, as muscular effort is labor of the body. But skill is capital. It is equally applicable to agriculture, as to manufactures; to the mechanic, or the useful, or fine arts. It is applicable to trade and commerce, to every pursuit and occupation of life.

[§ 5. ENTERPRISE IS CAPITAL]

It might seem quite unnecessary to say, in view of what enterprise has accomplished in and for this country, from the beginning of our history, that enterprise is capital. With slender means, it has evoked unbounded wealth from the long repose of a continent, and erected thereupon a vast national estate. No other species of capital has contributed so largely to this stupendous result. As the collective power of national enterprise is composed of individual enterprise, we find accordingly the same character in isolated conditions, chequering the whole surface of society with great achievements effected by single persons. There was capital enough in the soul of Washington, to humble the greatest nation, and to make another, with means that would have been laughed to scorn as a subject of prophecy. In all our history, and in the various walks of life, are to be found like miracles of enterprise, originating in the profound and inexhaustible wealth, and carried forward to consummation, by the invisible power of man's moral attributes. . . .

[§ 7. VESTED CAPITAL]

By vested capital is commonly understood money put to use for what is called interest or income. The most common forms of vested capital, are bonds, mortgages, negotiable notes, silent partnerships in business firms, stocks in banks, insurances offices, turnpike and railroads, canals, fishing companies, great commercial enterprises, steamboats and steamships, navigation companies, manufactories, state and government securities, and any undertaking that is beyond the ordinary means of individuals, and which requires the combined and aggregate capital of numerous persons having money to put to use. The capital of corporate companies or bodies, formed for these objects, is usually divided into small shares, which, being made negotiable, that anybody can buy or sell, are thence called *stocks*.

[§ 8. CORPORATIONS]

The object of corporations is to combine the surplus or spare capital of numerous individuals, for enterprises which are usually beyond the reach of single persons. Properly organized by the statute of incorporation, by a division of the capital into small shares, and securing to men of small means equal chances, they are well adapted to a democratic state of society, by bringing down the powers of government, distributing them among the people, and vesting them in the hands of all persons who can raise twenty, or fifty, or a hundred dollars, according to the price of shares. Few and large corporations, monopolizing power in their own specific spheres, are objects of popular jealousy, and justly so. But the multiplication of them, with moderate capital and powers, divided into small shares, spreads them out over the surface of society, and whatever powers they have, be it more or less, is so much resigned by the government, and vested immediately in the hands of the people, who are able and disposed to be owners of stock. It is a wider and more democratic distribution of power. The responsibility of the managers, is to the stockholders for the use of the capital, and to the government, and through the government, to the great body of the people, for the use of their powers. That is the best, most democratic, and most beneficent system of corporations, which enables and encourages laborers and men of small means, widows and orphans, and the more dependent and helpless portions of the community, to become interested in them, by the investment and application of their funds, which they themselves could not employ to advantage. For example:—Two men, in partnership, were joint-owners of mills of great value in the state of Maine, and one of them died, leaving a widow and several children. The widow and children, of course, could not manage such a business; but by an act of incorporation from the state, the widow and the guardians of her children became corporators and managers, and the joint-interest went on as before. It will be seen, that cases are constantly occurring in society, which require the aid of such privileges. All helpless persons, who have capital enough to support them, but who are unable to manage it, naturally resort to such helps provided by the state, in parental care, and by considerations of humanity, as well as for the general welfare. . . .

[§ 17. A False Notion]

It has been a prevalent and fatal doctrine in this country, with a certain class of statesmen, that it is always a safe policy and a duty in the government, to fight against moneyed capitalists, in whatever place or shape they lift up their heads, whether in banks, or in manufactories, or in any and all other forms and enterprises requiring associated capital. In this, it is not considered, that the employment and thriving of the people depend on the profitable investment of the moneyed capital of the country; nor that the wages and profits of labor, and the price of its products, depend on the profits accruing from the use of the moneyed capital which labor employs. Moneyed capital is regarded by this policy as a master, not as a servant and instrument; as a hostile power, not as a friendly auxiliary; as having in itself a faculty of independence, not as deriving all its value from labor; and as aiming to acquire a supremacy over society. But a little reflection, in view of what has been said, one would think, ought to show, that the condition of moneyed capital, in this country, is *passive* in the hand of labor, and not *active* to rule over it, and that it is not possible to change this relation of dependence in the former on the latter. Moneyed capital, in itself, is an *inert* power, and derives all its vitality from the touch of labor. For government, therefore, to open the way, by its policy, for the profitable use of money, is the same as to provide for the success and fair reward of industry and work; and that policy which destroys the profit of money, destroys the profit of labor. Let government strike at the rich, and the blow falls on the heads of the poor. . . .

[§ 19. A Comparative View of the Position of Labor in America and Europe]

We have told in the outset what we mean by labor. It is they who work—real workers, no matter *in* what, or *with* what, or for what *end*, if it be lawful and honorable work, to supply the wants of civilized man, or the increasing wants of advancing civilization. The more wants, the more work, and so much the better for all, where each chooses his own calling, and finds employment.

But the position of labor in this country is, in a variety of important particulars, a new one in human society. 1. It is *free*—with the exception of African slave labor. This species of freedom, which is a most important attainment in the progress of society, implies a practicable *alternative* to working on wages *at the price fixed by the employer.*

In Europe, for the most part, there is no such alternative, and the laborer is *compelled* to work at a price in which he has no voice, *or he must starve;* and for the reason that he has no voice in fixing his wages, they are too scanty for comfort, much more for bettering his condition, and often too scanty for subsistence. European wages are next to a state of *starvation.* At best, it is a state of *slavery, without hope.* But in this country, labor occupies *a high social and political position.* It is never *compelled* to work for wages fixed by employers, because there is always open to it the *alternative* of working *on its own hook.* American labor, therefore, does *not accept* a price imposed, but *commands* its own price. At least, it is always an *independent* party in the compact. It is made *freely,* and can be as freely dissolved, without insuring the doom of starvation or distressing want. 2. The *social* position of American labor is such, that none but workers are held in respect—and work is held in the highest respect. No power, in this country, can enforce respect for the man who has nothing to do, and who does nothing. Just in proportion as a rich man retires from society, to wrap himself up in selfishness, does he lose his influence, and the idle, lazy poor man gets little pity in his poverty. Our fathers brought with them both the necessity and spirit of work, and made it respectable. It has been transmitted as the highest recommendation, and the most honorable character. 3. The *political* position of labor here is all-powerful, and so long as it is so, it can not but be respectable. As a nation of workers, we *demand* from Government a security for the interests and rights of labor, and one of those rights is, that *free* American labor shall not be put on the same level with the *forced* labor of other countries, or any country. It is only necessary for the people of this country to understand correctly what the true interests and rights of labor are, and they are sure to have them secured at the ballot-box. No earthly power can hinder it. What more elevated or more commanding position, can labor possibly occupy? The free American laborer is the most powerful, and may well be the proudest of men. . . .

[§ 35. THE CAPACITIES OF OUR COUNTRY]

Well and rightly governed, it is capable, not only of astonishing the world, but of astonishing itself. If things do not go on well, it must be owing solely to the perversion of our institutions from their design. There is no sufficient apology, that our general prosperity should *ever* be interrupted. It is impossible that it should be, except by a violation or misapplication of the trusts reposed in our public functionaries. By a suitable protection of the interests of American labor and industry, from a self-sacrificing rivalship with a foreign, oppressed, and degraded pauperism, which is in no wise mitigated, but only aggravated and rendered more hopeless by the favor done to their oppressors; by a proper encouragement of the voluntary enterprises of our own citizens, the people of this country, with the rich and inexhaustible treasures of creation comprehended in our jurisdiction, are capable of producing amazing results. That almost astonishing height of prosperity, to which we had attained, under all the disadvantages of a defective tariff system, before the advent of the late Destructive Dynasty, is conclusive and impressive evidence of what this nation is capable of, under a wise and faithful administration of our public affairs. We had been put in a train, by which we were enabled to discharge with ease the entire and heavy debt incurred by the last war with Great Britain, and to overwhelm the public treasury with surplus funds; the public domain in the west was in such demand, that the sales of one year amounted to *twenty-four millions of dollars,* and although there were special reasons for this fact, which could not be expected to operate in perpetuity, to an equal extent, nevertheless, in a prosperous state of things, there would be a steady increase in those sales, which, under an equitable system of distributing the proceeds among the States, whose property they are, would relieve the burdens of the indebted States, and give the others a chance for such enterprises as might best promote their interests.

Providence has assigned us a rich, productive, and glorious heritage, and established among us and over us a new, regenerate, and admirable system of Government. It has been abused, indeed; but it is good. All we want is good and faithful men at the head of it. The wealth of the country is inexhaustible, and the enterprise of the people is unsubdued, notwithstanding all our late misfortunes. Give them a good Government, and they can not help going ahead, and outstripping every nation on the globe.

[§ 36. THE CHANCES OF LIFE IN THIS COUNTRY]

Ours is a country, where men start from an humble origin, and from small beginnings rise gradually in the world, as the reward of merit and industry, and where they can attain to the most elevated positions, or acquire a large amount of wealth, according to the pursuits they elect for themselves. No exclusive privileges of birth, no entailment of estates, no civil or political disqualifications, stand in their path; but one has as good a chance as another, according to his talents, prudence, and personal exertions. This is a country of *self-made men*, than which nothing better could be said of any state of society.

[§ 37. THE MUTUAL DEPENDENCE BETWEEN THE GOVERNMENT AND THE PEOPLE]

Nothing is more instructive to this point, than the chapter of our own history. Except as the Government, by its policy, shall enable the people to prosper, in a free country like ours, where tyrannical exactions can not be enforced, the Government itself can not prosper, but its finances will be embarrassed as soon as its own measures shall have brought embarrassment and distress on the people. A crippled and disheartened population, who have no money, either to pay taxes or buy luxuries, can not send money into the public treasury. While they are poor, the Government will be poor.

[§ 38. A RETROSPECT]

Understanding, as we now do, if what we have said is correct, the relation between the labor of the country and its moneyed capital, we must look back with astonishment at the policy of the Federal Administration, from 1829 to 1841, when the cry rung through the land, and never ceased—DOWN WITH THE BANKS! DOWN WITH MANUFACTORIES! DOWN WITH CORPORATIONS! DOWN WITH CAPITALISTS! It is a history that one can hardly believe in!

While memory lasts, and fathers are capable of telling the story to their children; while true Americans are endowed with concern for the welfare of the country, and have virtue enough to stand up for its interests; and while history may be relied upon to discharge its impartial functions, it will not fail to stand stereotyped in the minds of the American people, to be rehearsed to the listening and succeeding generation, and recorded in the annals of this nation, that, for the period above named, we had a *re*-lapse and *col*-lapse in our national welfare, never to be forgotten; that an unlucky star rose in our hemisphere, ascended to its meridian, and marched to the western hills, leaving an OMINOUS TAIL BEHIND; that the people were persuaded for a time, that it was the TRUE SUN, and were hard to be convinced of its eccentric and ill boding character; that it brought famine, pestilence, and death; that demagogueism was the rage of its season, innoculating the poor with a mania against the rich, and the laborer with jealousy against the moneyed capitalist; that the love of ONE MAN POWER, was the chief malady that afflicted the nation, and its ascendency the most remarkable occurrence of the time; that the long-established, simple, and democratic habits of the people, social and political, were superseded by the dictation of a Chief, and by the aristocratic assumptions of his menials; that new, unheard-of, and destructive doctrines were promulged for the government of the country; that a well-ordered system of currency was broken up and destroyed; that the useful relations between capitalists and the laboring classes, were violently assailed, and so far dissolved, as to bring great distress on the industrious and working population; that States and large corporations were first enticed to enlist in great enterprises, and then forced to suspend them, and to stop payment, by sudden changes in the policy and measures of the Government; that our credit at home was prostrated, and abroad became the by-word and scorn of nations; that the shameless doctrine of the Repudiation of debts, was for the first time avowed and sanctioned by legislative authority; that the superstructure and very foundations of society were shaken in the general convulsion; in short, that times, modes, customs, morals, and manners underwent a complete revolution, so that the republic that *was*, could hardly be recognised in the new state of things.

It was because the relation of labor to moneyed capital, was entirely mistaken and misrepresented, and a war of Government made upon the latter, as if it was the natural enemy of the former. . . .

[§ 40. Revolutions Never Go Backward]

Under our form of Government, other revolution than that of opinion, is impossible. Can anybody doubt there was a great revolution of this kind in 1840? And where is that feeling? Have the people changed their minds? They would not *act*, till the time of *rescue* should come, and the silly crew at the head of affairs, took the people's *disgust* as a compliment to their *treason!* The *banished* horde also took courage. But the sleeping fires have only been made hotter, by that respect for order which sealed them up, and for a time repressed them. The internal pressure tends upward, to open a place of utterance ere long, and cast its bright light on the dark upper sky, and thence to astonish those below. A free nation, once convinced of its wrongs, must be avenged, and wo to them who have done the wrong! BACKWARD? OR FORWARD? is the question for this nation to answer, and it will be answered . . . the cry is—ONWARD! . . .

41

Contrasting Styles and Values

(See Plates 17–24 following page 334.)

The paintings and engravings of the age of Jackson offer additional evidence of the uncertainties of belief and the conflicts between old and new styles of life as the American people were changing from the habits and values of an agrarian society to the techniques and goals of a society moving rapidly into an industrial stage of economy and into a new stage of mass politics. Plates 17–24 reveal some of the variety and contrariety in Jacksonian America.

PLATE 17. *Fruits of Industry*. Painted by F. Prentis and engraved by A. L. Dick. From *Godey's Lady's Book* (1842) XXIV, v.

This is a familiar form of moralizing in the Jacksonian generation. Material comfort, domestic felicity, and virtuous sons and daughters are the *natural* rewards for industry.

PLATE 18. *Fruits of Idleness*. Painted by F. Prentis and engraved by A. L. Dick. From *Godey's Lady's Book* (1842) XXIV, vi.

This is the other half of the moral drama of industry and idleness as conceived by the Jacksonian generation. The fruits of idleness are penury, domestic unhappiness, and dissolute fathers and sons.

PLATE 19. *Pat Lyon at the Forge*. Painting by John Neagle. Courtesy of the Boston Athenaeum. On loan to the Museum of Fine Arts, Boston.

John Neagle's painting of Pat Lyon, done in 1826, was one of the first paintings of an artisan at his work by an American artist. Pat Lyon seems to exemplify the sturdy moral independence of the blacksmith and other artisans like him in the Jacksonian generation.

PLATE 20. *Power Loom Weaving.* Engraver unknown. From George S. White, *Memoirs of Samuel Slater, The Father of American Manufactures, Connected with a History of the Rise and Progress of the Cotton Manufacture in England and America, with Remarks on the Moral Influence of Manufactories in the United States* (Philadelphia, 1836), p. 385.

This engraving in George S. White's remarkable history of early American cotton manufacturing is probably one of the earliest representations of the interior of one of the new textile factories. This is a very different world from that of Pat Lyon. Here we see the discipline of the machine and the subservience of the factory girls, rather than the good-humored independence of the master craftsmen.

PLATE 21. *The Exchange and Girard's Bank, Philadelphia.* Engraved by W. H. Bartlett. From N. P. Willis, *American Scenery,* II, 53.

There was still a great fondness in the early years of the Jacksonian era for a Greek style in architecture. Nicholas Biddle, the head of the Bank of the United States, was particularly enamored of Grecian standards in architecture, and influenced the construction of templed buildings in Philadelphia, including the United States Bank on Chestnut Street. The Exchange and Girard's Bank depicted in the engraving were designed by William Strickland. Strickland's use of the Grecian style is among the best of American architects of this period, and these two buildings have the dignity and graceful proportions that appealed to the gentlemen of Philadelphia who were the taste-makers of the 1820s and 1830s.

PLATE 22. *Iranistan.* Engraver unknown. From P. T. Barnum, *Struggles and Triumphs: or Forty Years' Recollections of P. T. Barnum* (Hartford, 1869) p. 263.

P. T. Barnum was a self-made man who had turned his hand to a variety of occupations before he became a successful promoter of various forms of mass entertainment in the later years of the 1830s. Having amassed a considerable fortune by 1848, Barnum yearned to have a home outside New York to which he might withdraw from the "whirlpool of business excitement." Barnum engaged an architect with instructions "to spare neither time nor expense in erecting a . . . tasteful residence." The result was "Iranistan," an "oriental villa" in Fairfield, Connecticut, where a thousand invited guests attended the huge "house-warming" in November of 1848. In this architectural folly, we can see some evidence of the uncertainties of taste that accompanied the rapid appearance of a new class of rich men in the Jacksonian era.

PLATE 23. *The United States Senate, A.D. 1850.* Engraver unknown. Courtesy of the Mead Art Collection, Amherst College.

This familiar painting of Henry Clay addressing the Senate represents the old style of politics which had been formed in an earlier generation. The scene depicted in this painting suggests high-flown oratory, senatorial dignity, and, above all, statesmanship.

PLATE 24. *Stump Speaking.* Hand-colored lithograph by Gautier after a painting by George Caleb Bingham. Courtesy of the Mead Art Collection, Amherst College.

One of the foremost painters of American life, George Caleb Bingham was a favorite with the Jacksonian generation, and his genre paintings were sold by the thousands in engraved reproductions. In *Stump Speaking*, Bingham portrays the new style of politics which has been given form by the Jacksonians. This painting suggests the new skills of demagoguery that were required for success in politics in the age of the common man.

Suggested Readings

The most comprehensive study of the economic changes in the Jacksonian period is George Rogers Taylor's *The Transportation Revolution, 1815–1860* (New York, 1951). Also useful for an understanding of new forms and functions in an emerging industrial order is Thomas C. Cochran's "Business Organization and the Development of an Industrial Discipline" in *The Growth of the American Economy*, Harold F. Williamson, ed. (New York, 1951). The problems of banking and currency that were so crucial to the Jacksonian generation are closely analyzed in Bray Hammond's *Banks and Politics in America, from the Revolution to the Civil War* (Princeton, 1957).

The most recent account of the political history of the Jacksonian era is Glyndon G. Van Deusen's *The Jacksonian Era, 1828–1848* (New York, 1959). The best study of the changes in the presidency during the Jacksonian generation is Leonard D. White's *The Jacksonians, a Study in Administrative History, 1829–1861* (New York, 1954). The early chapters in volume two of Moisei Ostrogorski, *Democracy and the Organization of Political Parties* (New York, 1902), contain a useful analysis of the new techniques of party organization and the new styles of political leadership. The most thorough localized study of the ethnic, religious, and economic patterns of Jacksonian politics is Lee Benson's, *The Concept of Jacksonian Democracy: New York as a Test Case* (Princeton, 1961). Richard P. McCormick's "New Perspectives on Jacksonian Politics", in the *American Historical Review*, LXV (January 1960), 288–301, is an indispensable addition to our knowledge of voting behavior in the Jacksonian generation.

For a comprehensive examination of the economic ideas of the Jacksonian generation, one should consult volume two of Joseph Dorfman, *The Economic Mind in American Civilization, 1606–1865* (New York, 1946). A handy collection of primary sources articulating social and economic ideas is *Social Theories of Jacksonian Democracy, Representative Writings of the Period, 1825–1850*, Joseph L. Blau, ed. (New York, 1947). Vernon Louis Parrington's *The Romantic Revolution, 1800–1860* (volume two of *Main Currents in American Thought*, New York, 1927) can still be read with pleasure and profit by anyone interested in the age of Jackson. Alice Felt Tyler's *Freedom's Ferment, Phases of American Social History to 1860* (Minneapolis, 1944), is a good account of the organizations and programs of the many utopian and social reform movements of the period.

There are many good books which offer interpretations of the Jacksonian period based on some of the broader perspectives of cultural history. Carl Russell Fish, *The Rise of the Common Man, 1830–1850* (New York, 1927) was an early effort to write a cultural history of the period. Frederick Jackson Turner used the insights of his frontier hypothesis in his *The United States, 1830–1850; the Nation and Its Sections* (New York, 1935). Arthur M. Schlesinger, Jr., stimulated a great many reappraisals of Jacksonian democracy with his provocative and popular *The Age of Jackson* (Boston, 1945). Two interesting reappraisals of Jacksonian democracy are "Andrew Jackson and the Rise of Liberal Capitalism" in Richard Hofstadter's *The American Political Tradition and the Men Who Made It* (New York, 1949), and the chapter on the Jacksonian democrats in Louis Hartz, *The Liberal Tradition in America: An Interpretation of American Political Thought since the Revolution* (New York, 1955). John William Ward has examined some of the key ideals and symbols of Jacksonian democracy in his *Andrew Jackson, Symbol for an Age* (New York, 1955). Many chapters of Henry Nash Smith's *Virgin Land: the American West as Symbol and*

Myth (New York, 1957) can help us get at leading characteristics of American mythology in this period. Marvin Meyers, *The Jacksonian Persuasion, Politics and Belief* (New York, 1960) is a valuable inquiry into the fears and hopes, the passions and beliefs that lay beneath the political loyalties of the Jacksonian generation. Of course, no one can afford to neglect Alexis de Tocqueville's classic commentary on America in the early nineteenth century. The Phillips Bradley edition of *Democracy in America*, 2 vols. (New York, 1945), will furnish the reader with critical notes to make him aware of some of the dangers of an uncritical use of Tocqueville's work.

Those who wish to look further into the historiography of the Jacksonian period should consult John W. Ward's essay on "The Age of the Common Man" in *The Reconstruction of American History*, John Higham, ed. (New York, 1962) and the excellent article by Charles Grier Sellers, Jr., "Andrew Jackson *Versus* the Historians," in *Mississippi Valley Historical Review*, XLIV (March 1958), 615–48.

ANCHOR BOOKS

AMERICAN HISTORY AND STUDIES

LITTELL, FRANKLIN H. From State Church to Pluralism, A294
LUBELL, SAMUEL The Future of American Politics, A71
LUKACS, JOHN A History of the Cold War, A322
LYNN, KENNETH S., ed. The Comic Tradition in America, A187
MC GEE, REECE J., & CAPLOW, THEODORE The Academic Marketplace, A440
MARTINEAU, HARRIET Society in America, ed. Lipset, A302
MASSEL, MARK S. Competition and Monopoly, A386
MAYER, MARTIN The Schools, A331
MELVILLE, HERMAN Selected Poems of Herman Melville, ed. Cohen, A375
MILLER, PERRY, ed. The American Puritans, A80
—— The American Transcendentalists, A119
—— The Legal Mind in America, A313
—— Margaret Fuller: American Romantic—A Selection from Her Writings and Correspondence, A356
PEEL, ROBERT Christian Science: Its Encounter with American Culture, A446
PETERSEN, WILLIAM, ed. American Social Patterns, A86
PIERSON, GEORGE W. Tocqueville in America (Abridged), A189
POWELL, SUMNER CHILTON Puritan Village: The Formation of a New England Town, A441
RAAB, EARL American Race Relations Today, A318
—— Religious Conflict in America: Studies of the Problem Beyond Bigotry, A392
RANSOM, HARRY HOWE Can American Democracy Survive Cold War?, A402
RIESMAN, DAVID Constraint and Variety in American Education, A135
—— Selected Essays from Individualism Reconsidered, A58
ROURKE, CONSTANCE American Humor, A12
ROZWENC, EDWIN C., ed. Ideology and Power in the Age of Jackson, AD1
SANFORD, CHARLES, ed. Quest for America, 1810–1824, AD3
SMITH, LILLIAN Killers of the Dream, A339
TAYLOR, WILLIAM R. Cavalier and Yankee: The Old South and American National Character, A351
VERNON, RAYMOND Metropolis 1985, A341
VIDICH, ARTHUR, & BENSMAN, JOSEPH Small Town in Mass Society, A216
WARSHOW, ROBERT The Immediate Experience—Movies, Comics, Theatre and Other Aspects of Popular Culture, A410
WASHBURN, WILCOMB, ed. The Indian and the White Man, AD2
WHYTE, WILLIAM H., JR. The Organization Man, A117
WILLIAMS, JOHN A. White Man, Listen!, A414
WILSON, EDMUND The American Earthquake: A Documentary of the Jazz Age, the Great Depression and the New Deal, A382
WOODWARD, C. VANN Reunion and Reaction, A83

AMERICAN FICTION

BARTHELME, DONALD Come Back, Dr. Caligari, A470
HARRIS, MARK Bang the Drum Slowly, A324
JAMES, HENRY What Maisie Knew, A43
JEWETT, SARAH ORNE The Country of the Pointed Firs, A26
MELVILLE, HERMAN Redburn, A118
WILDER, THORNTON Heaven's My Destination, A209

ANCHOR BOOKS

EUROPEAN HISTORY

A 6Aa

ANCHOR BOOKS

BRITISH FICTION

CONRAD, JOSEPH The Secret Agent, A8
—— The Shadow-Line, Typhoon *and* The Secret Sharer, A178
—— Under Western Eyes, ed. Zabel, A323
—— Victory, A106
—— Youth, Heart of Darkness *and* The End of the Tether, A173
KIPLING, RUDYARD The English in England: Short Stories by Rudyard Kipling, ed. Jarrell, A362
—— In the Vernacular: The English in India, ed. Jarrell, A363
MISH, CHARLES C., ed. Anchor Anthology of Short Fiction of the Seventeenth Century, AC1
SNOW, C. P. The Masters, A162
WEINTRAUB, STANLEY, ed. The Yellow Book: Quintessence of the Nineties, A421

CONTINENTAL FICTION

ALAIN-FOURNIER, HENRI The Wanderer, A14
CHEKHOV, ANTON Ward No. 6 *Six Russian Short Novels,* ed. Jarrell, A348
COLETTE My Mother's House *and* The Vagabond, A62
DOSTOEVSKY Three Short Novels of Dostoevsky, A193
FLORES, ANGEL, ed. Nineteenth Century German Tales, A184
GOGOL, NIKOLAI The Overcoat *Six Russian Short Novels,* ed. Jarrell, A348
JARRELL, RANDALL, ed. Six Russian Short Novels, A348
LERMONTOV, MIHAIL A Hero of Our Time, A133
LESKOV, NIKOLAI The Lady Macbeth of the Mtsensk District *Six Russian Short Novels,* ed. Jarrell, A348
MERWIN, W. S., trans. The Life of Lazarillo de Tormes, A316
SERGE, VICTOR The Case of Comrade Tulayev, A349
TOLSTOY, LEO The Death of Ivan Ilych *and* Master and Man *Six Russian Short Novels,* ed. Jarrell, A348
TURGENEV, IVAN A Lear of the Steppes *Six Russian Short Novels,* ed. Jarrell, A348

ORIENTAL LITERATURE

KAI-YU, HSU, trans. & ed. Twentieth Century Chinese Poetry—An Anthology, A413
KANG-HU, KIANG The Jade Mountain—Being Three Hundred Poems of the T'ang Dynasty 618–906, trans. Bynner, A411
MURASAKI, LADY The Tale of Genji, trans. Waley
Vol. I—A55
SCOTT, A. C. Literature and the Arts in Twentieth Century China, A343
TSAO HSUEH-CHIN Dream of the Red Chamber, trans. Wang, A159

ANCHOR BOOKS

GOVERNMENT AND POLITICAL SCIENCE

LIPSET, SEYMOUR MARTIN Political Man: The Social Bases of Politics, A330

——, TROW, M. A., & COLEMAN, J. S. Union Democracy, A296

LUBELL, SAMUEL The Future of American Politics, A71

MAC GAFFEY, WYATT, & BARNETT, CLIFFORD R. Twentieth-Century Cuba—The Background of the Castro Revolution, A433

MADGE, JOHN The Tools of Social Science, A437

MARSHALL, T. H. Class, Citizenship and Social Development, A432

MARTIN, ROSCOE C., MUNGER, FRANK J., et al. Decisions in Syracuse, A434

MARX, KARL, & ENGELS, FRIEDRICH Basic Writings on Politics and Philosophy, A185

MASSEL, MARK S. Competition and Monopoly: Legal and Economic Issues, A386

MILL, JOHN STUART John Stuart Mill: Essays on Politics and Culture, ed. Himmelfarb, A373

MILLER, PERRY, ed. The Legal Mind in America, A313

MUELLER, WILLIAM A. Church and State in Luther and Calvin, A454

NAMIER, LEWIS 1848: The Revolution of the Intellectuals, A385

NEGLEY, GLENN, & PATRICK, J. MAX, eds. The Quest for Utopia, A326

NEHRU, JAWAHARLAL The Discovery of India, A200

ODAJNYK, WALTER Marxism and Existentialism, A443

OSTROGORSKI, M. Democracy and the Organization of Political Parties—Volume I: England; Volume II: The United States, ed. Lipset, A388a; A388b

PETERSON, WILLIAM The Politics of Population, A452

PIERSON, GEORGE W. Tocqueville in America (Abridged), A189

POWELL, SUMNER CHILTON Puritan Village: The Formation of a New England Town, A441

RAAB, EARL, ed. Religious Conflict in America: Studies of the Problem Beyond Bigotry, A392

RANSOM, HARRY HOWE Can American Democracy Survive Cold War?, A402

ROOSEVELT, JAMES, ed. The Liberal Papers, A290

SERGE, VICTOR The Case of Comrade Tulayev, A349

SIBLEY, MULFORD Q., ed. The Quiet Battle: Writings on the Theory and Practice of Non-Violent Resistance, A317

SOMERVILLE, JOHN, & SANTONI, RONALD, eds. Social and Political Philosophy: Readings from Plato to Gandhi, A370

STERN, FRITZ The Politics of Cultural Despair—A Study in the Rise of Germanic Ideology, A436

THEOBALD, ROBERT Free Men and Free Markets, A447

TOCQUEVILLE, ALEXIS DE The Old Regime and the French Revolution, A60

VERNON, RAYMOND Metropolis 1985, A341

WASKOW, ARTHUR The Worried Man's Guide to World Peace, A377

WILSON, EDMUND To the Finland Station, A6

WOOD, ROBERT C., JR. 1400 Governments, A389

A 11Ba